Strategic Thinking

IISS Studies in International Security

Mats Berdal, Series Editor

Strategic Thinking

An Introduction and Farewell

Philip Windsor

EDITED BY
Mats Berdal & Spyros Economides

BOULDER
LONDON

Published in the United States of America in 2002 by
Lynne Rienner Publishers, Inc.
1800 30th Street, Boulder, Colorado 80301
www.rienner.com

and in the United Kingdom by
Lynne Rienner Publishers, Inc.
3 Henrietta Street, Covent Garden, London WC2E 8LU

Library of Congress Cataloging-in-Publication Data
Windsor, Philip.
Strategic thinking : an introduction and farewell / Philip Windsor ; edited by Mats Berdal and Spyros Economides.
p. cm. — (IISS studies in international security)
Includes bibliographical references and index.
ISBN 1-58826-048-8 (alk. paper)
ISBN 1-58826-024-0 (pbk. : alk. paper)
1. Nuclear warfare. 2. Strategy. 3. Cold War. I. Berdal, Mats R., 1965– . II. Economides, Spyros. III. Title. IV. Series.
U263 .W56 2002
355.02'17—dc21 2001048936

British Cataloguing in Publication Data
A Cataloguing in Publication record for this book is available from the British Library.

Printed and bound in the United States of America

The paper used in this publication meets the requirements of the American National Standard for Permanence of Paper for Printed Library Materials Z39.48-1984.

5 4 3 2 1

Contents

Foreword

Mats Berdal and Spyros Economides

Of the many subjects that stimulated Philip Windsor's intellectual curiosity and fertile mind, war and military strategy in the nuclear age are perhaps the ones for which he is most widely remembered. In countless interviews and commentaries for the BBC, especially in the 1970s and 1980s, he brought clear and characteristically jargon-free analysis to bear on the vicissitudes of East-West relations. To gatherings of military officers and diplomats around the world, he placed the phenomenal increase in the destructive power of modern weaponry and the very real possibility of nuclear Armageddon into sharp historical, political, and philosophical relief. But it was during his tenure as a teacher at the London School of Economics from 1967 to 1997 that his reflections on the evolution of what he called "strategic thinking" reached their widest audience.

The principal setting for these reflections was an annual series of lectures titled "Strategic Aspects of International Relations." Philip's fluent and brilliant delivery, richly laced with wit and insights drawn from outside the narrow confines of the social sciences, captivated and enthralled undergraduate and graduate audiences. His flawless delivery aside, it was above all the content of Philip's lectures that proved so enriching and intellectually stimulating to new classes of students each year. Recognizing this, friends and colleagues persisted in encouraging Philip to bring his lectures and thoughts on modern strategy and war together in a single volume. After much prodding, he eventually obliged, and the result was *Strategic Thinking: An Introduction and Farewell*. The initial draft of the book was completed in 1995. But the long, drawn-out process of preparing a final draft for publication, combined with illness, meant that he was unable to complete the project before he died in 2000. In preparing the manuscript for publication, we have made no substantive changes to the original save for some minor amendments, mostly of a technical nature.

Strategic Thinking traces the evolution of strategic thinking from its religious, legal, and political origins in medieval and modern Europe through to the demise of the Cold War. In particular, it examines the peculiar character and autonomy that strategy acquired in the nuclear age. From the dying Roman Empire to the nuclear era, the book is concerned with changes in the understanding of war and strategy resulting less from technological change per se than from the combined effects of technological, social, and political transformations, whose interactions over time contributed to major shifts in thinking about strategy and war. It was a process that culminated in the nuclear age when strategic considerations, in Windsor's own words, emerged as "the decisive force in the conduct of the politics of states and blocs."

It is highly appropriate that this book should be the first in a new series to be released by Lynne Rienner Publishers in association with the International Institute for Strategic Studies (IISS). Philip Windsor was closely associated with the IISS throughout his academic career, especially in the early years of the institute's history under the directorship of Alistair Buchan, with whom he also coauthored a book.[1] Between 1961 and 1965 he worked as a research fellow at the institute and in the 1970s and early 1980s he went on to serve on its council. He wrote frequently for the institute, including a characteristically incisive Adelphi Paper on Germany and the crises facing the Western alliance after the Soviet invasion of Afghanistan and the breakdown of détente.[2]

But far more important than its author's association with the IISS, *Strategic Thinking* sets a standard by the quality of its analysis and the clarity and lucidity of its style. Substance and style, as Windsor knew well, are not unrelated. Indeed, in describing much of the writings on limited war as "needlessly complicated," he was in fact pointing to a wider problem with the "strategic studies" literature, one that fed into and reinforced what he saw as a distinguishing feature of strategic thinking in the nuclear age: its self-referring and self-legitimating character.[3] It is against this background that *Strategic Thinking* sets out to reexamine the influence and validity of the assumptions—the "forms of thought," as Windsor called them—that came to govern strategic thinking and that gradually came to be taken for granted during the Cold War (including, as Windsor readily admits, by himself). In an important sense, therefore, this book is a reminder of the need, not only for students of international relations but also for policymakers and practitioners, constantly to question our mental assumptions about a given subject. As such, it raises questions and stimulates a mode of thinking about the role of force in international relations whose relevance goes far beyond the historical period with which this book is principally concerned.

This process of questioning, however, should never become a dry or clever intellectual exercise. The subject matter is far too important for that. And herein lies, perhaps, the deeper explanation for the appeal of Windsor's original lectures and the legendary status they acquired among a generation of students. It also explains why *Strategic Thinking* is such an absorbing read. Windsor was deeply and genuinely engaged by problems of war and peace in the nuclear age, and his passion shone through in his lectures and his interactions with students. The concluding paragraph in this book fittingly captures Windsor's appeal, and its inclusion here will hopefully stimulate the reader to start from the beginning, read through it all, and think afresh about the problems of war and peace:

> The trouble with strategic thinking is that it was too optimistic. Many of its proponents attempted to cling to that optimism even in the face of disaster. In U.S. political discourse, for example, the horrors of the Vietnam War have been treated not in the obvious terms of tragedy—hubris, retribution, and expiation—but as a "syndrome" that had to be "got over." The Gulf War, and the much-vaunted expectations of a "New World Order" that followed from it, provided indications enough that such optimism remained in place. But its opposite is increasingly necessary: not pessimism but a proper sense of the tragic—starting with the assumption not that war is abnormal but that peace is difficult to achieve. If that becomes the future orientation of strategic thought, strategic assumptions can no longer provide a quick-fix solution to the tragic nature of human existence in international society. Instead, the understanding of tragedy can still be what, from the composition of the very earliest tragedies, it was meant to be: an act of liberation.

* * *

The editors would like to thank Professor Michael Yahuda and his colleagues in the Department of International Relations at the London School of Economics for supporting the effort to publish this book. A special debt of gratitude is also owed to Jana Chanaa and Elisabeth Udgaard for their assistance in preparing the manuscript for publication.

Notes

1. Alistair Buchan and Philip Windsor, *Arms and Stability in Europe* (London: Chatto and Windus, 1963).

2. Philip Windsor, *Germany and the Western Alliance: Lessons from the 1980 Crises,* Adelphi Paper no. 170 (London: International Institute for Strategic Studies, 1981).

3. Set against the "strategic studies" literature to which *Strategic Thinking* directly or indirectly refers, one is reminded of Geoffrey Hawthorn's review of Leszek Kolakowski's *Main Currents of Marxism,* which he considered to be "of a far finer quality than almost all of that with which it deals."

Preface

This book is intended to introduce those who wish to understand the development of strategic thought during the period of the Cold War to some of its principal features—whether its readers are students of international relations or interested members of the public who have no specialized knowledge of the subject. It seeks as far as possible to avoid the technicalities of deterrence theory, the arcana of arms control, and the details of political wrangling between East and West. Instead, it tries to examine, and in part account for, the evolution of an extraordinary set of forms of thought, which many people, including me, took for granted for a very long time. Perhaps the moment has come for one to be able to sit back, reexamine them, and question their influence and the validity of their assumptions. This is what I have tried to do.

I have been encouraged in this attempt by many friends and colleagues, three of whom in particular I would like to thank. Leon Mangassarian was exceptionally helpful in reminding me of what I had said when holding forth on previous occasions, and in tracking down allusions that I could no longer remember. Spyros Economides gave of his time and energy, even when very busy, in many friendly discussions and in helping me to ascertain sources.

My biggest debt is to Kim Gale. The old saying "without whose help this book could never have been written" is literally true in this case. Not only did she type the entire manuscript, but she also kept me going when I was inclined to flag. In the words of Robert Graves, she "sweated out the whole damned term, bowed stiffly and went free."

—Philip Windsor

Preface

1

The Autonomy of Strategy in the Nuclear Age

There are two ways of bringing the nuclear age to an end. One is with a bang. The other is far from being a whimper. The first is to fight an all-out nuclear war, which would terminate history itself. The second is to make the possession of nuclear weapons irrelevant to the conduct of relations between states and peoples. It is just possible that this is beginning to happen—that humanity might be witnessing the beginning of the end of the nuclear age. It is a consideration that will be addressed later in this book. *Strategic Thinking* is being written, however, with one particular assumption in mind, which is that it is now possible to stand back and look at the nuclear age as a particular historical epoch with certain defining characteristics of its own. It was the age in which a particular mode of strategic thinking dominated the conduct of international affairs.

Three of the historical catchphrases of the nuclear age epitomize that dominance. First, "the Cold War." What this suggests is the reversal of the Clausewitzian dictum, that war was the continuation of politics by other means: politics had now become the continuation of war by all other means available. At the same time, however, politics conducted in such a manner depended on an incessant preparation for war itself, which helps to explain the second catchphrase: "the superpowers." What are superpowers? They are not necessarily empires: the Soviet Union was one, but the United States was not, in anything more than a metaphorical sense. They are not necessarily global powers: the United States was the preeminent global power at the end of World War II, but the Soviet Union did not develop any real global reach until nearly twenty years later; and indeed for much of that period Britain and France were far more active global powers than the USSR, though superpowers they were not. Nor do superpowers need to possess advanced and sophisticated economies: it was apparent to most of the rest of the world long before it became obvious to the peoples of the Soviet Union that their state was, economically speaking, remarkably backward.

What distinguishes a superpower from the rest is its ability to destroy the society of an enemy state, and eventually perhaps to wipe out the world. It has no other attributes. Its role in history and in international society is based on its ability to negate both; it is dangerous. Yet it is on the relations between two such entities that other states were bound to depend when charting or modifying their own policies and their own relations with each other. As the commanders of ships might have to, when steering a course in a busy channel between two monstrous icebergs. And that raises the third catchphrase, though it is one more frequently found in academic writing than in popular speech: "bipolarity."

The multiple complications of the international system that had prevailed before World War II were now thought to have been brutally simplified by a structure in which there were only two poles of attraction or repulsion: Washington and Moscow. The fact that this wasn't true at all, that China (after 1958) explicitly rejected any part in such a system, that the Non-Aligned Movement represented precisely an attempt to provide an alternative framework of international activity, only seemed for many years to demonstrate the all-powerful embrace of the bipolarity from which weaker states were struggling (and failing) to secede. It is frequently the case, and not only in academic writing, that contrary evidence is taken as proof of the original contention. There is no limit to the capacity of people to believe what they know isn't true.

Phrases such as those mentioned here have become so familiar that it must appear banal in the extreme to discuss the nuclear age in such terms. But one might say in retrospect that they represent the most astonishing feature of international relations in the period since 1945: the emergence of strategic considerations as the decisive force in the conduct of the politics of states and blocs. In particular, the imperatives of nuclear deterrence seemed to acquire not only a political dynamic but also an apparent intellectual cohesion of their own, and to provide, as it were, a set of rules that came to dominate the conduct of strategy, which in turn set the agenda for the conduct of international politics.

Certainly there were intellectual figures who challenged such assumptions, as for example Karl Jaspers in Germany, Raymond Aron in France, and Bertrand Russell in Britain. The fact that they could all do so from very different philosophical standpoints might indicate that there was a basis for a consensus against any automatic acceptance of the strategic paradigm—but it was this paradigm that prevailed. In a sense, one could see why.

If the rules of nuclear deterrence entailed the manipulation of catastrophic risk, it seemed realistic to most commanders and their political masters to minimize the risk by keeping the rules in place, and by hoping that both principal antagonists would agree on what these were. (That was the basis for arms control negotiations.) But the upshot was that realism in politics came to be equated with the autonomy and dominance of strategic thinking. Politics became comprehensively subordinate to strategy, and ultimately the articulation and survival of other values came to depend on the threat of committing genocide and risking suicide.

The ethics of nuclear deterrence will be considered later. Clearly, genocide and suicide were prospects implicit in the large-scale deployment of nuclear weapons, but the explicit purpose was the very opposite: the avoidance of war. In a famous memorandum that came to the attention of President Truman, the eminent American strategist Bernard Brodie wrote (originally in 1946) that the advent of nuclear weapons had changed the nature of strategy: in the past the supreme objective of strategy had been to win wars, but now it was to avoid them.[1] Brodie showed a certain prescience here. For many of his contemporaries, the atomic bomb was a cheaper and more efficient way of winning wars than the thousand-bomber raids that had been necessary to destroy, for example, Cologne. But by the time that nuclear deterrence had come to be officially accepted policy some four years later, the avoidance of war was the paramount aim; and since then it has still been possible to argue on that basis that deterrence serves a rational and ethical end.

But deterrence is not as straightforward as that, since there has always been the assumption that if deterrence "fails," the weapons would be used—and indeed it is only this threat that makes it even remotely realistic to suggest that deterrence does after all "succeed" in preventing a war. The imperative of nuclear deterrence therefore becomes one of showing that the threat itself is realistic. That was simple enough at first when only one power possessed the atom bomb. It became more complicated when that power's chief opponent acquired a similar capability, and as the atom bomb was succeeded by the thermonuclear or hydrogen bomb, and as aircraft gave way to missiles. A complex interaction of political and technological changes very rapidly created a process of continuous adaptation in the doctrines and arsenals of both superpowers, in an attempt to make the threat stick. The more difficult and unrealistic such a threat became, the greater it grew in importance. The less effective it became in the conduct of international relations, the more it came to dominate them. There is an analogy here with the neurotic mechanism at the level of individual psychology, whereby a person who finds a pattern of conduct inadequate or frustrating persists with increasing efforts to strengthen that pattern rather than asking whether there might not have been something wrong with it in the first place. As far as one can tell, the first political leader in office to address such a question openly was Mikhail Gorbachev some forty years after the first atomic bombs were dropped—though some earlier figures had done so once they had left office.[2]

How, one might ask, did it all get so complicated? Nuclear weapons now appear to exist only in order to prevent nuclear war. That is a classic example of a contradiction in terms—or as Hegel might have preferred to call it, a case of a phenomenon negating its own existence. If that had been recognized as the case from the outset, there would have been no problem. Even two antagonistic countries could be quite content with a modest stockpile, secure in the knowledge that neither would dare attack the other so long as each could retaliate. Once they had reached that stage, there would of course be no point in having nuclear weapons anyway; and if adequate inspection procedures were agreed, the weapons could simply be dismantled.

This is exactly what Gorbachev argued at his summit meeting with President Reagan in Reykjavik in 1986. But the problem is that the system of nuclear deterrence was never invoked, and never has been invoked, only to ward off a nuclear threat. On the contrary: deterrence as a policy grew up through attempts to prevent other kinds of attack, and it has always been the central preoccupation of strategists in the nuclear age to convince their opponents that in certain eventualities (a conventional attack across the frontier of an alliance, for example) nuclear weapons would indeed be used. In other words it is the problem of credibility at lower levels that has created the complications at higher levels. So much so, that in order to maintain their credibility, the superpowers had between them amassed by the mid-1980s the explosive equivalent of about one million Hiroshimas.

This pattern of development, this "mad momentum," as the distinguished U.S. secretary of defense Robert McNamara called it, is not only an astonishing phenomenon in itself but also a startling contrast to earlier patterns of strategic thinking. They had been characterized by their attempts to bring war, and the threat of war, under control. Strategy was not seen as autonomous, nor did it enjoy the causal status in international affairs that was its hallmark in the nuclear age. On the contrary, strategy was regarded as subordinate to other considerations that it was bound to serve if military activity were to make any sense at all. There were three traditions of thought that were in part historically successive, and have in part overlapped. In the first tradition, that of "Just War" thinking, the attempt was made to bring strategy under moral control. In the second, the framework of control was legal. In the third, associated particularly with the name of Clausewitz, it was political. To understand the peculiar nature of the nuclear age, it is necessary to appreciate something of these traditions.

Notes

1. Bernard Brodie was to expand this argument at considerable length in his classic *Strategy in the Missile Age* (Princeton: Princeton University Press, 1959).

2. See, for example, McGeorge Bundy, George Kennan, and Gerard Smith, "Nuclear Weapons and the Atlantic Alliance," *Foreign Affairs* 60, no. 4 (spring 1982).

2

The Just War

The beginnings of the Just War tradition can be seen as part of the intellectual and spiritual challenge with which Christianity confronted the dying Roman Empire. That empire had not been noted for its restraint in the conduct of military operations: the total destruction of Carthage and the genocide of its citizens was one of its more notable exploits. Indeed, a modern religious philosopher, Simone Weil, has compared the ancient Romans to the Nazis. That is more than somewhat unfair, since the Romans had no driving ideology, were prepared to allow a man of any race to become a Roman citizen, and had no conception of total war. Yet they did regard themselves as a people destined to rule the world and were implacable in their resort to any means deemed necessary to extend and preserve their rule. But when their power buckled under the successive onslaughts of equally implacable barbarians, their social and political system had also to face a different kind of crisis.

The central tenets of Christianity would have been unrecognizable to any right-thinking Roman. Instead of assuming that the City was eternal and that individuals were merely its transient inhabitants, Christianity taught that all earthly things, even Rome itself, would ultimately perish and be consumed, and that it was the individual soul that was eternal. In this context, Christianity also laid great emphasis on the importance of forgiving, rather than slaughtering, one's enemies, and stressed that the meek would inherit the earth. Its teaching offered the ethical coherence of a universal faith, borne out by the central beliefs of the Crucifixion and the Resurrection. In that sense, early persecutions and martyrdoms only served to reinforce the faith. But in the best dialectical tradition, the more powerful the faith became, the greater the difficulties it encountered in maintaining the coherence of its beliefs.

By the time that the emperor Constantine converted to Christianity, the cross was already becoming a symbol of military might: according to tradition, the words that he heard in his vision were, "In this sign shalt thou conquer"—and that also became part of the tradition of Christianity, leading subsequently to the Crusades. How was it possible to reconcile the teachings of the original faith with the political and moral dilemmas that power brought with it? This is what the Just War tradition of thought attempted to do.

It began, appositely enough, in Carthage, where a pagan convert to Christianity eventually became bishop. Saint Augustine was born a few years after Constantine's death, and therefore into a world in which the Christian religion was now official. He is one of the least attractive of the prominent early Christian figures (how could *anyone* describe the Crucifixion as the mousetrap set by God to catch the Devil?), and much of his doctrinal teaching appears both tortuous and authoritarian. But he did try seriously to come to terms with the central question of how to reconcile ethical coherence with the knowledge that princes and powers could break the faith, and that retribution might have to be invoked. For Augustine, military considerations were at the bottom of an intellectual and moral hierarchy, in which the military was subordinate to the political, the political to the legal, the legal to the moral, and the moral to the theological. It was only when that whole hierarchy had been worked out and drawn together that wars could ever be justified. The immediate implication is clear: there could never, in these terms, be such a thing as a purely military decision. The contrast with modern strategic thinking is also clear: witness President Truman's 1945 telegram to General Eisenhower in response to a request for guidance as to whether to continue with the "broad front" strategy that Eisenhower favored in the latter stages of World War II, or to make a dash for Berlin. That, replied Truman, *is* a purely military decision.[1]

Augustine's primary concern, however, was with the question of when and in what circumstances it is justified to go to war, and only secondly with how to wage it. This became one of the twin pillars of the Just War tradition, namely jus ad bellum, which is sometimes misinterpreted, particularly by international lawyers of a Germanic variety, but also by others, who see in it a *right* to go to war. It could even be argued in terms of such misinterpretations that all states are inherently endowed with the right to make war. That, however, is precisely the opposite of what the Just War tradition holds—which is that war is always exceptional and abhorrent, and must have a strong moral justification before it can even be contemplated.

Between the time of Augustine and that of medieval philosophers, notably Saint Thomas Aquinas, the criteria of jus ad bellum were to be considerably elaborated, but they can be summarized here under six main points. The first, revealing in terms of the political chaos attendant on the collapse of the Roman Empire, was that of "legitimate authority." A war could be justified only if it was waged by a ruler whose rights to rule were duly recognized by papal authority and by other sovereigns. Later, in the eras of the Enlightenment, this concept of legitimacy was to become part of the political and legal fabric of European civilization, divorced from moral considerations or the authority of the pope—but it has its origins in the moral quandaries that the Just War tradition attempted to address. And today one can still see such considerations at work.

The legitimacy of the State of Israel was established by UN recognition in 1948 (though some states had recognized it before that), but what of the Palestine Liberation Organization (PLO)? It was established under Egyptian sponsorship in 1964, but its various factions were not recognized as representing anything much until the League of Arab States recognized it as the "sole legitimate representative of the Palestinian people" ten years later. Subsequently, it was given observer status at the United Nations.

That might be said to be the point at which the PLO would eventually become capable of transforming itself from what was regarded by many governments, including the United States, as a bunch of terrorists, into an organization that was eventually prepared to offer Israel coexistence. It is in this process of transformation that one can still see the contemporary importance of the old principle of "legitimate authority." It is seldom that those who have no recognized right to rule are capable of making peace.

The second criterion was that of "last resort," namely that war should never be lightly entertained as an option. All other means of resolving a dispute—diplomacy, negotiation, or in modern parlance, sanctions, should be exhausted first. The principle of last resort can be more complicated than it looks: it is difficult to know for example when an unprincipled dictator might simply be using the procedure of negotiation to consolidate his hold on territory he has already seized, or whether sanctions can ever work unless they are backed up by the visible threat of military force. To digress for a moment, it is frequently said that sanctions never work, that they merely invite the solidarity of a people with a previously unpopular government, encourage a policy of import-substitution, and help to broaden the industrial base of a country that would otherwise have been happy to remain part of an interdependent network. That is not quite true. Germany was unvanquished in military terms in World War I, but was brought to sign the articles of surrender by an economic blockade; and the government of Rhodesia was brought to its knees by sanctions, bearing in particular on the lack of spare parts for the helicopters it had previously been able to use to keep African guerrilla forces at bay. But in both cases, sanctions were not treated as a substitute for military force: they were applied in conjunction with it. It is when sanctions *are* seen as a substitute that they seldom or never work. But to end the digression, many social, political, and international debates over the applicability of sanctions in the contemporary era have shown how far the traditional criterion of last resort in Just War thinking remains apposite today.

The third criterion of jus ad bellum was that of what is frequently termed "restoration," but which might be more aptly termed, perhaps, "restitution." This is to say that the war must right an injury inflicted by one state upon another, or restore territory that has been wrongly seized. In a sense, this is simple. If a manifest wrong has been done, and if the intention is to put it right as far as possible, then the exceptional act of war can be morally justified. It might even be a manifest duty—much of the public debate in 1990 about whether the United Nations could be justified in using military force to expel the Iraqi invaders from Kuwait was couched in these terms. But restoration was also linked to the fourth criterion of jus ad bellum, namely that of "right intent." This is to say that the ruler (or state) who decides to go to war is concerned with the advancement of good and the avoidance of evil, rather than with taking advantage of a particular international situation to indulge the lust for power or sheer self-gratification. The trouble here is that right intent can frequently be adduced under the rubric of restoration, and that intervention with military means in a state's affairs by an external power can frequently be interpreted as so-called restoration without there being any right intent in the first place. The Vietnamese invasion of Cambodia in 1978 might be considered a case in point.

In addition to the above considerations, there was a fifth criterion, that of "proportionality"—namely that the evil consequences of going to war could not outweigh the evil that the war was meant to redress. This is of course a question that is seldom possible to answer in advance, but is one that, in the Just War tradition, had to be in the forefront of the minds of those whom the modern jargon calls "decision-makers." It also raises questions of practicality that were at first peripheral to thinking about jus ad bellum but that later became more central to it, particularly perhaps after the experience of the Crusades.

Thereafter, the sixth and last criterion to be incorporated into the tradition of jus ad bellum was prudential rather than moral in nature: there could only be a justification for going to war if there was a reasonable prospect of victory.

The second pillar of the Just War tradition, later to be expanded by Hugo Grotius and others in a juridical context, was that of jus in bello, or right conduct in war. The intent might be right, the cause just, and the prospect of success quite reasonable without entailing the risk of inflicting disproportionate evil. But if the conduct of the war itself broke the moral rules, then the war could no longer be just. In other words, it was not only considerations of strategy that were to be subordinate to moral considerations, but also those of military tactics. Later, during World War II, Churchill was to write in a memo: "It seems to me that the moment has come when the question of bombing German cities simply for the sake of increasing the terror, though under other pretexts, should be reviewed . . . the destruction of Dresden remains a serious query against the conduct of Allied bombing."[2] A serious query indeed, but in what framework?

If the Allies had had any notion of the ethical coherence that the Just War tradition had attempted to define and maintain, they would never have undertaken the bombing of Dresden. The jus in bello principle is quite explicit here: discrimination must always be maintained. Primarily, it refers to discriminating between combatants and noncombatants, but it might also be relevant to such matters as the selection of targets. That raises a difficult question, however, and one on which the Just War tradition is less coherent than it is on most points. If a military commander is seeking to attack a target that might be of considerable tactical significance, but also knows that any such attack would mean death and injury for civilians in the area, should he go ahead? The principle of "double effect" seeks to address this question by arguing that the attack could be justified if the intention is only to capture or destroy the military target and if any other deaths or injuries are only an undesired side effect (what is nowadays called "collateral damage"). An attack is not justified if the intention is also to cause such deaths and injuries. There are echoes here of the arguments of "right intent" and "proportionality" adduced in considering jus ad bellum, and one can see the kind of problems that the Just War theorists were grappling with when it came to applying their principles in bello. Nonetheless, the resort to "double effect" verges on casuistry, and opens the door to the unscrupulous. The use of precision-guided missiles against very carefully selected targets in Iraq during the Gulf War of 1991 might show an honest attempt to apply the idea in practice. On the other hand, it is not unknown for proponents of nuclear deterrence to argue that if a nuclear missile is directed against a military target, and if the deaths of a couple million people unfortunately ensue, without that being the prime intention, and if the adversary knows that such would be the case, then nuclear deterrence works—and works without breaking any moral laws. In other words, you can do what you like with "double effect," and it is the weakest part of the Just War tradition.

In all, however, the tradition represents a serious attempt, in reaction against both earlier Roman military assumptions and the experience of barbarian invasions, to bring strategic conduct into an ethical framework, and indeed to bring even the exceptional and abhorrent phenomenon of war within the compass of a theological whole. By the time that Saint Thomas Aquinas came to write his *Summa Theologica,* the attempt, precisely, to establish that theological whole against the challenges of Islam and of the heretics, he had devoted considerable attention to the Just War. But was it of any practical relevance to kings and commanders? The answer is twofold.

The first part of the answer is that the practical application was limited because the Just War applied only to conflicts between Christians. Its provisions were not applicable to crusades against the infidel or the heretic. The second part is that it could be surprisingly effective because of the established authority of the church. One can illustrate both points in a single historical instance. When Simon de Montfort was leading the forces of the king of France against Count Raymond VI of Toulouse in what was a protracted power struggle extending over many campaigns, both he and the king frequently attempted to persuade the pope to declare their campaign a Crusade. De Montfort had been frequently irked and frustrated by the restrictions placed on his operations, particularly because he had to call them off if the count could persuade a bishop to declare that the cause wasn't just. But the Cathar heresy was spreading in the count's territories at the time, and the count was accused of protecting the Cathars. The result was that in the end the pope made the required declaration, and the full horrors of the Albigensian Crusade were unleashed on southern France.

One would not wish to exaggerate the degree to which medieval military commanders studied and adhered to the principles of the Just War—of which a good many of them had probably never heard. But these principles were nonetheless a part of the immense moral authority of the *ecumen,* the universal church, which had important political implications. For the universal church was not just a church in the modern sense; it was also a powerful bureaucracy and political authority. If the most powerful emperor in Europe could come and do penance before the pope, shivering in the snow at Canossa, it was also true that the most obscure peasant could not be married or buried without the services of a priest. And if a prince were excommunicated, and his subjects continued to obey his orders, the territory could be laid under an interdict and those services withdrawn. That could play havoc with property rights if all children born during the period of the interdict were bastards; and it could also lead to epidemics caused by delays in burial. Indeed, the Republic of Venice at one stage suffered an outbreak of plague because bodies were not being buried while an interdict was in force. Rulers thus had very powerful incentives to obey the commands of the church, even where they might challenge the political power of the pope. And the moral laws were the same everywhere the church held sway.

The universality of moral rules had another implication—that there was no body of international law. International law only developed slowly as disagreements arose over the moral rules. Indeed its very existence is a testimony to the absence of any such agreement. For example, in the fourteenth century a knight could be tried and executed in France for the universal crimes of rape and pillage committed in Poland without raising any questions of extradition or national jurisdiction. But as disagreement arose over the authority of the church itself, it would become necessary to rethink the question of restraints on war, and the context in which strategy could be said to have served any ends other than those of efficiency in slaughter.

It is perhaps permissible in a book of this kind (which does not purport to be a work of history) to select certain historical "moments" as representative of a more complex historical process. The Reformation was one such moment. It was not the cause of the Christian challenge to the authority of the universal church, but the outcome of developments within the church itself and of many years of social as well as intellectual change. It was not an event, but a complex and long, drawn-out process. Yet one might say that the Reformation epitomized the collapse of the *ecumen* and led to a new kind of conflict in which Christianity was at war with itself. That conflict came to a head in the Thirty Years' War (1618–1648), which was one of the most brutal and horrifying in European history. It brought together many forms of power struggle, both economic and political, but it was also a war of religion, of Protestant against Catholic. It represented the politicization of religion, which was nothing particularly new (the Protestant Henry of Navarre had already declared that Paris was well worth a mass), but it also represented a religious definition of politics. In those terms, it was a war about everything, which is no doubt why it was so difficult to conclude. And it was also a moral war.

A war that is fought about the nature of God and of belief, about the eternal destination of one's immortal soul, is obviously difficult to conclude in a compromise peace. The combatants cannot simply sign an agreement that God shall be a Catholic on Mondays and Wednesdays and a Protestant on Tuesdays and Thursdays. The war must be fought to an end or else terminated by sheer exhaustion—as ultimately it was. It is also a moral war in the sense that the moral nature of the cause is invoked to justify even the most brutal and ruthless means of destruction. In itself, that perhaps continues a part of the Just War tradition, in which the criteria of restraint and proportionality had not applied to wars against the infidel or heretic, since it was a good end in itself to exterminate heresy or to drive out the infidel from the Holy Land. One can also see traces of the same assumptions in later wars, particularly those of this century, when moral ends were used to justify the most barbaric means. In these terms, the Thirty Years' War might be said to stand within a continuous tradition of Western conduct. But it also represented a sharp break with the tradition of Just War thinking. For previously, in terms of that tradition, the rules of the conduct of war were grounded in a universally valid morality (which was why "anything went" against those who denied such a universal proposition), whereas the Thirty Years' War was fought precisely to establish which grounds of morality were to dominate. In that sense, it ended in a defeat for all parties: nobody's morality was to triumph over anybody else's. The Peace of Westphalia, which ended the war in 1648, established what was to be the cardinal rule of international relations for the following centuries, namely that no state (or prince) had the right to interfere in the internal affairs of another. It confirmed and extended the principle of *cuius regio eius religio*—literally, "whose region, his religion"—which had first been laid down at the Religious Peace of Augsburg in 1555. In other words, a Catholic ruler would be able to decree all his subjects Catholic, and a Protestant ruler would be able to act in a similar fashion. One can only conclude that in respect of that for which it was ostensibly fought, the ferocity and horror of the Thirty Years' War had been all about nothing.

Augsburg and Westphalia did not altogether bury the Just War tradition. In fact it has found a new vitality in recent years, as attempts have been made to grapple with the ethics of war and of deterrence in the nuclear age. But they did mark the end of an age-old series of assumptions whereby the control of strategy and of the conduct of war had lain in the appeal to moral principle. The collapse of moral principle was now to have two contradictory results. The first was that a new framework, which had already begun to evolve in the period before the Thirty Years' War, would now become predominant. This is to say that the codification and acceptance of legal rules and restraints, sometimes implicitly and sometimes explicitly agreed, among the rulers of Europe, would supersede the older appeal to moral authority. This was made all the more possible by the prevailing social and political conditions in the latter half of the seventeenth century and the first three quarters of the eighteenth. These conditions will be considered in the next chapter. But among them was the fact that the secular power of Europe's monarchs now grew enormously and that the authority of the church was increasingly marginalized. That led to the second, and contradictory, consequence. Under the *ecumen,* the prince had derived his authority from God, and maintained it so long as he had the blessing of the church. But the principle of *cuius regio eius religio* now meant that in effect God derived His authority from the prince. It would not be long before the bolder spirits of the Enlightenment began to ask where, in that case, the prince's authority came from. Ultimately, such questions were to lead to the French Revolution and in consequence to the emergence of new kinds of war driven by nationalism and ideology. In a sense the old joke about it being too early to assess the consequences of the French Revolution is still true; but one can certainly say that among those consequences was the absolutism of strategy in the nuclear age, in its own terms peculiarly enlightened but also as peculiarly despotic as any eighteenth-century monarch.

Notes

1. Harry S. Truman, *Memoirs,* vol. 1, *Year of Decisions, 1945* (London: Hodder & Stoughton, 1955).
2. Quoted in Max Hastings, *Bomber Command* (London: Pan Books, 1979), pp. 414–415.

3

The Legal Tradition

The French Revolution might have been the historical turning point from which the ideological conflicts of the modern world ultimately derive, and it did in itself represent a new form of conflict that precipitated a revolutionary nation against the "legitimate" order of the European monarchs. Yet it did not seem at the time to indicate a breakdown of the common civilization to which all Europeans held. After Napoleon's retreat from Moscow and in the wake of his defeat at the Battle of Leipzig in 1813—grandiloquently known to contemporary annalists as the Battle of the Nations—the French emperor nonetheless still found time to make a detour to Weimar, where he invested the aging Goethe with the insignia of a chevalier of the Legion of Honor. It is worth perhaps recalling that Goethe held a political office: he was chief minister of state of the Grand Duchy of Saxony-Weimar-Eisenach, yet no one appears to have thought him a traitor for accepting this distinction. The assumptions of sharing a common civilization were still very strong indeed, and they persisted right up to World War I. So much so, that when the great French soldier and administrator Maréchal Lyautey heard of the outbreak of that war when he was in the depths of Morocco, he exclaimed: "My God! This is a European civil war."

To generalize: the framework of a common morality had broken down under the pressures of warring interpretations of the Christian faith, but had given way to the framework of a common civilization, in which international law was beginning to emerge and, more importantly perhaps in a discussion of war and strategy, common codes of conduct were being established. The idea of the "officer and gentleman" dates back to these codes, but they were not merely concerned with behavior on and off the battlefield; they were concerned with battle and with war itself.

Much of what is involved here was prearticulate. This is to say that there were no international agreements, no explicit recognition of a set of rules, and surprisingly little writing about the conduct of war. Yet one can see a consensus forming among rulers and commanders, probably unconsciously for the most part, after the Religious Peace of Augsburg. The main elements of this consensus really derive from the principle of *cuius regio eius religio,* in that it represents an agreement never to fight about religion again. Moreover, wars, no longer concerned with universal principles, came to be fought for the interests of states. The Austrian Empire was an exception, but France, Prussia, and Britain were emerging as recognizable states in the modern sense. Russia played very little part in the European system, preoccupied as it was with expansion to the east and south; and neither Spain nor Sweden was any longer a major force. In this context wars were fought over important but limited questions—the furtherance or prevention of a dynastic marriage, the control of a mercantilist trading advantage, a territorial settlement. In other words, they were fought over issues that war could actually decide rather than the imponderables it could not. In consequence, while they could drag on for long periods of time, they were yet limited in scope. And that limitation was the first major element of the prearticulate consensus of a common civilization.

The second major element was that of the limitation of the means of war themselves. Armies and navies were small, manned for the most part by professionals or mercenaries (the majority of the British forces who surrendered to the Americans at Yorktown during the American War of Independence were actually Hessians), and it was very much in their interests to avoid heavy losses. Campaigns were campaigns of maneuver, in which the avoidance of battle in unfavorable circumstances was just as important as being able to impose battle on the adversary when conditions were right. Indeed, one of the qualities that Clausewitz admired in Frederick the Great was his ability to outmaneuver the enemy and avoid giving battle. When battles did occur, they were bloody enough—there has never been a golden age of warfare—but by modern standards the level of destruction was remarkably limited. That is no doubt due in large part to the inefficiency of the weapons employed, but it should not be forgotten, after all, that those used in the Thirty Years' War had been even less efficient, yet the level of destruction and slaughter was vast. The contention here is that there was no inevitable relationship between the technological ability to destroy and the rate of destruction: a great deal depended on the way the opponents saw and understood each other. And mutual understanding was a distinct feature of the eighteenth-century war. At the Battle of Fontenoy in 1745, the French commander could gallop over to the English lines, doff his hat, bow from the saddle, and utter the immortal words: "Messieurs les Anglais tirez les premiers." As with many elaborate displays of French courtesy, there was sound tactical calculation involved—he needed to know more about the English order of battle—but the point is that he could come over and ride back without being shot at. Some years later, during the Napoleonic Wars, a British regiment earned the sobriquet "The Cherry Pickers," by which it was known until its forced amalgamation under the 1967 Defence Review, for pausing in the middle of hostilities to pick cherries. Yet battles were not frivolous affairs: not only were they bloody, but they were also regarded as decisive in settling issues and in determining the relations between states.

This indicates the third major element of the unspoken agreement that governed the conduct of strategy in this period. It was that states abided to a remarkable degree by the outcome of the battle. A major campaign would seldom have more than three or four battles to record; and once one or another army had been decisively defeated in the last, the war was over, and the losing power was ready to negotiate peace. It was a state of mind aptly summed up by the emperor Joseph II of Austria when he declared: "I have lost a battle, I must pay with a province." In retrospect, this willingness to accept battle as the arbiter of relations between contending states seems absolutely extraordinary. There was nothing to stop a defeated country from raising new forces and fighting on. Why should a defeat of one small professional group by another determine the conduct of state policy? That question can probably be answered at several levels.

The first view goes back to the limited nature of the objectives for which wars were fought at the time. It was probably cheaper and more expedient, if a state took a long-term view of its interests and its relations with others, to accept defeat over a less-than-vital matter, than to go on fighting. Such a view, of course, must have a corollary: namely that the victor would not seek to press the advantage home until the really vital interests of the vanquished were threatened. Again, this presupposes some kind of unspoken consensus; but it also has another name that characterizes a different level of answer: it is the "balance of power." As balance of power came to be recognized as a guiding principle of international relations, it became increasingly clear that the major competitors in the system had an interest in preserving each other's existence. Today's victorious enemy in a limited engagement might be tomorrow's valuable ally against a third party whose ambitions had become too threatening. In those terms, the acceptance of defeat was as necessary to the preservation of the system as a whole, as was moderation in victory. But there is a third level of explanation.

It has been argued above that most of the active powers in European affairs were now coming to resemble states in a recognizably modern sense. That is true, but they were also states with rulers, whose power for the most part was largely autocratic; and this power was grounded in the principle of legitimacy. However enlightened a despot might aspire to be in the Age of Reason, he or she did not push that aspiration to the point of questioning an inherent right to rule over subjects who had an inherent duty to obey—rather than participate in the conduct of affairs. The ruler's legitimacy was hardly threatened by small armies made up of professionals and mercenaries, but it could easily become much more vulnerable if the masses of the nation were conscripted into large fighting forces.

What this amounts to is that this kind of unspoken and probably unconscious consensus, which determined the conduct of war and allowed the battle to play such a decisive role, was grounded in a *social* consensus that was highly conscious and in which all the European rulers, with the partial exception of His Britannic Majesty, had a common stake—however competitive their relations might otherwise have been. It is interesting that the articulation of their common concerns lay in the emphasis that was given both in practice and in some of the influential writings of the late seventeenth and eighteenth centuries, to the formulation of the rules of diplomacy. Already in 1681 Abraham de Wicquefort had published his work on *The Embassador and His Functions,* a work that sees the European state system as a kind of society with recognized practices and rules of conduct.[1] In this sense the emergence of the state also meant the emergence of legal restraints on the powers of sovereigns vis-à-vis each other; and diplomacy was not merely diplomacy but also the application of international law, or the "Law of Nations" as it rapidly came to be called in the eighteenth century. Restraint on uninhibited power had passed from one domain of authority to another—from the spiritual authority of the church to the temporal authority of law itself. Even well into the eighteenth century however, most writers on this question did not regard such a transition as a clear break: they were anxious to convince themselves and others that the Law of Nations held an intermediary position between natural law (clearly a part of the Christian tradition), which applied to all mankind, and civil law, which applied to a particular state. But the point here is that, even in writing about diplomacy, attempts were being made to ground diplomatic conduct in a more general system of rules and restraints that applied to war as well as peace—and in that sense, a system that applied in practice some of the more general rules that had been enunciated in Hugo Grotius's classic work *De Jure Belli ac Pacis,* published in Paris in 1625.

Grotius has had several reputations over the past couple of centuries. In his own day his reputation arose from his writings on Christianity. Toward the end of the nineteenth century he came to be regarded as "the father of international law"—though in fact the grounds for such an accolade are slight, and in the opinion of one scholar seem to owe more to a zealous search late in the nineteenth century for a prophet of internationalism than to any distinctive contribution on Grotius's part.[2] More recently, political scientists and writers on international relations have seen in him the first founder of the tradition of rationalist thought and of the concept of "international society."[3] One can perhaps find pretty well what one likes in Grotius: his work appears interminable anyway. But his importance in this context lies in the fact that he extended the applicability of law to warfare. It was this principle that was extended in the middle of the eighteenth century by a writer who had been a practicing politician and diplomat, Emerich de Vattel.

Vattel's book, *The Law of Nations,* is in some respects an elaborate attempt to ground international law securely within natural law; and his manner of extending the principles of international law to the rules of warfare shows a continuing concern with the criteria of the Just War.[4] In that respect he could hardly be said to be a revolutionary thinker. Yet he does make a courageous and honest attempt to argue on both moral and practical grounds that what he calls "the voluntary Law of Nations" (the argument behind this choice of phrase is complex but irrelevant here) should be extended to states at war and armies engaged in warfare. Only if war is conducted within the context and under the control of wider legal and humanitarian considerations can it actually settle a dispute and limit the suffering it inflicts. Vattel is openly humanitarian (he was Swiss, and it is indirectly to him that we owe the Red Cross), but for him there was no conflict between the end of strategy and considerations of morality unless strategy were to be regarded as an end in itself.[5] That was not his idea of what was meant by a "society of states" or "voluntary Law of Nations."

His work epitomizes the fusion of the intellectual and social conditions that came to prevail under the ancien régime. A general international acceptance of the rules of legitimacy, which was the foundation-stone of a society of states, came to be articulated in practice by the conduct of diplomacy. The object of diplomacy was clearly to further the interests of one's own particular state, but it was also to preserve the society as a whole, and it accomplished that through the mechanism of balance of power. Equally, the objective of the balance of power was not to avoid war: on the contrary, war was an acceptable instrument of preserving the balance. (That is one reason why Kant was later to argue that a perpetual peace could only be brought about among states with republican constitutions—he saw very clearly the connection between the balance-of-power system and the self-interest of Europe's various dynasties.) But even if war was acceptable to the representatives of legitimacy, they also accepted the rules, chief among which was the decisiveness of battle. In the end, Europe was to discover that "legitimate" despots were not necessary to a society of states, but only at the price of discovering that battles were not necessarily decisive. Wars in consequence would become vastly more destructive and at the same time far less successful in settling anything. The philosopher and soldier who foresaw these dangers and argued that, in order to avert them, war would have to be conducted under strict political control was Carl von Clausewitz.

Notes

1. Abraham de Wicquefort, *The Embassador and His Functions* (Leicester: Leicester University Press, 1997).

2. See Maurice Keens-Soper, "The Practice of a States-System," in Michael Donelan, ed., *The Reason of States* (London: Allen & Unwin, 1978), p. 41.

3. Both Martin Wight and Hedley Bull are scholars in this tradition, the latter particularly in *The Anarchical Society: A Study of Order in World Politics* (Basingstoke: Macmillan Press, 1977). On Grotius and the study of international relations, see also Hedley Bull, Benedict Kingsbury, and Adam Roberts, *Hugo Grotius and International Relations* (Oxford: Oxford University Press, 1990).

4. Emerich de Vattel, *The Law of Nations: or, Principles of the Law of Nature, Applied to the Conduct and Affairs of Nations and Sovereigns* (New York: AMS Press, 1982).

5. Vattel also added a new criterion to the Just War tradition—namely that under jus in bello, war should not destroy "the work and monuments of civilisation." Later, in the twentieth century, that argument was advanced by some to justify the deployment of the "neutron bomb"!

4

The Political Context of Strategy: Clausewitz

The social and intellectual conditions that were sketched in the last chapter—an extraordinary confluence of Enlightenment reasoning and ancien régime legitimacy—might seem at first sight to suggest that by the time Emerich de Vattel was writing, war had already come clearly to be seen as a servant of politics. In a sense, that was true: war was not pushed beyond the limits of what the society of states as a whole could sustain; and even if the society of states was defined at times with a breathtaking cynicism (witness the successive partitions of Poland), there was still a fundamental agreement on the balance of power, which war served and which even the Polish partitions could be said to have maintained. But if within this context war could be said to have been the instrument of a general political system, it was also true that it lacked political direction.

What is meant here is that war was what happened when diplomacy had failed. Effectively, part of the implicit agreement that governed the emerging state system was that if political accommodation could not be reached, an issue in dispute was left to be resolved by war. Ambassadors asked for their passports and were escorted by the belligerent power to which they had been accredited to the frontier of the nearest neutral state. The military commanders then took over, and the dispute was resolved by force of arms. The ultimate military commanders were in any case frequently the monarchs themselves. Frederick the Great is the most notable example, but George II was also the last British king to command his troops in battle. There was more than an echo here of older assumptions that a ruler had to demonstrate his worth—indeed his "legitimacy"—by showing skill and courage in the field. But whether it was the monarch or some less sacrosanct figure who was in command, the main point is that politics had now been suspended and war had taken over. Careful and, generally speaking, restrained war, to be sure, but nonetheless war as the arbiter of political disputes, in which as suggested earlier, the decisive battle was also the arbiter of war.

Among aspiring officers, and in such military academies as existed, the histories of earlier campaigns were studied not to gain any insight into the interaction between military decisions and political consequences but to learn the tactical tricks of the trade in order to apply them the next time a military confrontation arose. Perhaps that helps to explain the extraordinary paucity of writing about war and strategy in the eighteenth century. Such writings as there were, as for example the works of Saxe and von Bülow, were not very much more than glorified military manuals, teaching the commander how to win. The discussion of war made extensive use of the arcana of French military terminology, as if to preserve its mystery and uniqueness, in the manner so effectively parodied by Laurence Sterne in *Tristram Shandy*. It was against this whole habit of thought that Clausewitz was to rebel, and it was indeed to von Bülow that he explicitly addressed his tract *The Warning*.

From the near-desert of the preceding discourse, Clausewitz's work emerges like a sudden and torrential river. That was not what he was aiming for. He aspired to a rigor and economy of presentation within a logical framework; and indeed he achieved that in book 1 of his masterpiece, *On War*. But that was the only part of his work that he was able to revise before his death in the plague of cholera of 1831, which also carried off Hegel, a philosopher with whom Clausewitz had many points in common. It would be erroneous to argue, though many have, that Clausewitz was in some sense a Hegelian, but both were concerned with the impact of the French Revolution on German society, both were anxious to reorder and held to redefine that society in terms of its own response not only to the Revolution itself but also to the emergence of the romantic historical consciousness. Yet Hegel, in a famous phrase, characterized Napoleon as "that World Spirit . . . dominating the entire world from horseback," whereas Clausewitz was passionately opposed to Napoleon as the principal threat to a European state order that was vital to preserve. Why should that be so?

An attempt to answer that question might help to elucidate the richness and variety of Clausewitz's thought, even though, with the exception of book 1, it is frequently incomplete, sometimes works at different levels—so that what he says about military operations can suddenly be seen to have wider and more general implications about both society and war—and can sometimes be downright inconsistent. That is why his dicta, usually taken out of context, have been adopted by military commanders and even political leaders of many different persuasions, and why he has attracted the opprobrium on the one hand of such people as the great British strategic writer Sir Basil Liddell-Hart (who denounced Clausewitz as an "apostle of mass slaughter") and the admiration on the other hand of the still greater and indubitably humane French philosopher and sociologist Raymond Aron (who called him a "noble soul"). In a sense, to use a sexist phrase, to every man his own Clausewitz. What follows here will be one person's attempt to portray the pattern of Clausewitzian thought in addressing the question indicated above. First, it is worth remarking that Clausewitz's whole life was dominated by wars of the French Revolution (he took part in his first battle at the age of thirteen) and by Napoleon's subsequent career. It is important to appreciate what those wars and that career did to the social and strategic assumptions of the eighteenth century.

The wars of the French Revolution were not those of one state against others within a society of states; they were the wars of a new society against the principle of legitimacy, which held the other society together. In fact, it was the monarchs of the old society who first attacked France in the name of that principle; but they were defeated. Subsequently, it was France that attacked Austria for internal political reasons of its own, and so embarked on a career of conquest that would eventually lead Napoleon to Moscow and ultimately to Waterloo. But the French armies, which won so many battles in between, were not the professionals and mercenaries of the ancien régime: they represented a nation in arms. One of the most misunderstood French phrases (particularly by Germans) is "la grande nation." Even today one can hear Germans quoting this phrase, usually with a resigned smile, whenever they are discussing some piece of outré behavior by the French, as if it referred to a self-image of France as a nation set apart from and superior to all the others. The fact that most French people do have this self-image is beside the point: what the original phrase referred to was the greatness of the nation as opposed to the pettiness of thrones. It was their readiness to spill their blood as the citizens of a liberated nation that did much to carry the French armies to so many astounding victories, even after Napoleon's crowning of himself as emperor in 1804 had made a nonsense of the ideals of liberty, equality, and fraternity.

In these terms, the wars of the French Revolution were the first ideological wars, and prefigured the atrocious ideological conflicts of the twentieth century. Napoleon himself attempted to preserve the European state system, even going so far as to marry into the Austrian imperial family; but that very act indicated that his attempt at preserving the system was predicated on making its other members subordinate to France. He was to discover, however, that it was impossible to preserve the system while destroying the balance of power. It was this combination of revolutionary fervor and the attempt to impose French hegemony that Clausewitz saw as a threat to the European state order itself.

There was a further consequence of the eruption into history of a nation in arms. Armies were now to become bigger than ever before. Not only did that change the nature of tactics, it now meant that whole societies would be fighting each other, and simultaneously that it would be harder and harder to define what they were fighting for unless, again, it was their beliefs. Strategy was to acquire a social base that, when galvanized by ideology, would make war more and more difficult to control—or stop. That helps to explain why Clausewitz insisted on the political control of war.

Within this general context, it will perhaps now be possible to get to grips with some of the central tenets of what Clausewitz was arguing. What sets him so apart from other strategic writers is that he is not primarily concerned with the conduct of war (though he certainly confronts it) but with the phenomenon of war itself. Others took war for granted. He asked what it was. It is for this reason that Raymond Aron called him the "philosopher of war."[1] His answer to his own question is twofold—and that duality has, it seems, given rise to many of the misunderstandings of what he was advocating.

First, he considers war as a principle or an idea, much as a classical Greek might have asked, "What is justice?" And in principle war is an act of unbounded violence by which one seeks to impose one's will on the enemy. The logic of war so considered points to the use of all means that are necessary to win, and its aim is the total destruction of the enemy's ability to resist—even, perhaps, the total destruction of the enemy itself. To this logic there are no limits. Clausewitz's detractors usually quote his discussions of the logic of war to conclude that he was indeed the ruthless apostle of mass slaughter. But that is to miss the point, which is that "Absolute War," as Clausewitz termed it, does not happen, and that in the wars that do happen, they do not obey that logic. Why?

The answer lies in his most famous aphorism (usually misquoted): "War is a continuation of politics with an admixture of other means." Those other means, to be sure, are force and violence; but one can already see how far Clausewitz had gone beyond the conventional thinking of the ancien régime, in which war represented a suspension of politics, and politics was resumed when the war was over. Clausewitz on the contrary considered war a ceaseless act of political communication, even between enemies, for the achievement of political ends. One can see here how important to his thinking was the idea of an underlying political order, as opposed to the sheer destructiveness of Absolute War. Absolute War had been waged in the past—in the destruction of Carthage by Rome or, in some senses at least, in the Thirty Years' War, but it did not represent the achievement of political ends for which Clausewitz was arguing.[2]

That raises a general difficulty with the study of Clausewitz. It has just been said that a principal contention of his was that wars do not obey the logic of Absolute War—but also now admitted that Absolute War has not been unknown. The question that follows is whether Clausewitz was writing a descriptive analysis of war or whether he was engaged in something more prescriptive: namely an analysis of what should be the prime considerations in the conduct of war if it were ever to make sense or be justified at all. The question is probably impossible to answer—again partly due to the incomplete nature of Clausewitz's work, and partly due to the fact that different parts of it were written at different times at which varying considerations, not all of a piece with each other, seem to have been uppermost in Clausewitz's mind. At some moments, particularly when he is concerned with operational analysis, he seems to be saying, "War is . . ."; at others, it seems clear that he is saying, "This is how we should think about it . . ." It is impossible to read him, or even try to write about him, without being aware of the tension between these two intentions and interpretations; but in moving from the considerations of Absolute War to those of war in the political context, it is not too misleading to present Clausewitz primarily as a prescriptive analyst. And there are indeed moments at which he seems to have been Hegelian enough to try to argue from the "what is" to the "what ought to be." That aside, he does adduce a number of purely descriptive forms of analysis when contrasting the logic of Absolute War with war as it occurs in the political context and in the real world. These can be summarized by the term "friction."

Clausewitz was in many ways a child of the Enlightenment, and heir to the assumption it had engendered that the axioms and achievements of science lay within the reach of any educated person. Gentlemen of the generation preceding his were fond of doing amateur optical experiments in their libraries with the aid of prisms, or of inventing cumbersome gadgets. It was natural for Clausewitz to think in terms of an analogy with physics; and what he meant by "friction" was just such an analogy—the "drag" encountered by a moving object, and that reduces its momentum, as it passes over a surface or through a medium such as air or water. The logic of Absolute War was in his view subject to just such friction; and it impedes the race to extremes that would otherwise characterize the actions of the adversaries.

Friction is not a single phenomenon: it takes many forms. In any society, there are conflicting economic demands to those of the war itself; and in most, the resources devoted to the "war effort" have, until the total wars of the twentieth century, been surprisingly small. The need for political support in prosecuting war, which any government requires, can impose its own form of friction: people are not willing to make indefinite sacrifices unless they regard the war as worthwhile; and in a strikingly modern phrase, Clausewitz says that "war can not be sustained without the enthusiastic support of the masses." That raises questions not only of politics but also of morale. In the course of World War II, and in his attempts to expand armaments production, Hitler's armaments minister, Albert Speer, advocated the conversion of German lipstick factories for the production of munitions: both needed cartridges. But he was successfully opposed by Josef Goebbels, the propaganda minister, who declared that he was not prepared to sacrifice the morale of German women in this way. And that was in the middle of what Goebbels himself repeatedly called "totaler Krieg." Clausewitz, incidentally, never refers to "total war," and this is one more indication of the fact that he regarded Absolute War as an intellectual proposition; but the forces of friction that he recognized do help to determine the nature of real war in the real world.

They operate, moreover, not only in a society at war but also in the conduct of the campaign. Like Napoleon, Clausewitz recognized the supreme importance of morale among the soldiers, particularly when the unexpected occurs or military planning goes astray—both of which are inevitable in any war. War, he says, is an activity in which even the simplest things become difficult, like walking underwater. And there is one further consideration that does not strictly belong to those of friction but that is convenient to raise here: the role of chance.

Clausewitz is almost impassioned in his emphasis on the importance of chance—an unexpected change in the weather, a breakdown in communication, faulty or misleading intelligence, the failure of reinforcements to arrive: any of these can shape the outcome of a battle. In one sense that is obvious; but in another, Clausewitz is stressing what the other strategic writers of his time, such as von Bülow or Jomini ignored. Their writings tend, as has been suggested, to set out the rules on how to win. Clausewitz emphasizes that there cannot be any such maxims. "Pity the poor soldier," he says, "who is condemned to crawl about amid the ruins of their rules."

The interplay of the forces of friction, the role of chance: these create the climate for what Clausewitz called the "fog of war"—a phrase that by now has been quoted almost to the point where its meaning is extinct, but that when he coined it was clearly meant to stand opposed both to the rationalist models of war put forward by other writers and also to the apparently implacable logic of Absolute War. If the logic is only apparent and if the rationalism is illusory, what does Clausewitz propose in their place? The answer is what he calls the "grammar of war"—which is the grammar of the political discourse between opponents to which military activity must be subordinate.

That helps to clarify what war in the real world, as opposed to the intellectual principle of Absolute War, consists in. Clausewitz ascribes a triple nature to war. At the first level, war can clearly not be fought without what he calls the "primitive violence of the people": the ability to take risks and the willingness to kill. Many take the view that such violence is endemic in human nature; and if they are right, war is not a particularly exceptional activity. But in the Clausewitzian schema, it is, because at the second level war requires this violence to be disciplined and directed. It is the commander who must make sense of the violence of war to achieve rational military goals. But the commander's definition of what constitutes such goals is itself determined at the third level by the political imperatives of the government he serves. Obviously, there is a certain tension between the first level and the second, and between the second level and the third; but taken together they constitute the triple nature of war, and can also help to elucidate its grammar.

Central to the interpretation of that grammar is the distinction that Clausewitz draws between two German words: *Zweck* and *Ziel*. In general terms, the first means "purpose," but in this context more specifically refers to the political objective for which the war is being fought. *Ziel*, generally speaking, means "aim," but again in context refers to what the military commander is trying to achieve. Clausewitz argues that the *Ziel* must always be defined in the context of the *Zweck* and be subordinate to it. At any military or indeed political briefing, when one hears a public relations representative of the armed forces or the government declare, "Our objective is . . . ," it is always worth asking oneself whether Clausewitz would have translated that as *Zweck* or *Ziel*. Brilliant victories are not necessarily very useful in themselves—as in contemporary history the Israeli forces have discovered on a number of occasions.

What then is victory? Certainly victory on the battlefield is indispensable—Clausewitz emphasizes that—but it is not the whole story. It *was* the whole story within the social and legal context of the ancien régime, whose unwritten compact was that one ruler or another would agree to abide by the outcome of the battle; and in those terms it was quite natural to assume that victory was *causal* in status. But in the absence of any such social agreement a victory on the battlefield can only be consequential in status.

To be more explicit: Napoleon was an innovator in many respects, political as well as military. He was a tactician of genius who handled larger bodies of men in battle than had probably ever been seen before, at least in Europe. His armies carried with them an implicit revolutionary message. Yet ultimately—as a strategist—he was a hidebound traditionalist whose success depended on the acquiescence of even more traditionalist princes in the old rules of the game. They were ready, when the rules dictated, to concede victory. For these reasons, perhaps, Napoleon did not recognize the full import of what he was doing when he led the armies of *la grande nation* against the European monarchy—until he got to Moscow. When he did so, the implicit political dialogue went as follows: "I have won." "Oh no, you haven't." "But I have beaten your armies in battle, and I've occupied Moscow." By all the traditional rules this should have been the end of the dialogue. But the riposte of the feckless, stubborn Russians was to say: "Very well, then, we'll burn it down." In the end Napoleon was forced to retreat, and the Russians had won the war of one society against another that the French had initiated in the first place.

In other words, victory, far from being causal in nature and imposed by one side upon another, is after all consequential. It depends upon the other's willingness to *accept* defeat. This was a lesson relearned by the forces of the United States after their series of victories during the campaign of the Tet offensive in Vietnam in 1968: the Viet Cong did not accept defeat, and ultimately the Americans went home.

What follows from this is not an account of what Clausewitz actually said, but it is derived from the many passages in his work that show how thoroughly he grasped the consequential nature of victory, and what victory thus meant in relation to the *Zweck.* If victory on the battlefield is to be translated into the attainment of a political objective, and if the victory of one side depends on the agreement of the other to lose, then that agreement will in turn obviously depend on what the stakes are. If the survival of a society is at stake, it is very hard to imagine that it would agree to lose. If it is a question of some matter of national interest—important to be sure, for otherwise why go to war, but not vital—then the loser in battle will in all probability begin to weigh up the costs and consequences of continuing to fight against those of sacrificing a particular interest. In such circumstances, a government might very well conclude that it is better to give way than to continue the struggle, and will accept defeat. But only if it knows that the political objectives of its opponent are limited. Thus, in terms of the grammar of war as opposed to the logic of war, *the best victory is a limited victory*—one with which both sides can live when the hostilities are over and the international state order is restored. Ideally, the best victory can lead to a lasting peace.

In October 1973, President Sadat of Egypt launched a surprise attack on the Israeli positions along the Suez Canal and in the Sinai Peninsula, in conjunction with the Syrian forces that were simultaneously attacking Israel from the north. President Sadat angered the Syrians (and some of his own generals) by not pushing forward once he had captured the initial Israeli positions. But his refusal sent a clear signal to the Israeli government that what he was interested in was regaining Egyptian territory, not in destroying the State of Israel. The result was that after some weeks of fighting and much complicated diplomacy, Israel agreed effectively to accept defeat, even though by then it was in a greatly superior military position. It agreed first to successive disengagements between the Egyptian and Israeli forces in the Sinai, and subsequently to returning the whole peninsula to Egypt in exchange for a peace treaty. This was a classic example of how a limited objective can be translated, even through battle, into a stable political relationship; and Clausewitz would have thoroughly approved.

The notion that the best victory is a limited victory also has operational implications. In book 6 of *On War,* Clausewitz discusses the relationship between the offensive and the defensive. He argues that the defensive is inherently stronger (a proposition of which the validity has perhaps somewhat fluctuated since) and goes on to suggest that the culminating point of victory comes when the commander can move over from the defensive to the offensive. It is, he says, the supreme genius of the commander to be able to recognize the culminating point of victory. But he then goes on to warn that this culminating point should not lead to new temptations. The prospect of more and more military successes might be so alluring that the commander might very well allow the war to run away with him. Operationally, this can be disastrous. Lines of communication can be overstretched, whereas those of the enemy become more compact; each new victory is purchased at a higher cost; and ultimately the initially successful commander might even end up facing defeat. History has many examples, ranging from the disastrous dispersal of Rupert of the Rhine's cavalry after the first phase of the English Civil War to Napoleon's momentous decision to advance on Moscow. But if one confines the discussion to military operations themselves, the culminating point of victory can be seen pretty well as a military form of cost-benefit analysis. The implications go beyond that, however.

When the North Korean forces invaded South Korea in June 1950, the response of the United States was swift. It intervened, and secured UN backing for an operation to liberate South Korea and drive the North Koreans back behind the thirty-eighth parallel. That was the original objective, and the wider *Zweck* might be said to have been to establish U.S. credibility in containing the forces of Communism worldwide. The intervention was effective: within a month of the Inchon landings, Seoul was liberated (though at a very heavy cost in casualties) and before long the North Korean forces were in full retreat. The immediate objective had been attained and U.S. credibility established. It was at this point, however, that the United States decided to widen the scope of the operations by invading North Korea so as to bring about Korean unification—and that turned out to prove a classic case of going beyond the culminating point of victory. China had, through various channels, given out a warning that it would regard a U.S. invasion of North Korea as a threat to its own security. In turn, it duly intervened, and it was not long before U.S. and other UN forces in North Korea found themselves being driven remorselessly back. It is often remarked in the United States that it was Vietnam that represented America's first defeat. It was not. That came in the second phase of the Korean War—and there could be no clearer evidence that this was so than MacArthur's desperate demand for the use of nuclear weapons—for which he got the sack. The Chinese "volunteers" were successful in driving the U.S./UN forces back down to around the thirty-eighth parallel, but it was now they who threatened to go beyond the culminating point of victory and invade South Korea even while the Panmunjon truce talks were taking place. It was only when President Eisenhower threatened that the United States would after all contemplate the use of nuclear weapons if the Chinese persisted, that a truce was agreed—one that still holds today and one whereby North Korean forces on the one hand and South Korean and U.S. forces on the other hand are separated by a rather wavy line running more or less along the thirty-eighth parallel.

What had happened here? First, MacArthur had allowed the war to run away with him, and in doing so had turned it from an operation originally designed to rescue South Korea and establish U.S. credibility into a major confrontation between the United States and China—in which neither side could afford to lose. That implied the possibility of nuclear war, but this was originally rejected by President Truman; and in effect, the United States retreated to the terms of its original objective. But when China tried to push beyond the terms of its original objective, President Eishenhower did after all invoke the nuclear threat. In each case, one of the contending parties, having moved from the defensive to the offensive, then allowed itself to pass the culminating point of victory and in so doing changed the original character of the war, on both occasions with potentially disastrous consequences.

What emerges from this particular instance is the advice that Clausewitz might have given, couched in more general terms than those of a purely operational analysis of the culminating point of victory. It is: Even at the height of success, stick to the war you were originally fighting, always bear in mind your original *Zweck,* and do not let some new, tangential military *Ziel* take over and transform it into another war. The consequences can be totally unpredictable.

At this point, it might be useful to summarize. Clausewitz sees war as a continuation of politics with an admixture of the means of force and violence. Within the context of international state order, this means that war, if it is to make any sense or have any justification, must be able to resolve a dispute and allow the contending parties to coexist thereafter. The fact that victory is only victory when one party agrees to lose means that victory is most effective when it is limited in scope. That reemphasizes the primacy of the political *Zweck* over the military *Ziel*. In those terms, it is vital for political as well as operational reasons not to pass the culminating point. So far, so good; but given the inherent difficulties of the fog of war, how does one attempt to achieve victory in the first place?

The answer lies in the Clausewitzian concept of the "center of gravity"—another analogy with elementary physics. Again, *On War* discusses this primarily in operational terms, but again it has wider implications. Operationally speaking, the center of gravity is the point on which the success of a military action will depend. Its nature will vary—Clausewitz gives no rules here, either. It might be the point at which the forces of two members of an alliance or coalition had planned to join together for an offensive. It might be the enemy's lines of communication, which, once cut, would cost the adversary the ability to fight on. (This can mean that wars can be won without epic slaughters. Later, Liddell-Hart was to elaborate on this as the "strategy of the indirect approach"; but for all his hostility to Clausewitz, such a concept is thoroughly Clausewitzian.) To strike at the *Schwerpunkt* is in this sense a question of economy and efficiency in warfare. But in a wider sense, and bearing in mind that war is a continuation of politics, one must ask the question: What is it that enables the enemy to fight this particular war?

To give a couple of examples: an extensive and sophisticated empire of some twenty million people was once conquered by a band of about four hundred scrofulous and semi-starving marauders. On the face of it that would seem impossible; but Pizarro's Spaniards had correctly identified the center of gravity of the Inca Empire as the sacred person of the Inca himself. Once he was killed, the Inca system of belief collapsed and the empire lost the will to resist. On the other hand, the mass bombing of Germany that was carried out by the U.S. and British air forces seems only to have reinforced the center of gravity of the Third Reich, which was the identification of the Nazi regime with the German nation, and stiffened German determination to resist. It might even have prolonged the war. One can certainly argue that the demand for unconditional surrender, of which the strategic bombing was the military expression, made it very difficult for the German armed forces to contemplate getting rid of Hitler and offering peace—though a few brave souls did try in 1944.

These two examples, one of success in identifying the center of gravity, and one of the consequences of the failure to observe it, indicate how far Clausewitz's thought about war went beyond the operational phenomena of warfare. For him, war was not only a continuation of politics; it was also an activity that took place within a social context—and about that he was highly explicit. He recognized that the armies of the French Revolution and of Napoleon could not be defeated by the old sweats of the ancien régime. Success in resisting Napoleon and in restoring the European state order would also depend on transforming the nature of that order and of the societies that it comprised. To this end, Napoleon made himself an ally of those who argued for political and social reform in Prussia—and many of them, like Scharnhorst, also saw military victory and social reform as interdependent. The king of Prussia temporarily and reluctantly agreed to certain measures of reform, but much of what was undertaken was rescinded after the victory of the anti-Napoleonic coalition. More generally, the consequences of that victory were contradictory. On the one hand, it did lead to the reestablishment of an international state order without any single dominant power, which was enshrined in the Concert of Europe. On the other hand, it led to a reassertion of the principle of legitimacy as enshrined in the Holy Alliance between Russia, Austria, and Prussia, explicitly dedicated to suppressing the forces of liberalism.

The state order more or less ensured peace for many years after 1815: a few balance-of-power wars were fought in Europe, but nothing of any great moment until German unification in 1871 shattered the balance. At the same time, however, the social transformations triggered by the French Revolution could not be suppressed even by the best efforts of the Holy Alliance. The result was that war was, so to speak, taken out of its social context. Yet vast changes in both society and technology were to transform the character of warfare and to belie the simple assumption that it could be seen as a political instrument without reference to the societies engaged. The consequences would not be fully appreciated until 1914.

This chapter has focused on Clausewitz because he represents the most comprehensive as well as the most valiant attempt to establish a framework for bringing strategy under political control. After his death he was widely regarded as exactly the opposite of what he would have wished to be: the logician of war, who laid down precepts on how to fight and win. Most of the commanders in World War I regarded themselves as in some sense or other Clausewitzians (except for the British, who tended to think of that kind of thing as Continental and far too intellectual). Yet they fought a war in which there was precious little remnant of any of the moral controls of the Just War tradition, only partial observance of legal constraints, and no semblance of a Clausewitzian *Zweck* at all. War itself, as Edmund Blunden wrote, became a God,[3] and in doing so created the conditions for that autonomy of strategy briefly discussed in Chapter 1, whereby the threat to destroy the world became the only apparent means of saving it. How this came about will be examined in the following chapter.

Notes

1. Raymond Aron, *Clausewitz: Philosopher of War* (London: Routledge & Kegan Paul, 1983).

2. Clausewitz had studied the Thirty Years' War and in particular the campaigns of Gustavus Adolphus.

3. Edmund Charles Blunden's poem "Report on Experience," reprinted in *Poems of the Great War, 1914–1918* (London: Penguin Books, 1998), p. 79.

5

The Transformation of War

Napoleon's march on Moscow was regarded at the time, and has gone down in history since, as an undertaking of epic proportions. Yet Napoleon never marched his armies over anything like the distances covered by Alexander the Great. The point here, however, is that the armies of both conquerors still marched; and in spite of the fact that warfare had seen many technological innovations in between, from the introduction of the crossbow to the use of artillery, there was a remarkable continuity in its essentials. Horses and shanks' pony were the only means of locomotion. The baggage trains either trundled behind, or an army lived off the country. For all the difference made by gunpowder, battles were still usually decided by the charge and by close combat. But warfare was soon to be transformed: Clausewitz and Napoleon lived at the end of an age of technological stability, and neither could foresee the effect of the technological changes that were beginning even in their lifetime. It is again one of Clausewitz's strengths that he did not lay down rules—they would not have lasted long if he had. The first technological innovation that was to lead to a transformation of warfare was an eminently peaceable development: the railway. What is generally recognized as the world's first railway was built between Stockton and Darlington in England in 1825 and was twelve miles long. By the time of the U.S. Civil War, less than forty years later, it is estimated that there were some forty thousand miles of railway in the world, much of it in the United States. The rapidly spreading network of railways was to mean that armies could now be transported to battle more swiftly and efficiently than had ever been imagined. Moreover, they could take their own supplies of munitions, food, and medicaments, in large quantities, so their size was no longer constrained by dependence on the baggage train or on foraging parties. Large armies would be able to confront each other very quickly and that in turn meant that logistics could be decisive in determining the battle. The pressures grew on General Staffs to plan the most efficient use of the railway systems—so much so that, as Michael Howard has pointed out, the commanders in chief of all the contending armies when World War I broke out were logisticians.[1] All, that is, apart from the Russians; and perhaps it's no accident that the Russian railway system was woefully inadequate. It was this very inadequacy that made it difficult for the Russian forces to stand down once they had been mobilized, and so helped to precipitate the war.

While the railway made it possible to get far greater numbers of men to the military theater far more quickly than ever before, another innovation made it possible to slaughter them far more efficiently. In the days when the standard small-arms drill was "Load, Aim, Fire," the gun was a pretty inefficient weapon. Snipers could kill people in exposed and static positions; but fast-moving targets were difficult to hit, and it is probably true that it took hundreds of rounds to kill or disable a single enemy soldier. The machine gun changed all that. As the rounds clattered through the breech, and as the gun swiveled back and forth on its mounting, the old drill was replaced by an action that was more like hosing down the garden. The machine gun represented an exponential leap in the lethality of battlefield weapons. As the saying went:

> Whatever happens, we have got
> The Maxim gun and they have not.

The effect of this new lethality was of course that as more and more soldiers were killed, more and more replacements became necessary, and the railway was happy to oblige. But that was to have profound social consequences. If the replacements are volunteers, they must believe in what they are fighting for, and it is very hard to appeal to such belief in terms of narrow state interests. The recruiting sergeant would not get much of a response were he to ask who was plucky enough to risk his life in order to maintain the neutrality of the Scheldt Estuary. And even if the replacements are conscripts and have no choice but to board the train, they must still be, as the modern jargon has it, motivated enough to take that risk when they arrive at the scene of the battle. The result was that the more murderous wars became, the loftier were the principles in whose name they were fought. In the British case, what began in 1914 as an expeditionary intervention in France after Germany had violated

Belgian neutrality, had become by 1917 "a war to end all wars" and by 1918 a war "to make a land fit for heroes to live in"—with its implicit promises of radical social reform. Some of the implications of such developments will be considered later.

Meanwhile other innovations were coming about, which also helped to change the character of war. Two of them derived from the huge cattle ranches opened up in the mid–nineteenth century in the United States and Argentina. The first was barbed wire, in its rudimentary form a device for keeping rustlers out and cattle in. But by the time that it was being mass-produced in great rolls in the early twentieth century, it did not take long to see its military implications. Here was a fortification far more efficient than any crusader's castle. In the end, even the stoutest castle wall will succumb to modern artillery fire. The rolls of barbed wire merely bounced. And these terrible bouncing walls had a lethality of their own: they were excellent at catching and holding, until they were bayoneted or simply died, such survivors as had made it across the murderous fire of no-man's-land. During World War I, barbed wire helped to ensure the supremacy of the defense—but on both sides. That was something Clausewitz had not envisaged: for him, war was much more categorically divided between the offensive and the defensive, and the culminating point of victory occurred when the commander was able to move from the latter to the former. Repeated attempts to make that transition during World War I only led to successive culminating points of defeat.

How then could the war have lasted so long? The fundamental answer lies not only in the supremacy of the defense but also in the fact that, as its principles became more grandiloquent, so it became increasingly difficult to define what the war was about and thereby to negotiate a peace. But an incidental answer was also provided by the cattle ranches: corned beef. This primarily, and also other forms of preserved food, made it possible to offer reasonable nourishment for years on end to very large numbers of men. Cattle became the fodder for the cannon fodder, and the tins of corned beef of that period were precursors of the "meals ready-to-eat" that have been staple to more recent campaigns.

In fact, first through the freewheeling activities of commerce and industry, and then increasingly through the direct intervention of the state itself,[2] Western society in the late nineteenth and early twentieth centuries had begun to develop a complex of technological changes that completely changed the character of war, making it easier to fight on and on, and harder and harder to win. Three more military innovations seemed to offer the chance of some kind of breakthrough in these circumstances. Each was to have enormous implications for the future, but although all of them were put to use in the years 1914 to 1918, they did not significantly affect the nature of the conflict.

The first was the aircraft—first flown in North Carolina only a few years before the war began, but nonetheless available in significant numbers by the time it was being fought. It accomplished nothing very much: light and vulnerable airframes, limited range, and minimal payloads ensured that it would be used primarily for reconnaissance and to engage in dogfights with other aircraft on similar missions. But a portent of things to come lay in the sporadic raids carried out over cities a long way from the front.

The second was the tank, first developed in Britain during the course of the war itself. It had certain obvious advantages on the battlefield: its armor plating was largely impervious to machine-gun bullets, and its caterpillar tracks could crunch up barbed wire. But limited production and unimaginative tactics ensured between them that its role would be very limited. It did not, as in World War II, prove a decisive factor in any military engagement.

The third, in a different strategic environment, was the submarine. In fact, a submersible boat had first been used during the U.S. Civil War; but it was not until the turn of the century that naval staffs in various countries had begun seriously to develop submarine programs. Their effect on the war was pretty negligible because there was no real war at sea—except in two respects: it was the British success at the Battle of Jutland in 1916 that enabled the economic blockade of Germany to continue, and it was the German torpedo attack on the *Lusitania* that brought the United States into the war in 1917.

The significance of these innovations in the context of World War I was this: that war demonstrated both efficiency in slaughter and the supremacy of the defense. It was a terrible combination that doomed millions to die for utterly futile reasons. The memory of that experience ensured that in the future, the attempt would be made to win quick, decisive wars. The German blitzkrieg tactics of World War II, using a ruthless and masterly combination of the tank and the aircraft, were a direct outcome of the prolonged indecisiveness of World War I. But the terrible irony is that the very success of the blitzkrieg, which ensured Hitler's mastery of Europe also ensured that in an attempt to break his hold, the Western allies would resort to the destruction of civilian populations from the air in a way that not even the most hardened World War I politician or general would have contemplated. That was partly an indication of sheer desperation, but it also indicated a major shift in the social and mental context of strategic thinking.

In 1937, when German "volunteers" fighting on General Franco's side in the Spanish Civil War deliberately bombed the civilian population of the small town of Guernica, public opinion worldwide was one of horror at this massacre from the air. It created such a resonance that it is probably still true today to say that Picasso's painting in response to the event is the most famous painting of the twentieth century. Yet only eight years later the official communiqué issued by the U.S. and British commands after the Dresden raids read in part: "The raids on Dresden were undertaken in order to impede German military movements. The fact that between 300,000 and 500,000 civilian refugees were in the city at the time must be regarded as a bonus." This was the voice of the champions of freedom and democracy, and it says much about what had happened to civilization by then. So does the fact that the British successfully maneuvered in the course of the preparations for the Nuremberg Trials to prevent Stalin from including the mass bombing of Soviet cities in the indictment of the Nazi leaders for crimes against humanity. How could it all have come about?

There are two answers, one "purely" strategic, the other relating to the more general context within which strategic developments had occurred. The strategic answer is that technological developments had made both the tank and the aircraft relatively efficient by 1940; and certain military thinkers had begun to explore their potential for future war. In the case of the tank these were Basil Liddell-Hart in Britain in particular, and also Charles de Gaulle in France—both prophets without much honor in their own country at the time. They envisaged wars of rapid maneuver, in which the nature of the maneuver would be able to dictate the nature of the battle and also reduce the appalling casualties of the set-piece engagements of World War I. What they do not seem to have envisaged, however, is that such tactics could be applied within the strategic context of total war and that much more than the outcome of a battle would be at stake. The greater the pity in such circumstances that while Liddell-Hart was virtually ignored in Britain, he was widely studied and admired in Germany—by none more so than General Guderian, who after he had conquered France in 1940 publicly declared that he owed his victory to Liddell-Hart.

In the case of the aircraft, the military thinker most commonly associated with its applicability to future war is the Italian airpower enthusiast Giulio Douhet, whose book *The Command of the Air* argued that wars could henceforth be won from the air. There is not in fact much evidence that Douhet was particularly influential, even though he was translated, but he did articulate, more coherently than most, many of the strategic assumptions that were then gaining ground. In one sense his work can be seen as a long extrapolation of Stanley Baldwin's saying that "the bomber will always get through." But whereas Baldwin said this in tones of near despair, Douhet was almost gleeful. If conflict was approaching, he advocated a surprise attack without declaration of war to destroy the enemy's air force on the ground. If the enemy did not have the good sense to surrender immediately, this was to be followed up by large-scale attacks on military and industrial targets so as to cripple the enemy's capacity to resist; and if that did not do the trick, then cities were to be bombed and civilians terrified by a mixture of incendiary and high explosive weapons (gas optional). In reality, Douhet was wrong on just about every count. It is very difficult to launch an effective surprise attack from the air (admittedly he wrote before the development of radar); it is even more difficult to destroy industry from the air (German industrial output in 1943 when the Western allies had secured command of the air was considerably higher than in 1940); and the bombing of cities stiffens the civilian will to resist.[3] What he said simply did not apply to the aircraft, though it might well have applied in later years to the first-strike missile (of which more later). Nonetheless, his pattern of thought is reasonably indicative of what first Germany and then Western allies attempted to do in World War II.

They would not have done so, however, had it not been for the change in the mental and social climate already mentioned. How can that be characterized? It is here that the escalating moral imperatives of increasingly murderous wars come back in—but they do so in stages. The first stage was probably one of pure propaganda: motivate the soldier and keep the home fires burning by emphasizing the nobility of the cause. But such propaganda confronts inherent and growing difficulties as rhetoric comes face to face with reality, and as the soldier himself becomes aware of the futility in which he is engaged and for which he is as like as not to give his life or face a permanent disablement. The language of ardent exhortation gives way to that of bitter disillusionment[4]—as not only the war-poetry of Wilfrid Owen or Siegfried Sassoon came to testify, but also as the demotic reactions of army songs on all sides, and of subsequent recollections, agreed. In the case of Britain and France, such reactions led to a profound distrust of the old ruling class, deepened by the failure of their victorious governments to deliver the kind of radical social reform that Lloyd George had implicitly promised when he spoke of "a land fit for heroes to live in." The subsequent upheavals in both societies can in large measure be attributed to the experiences of the war, but they were as nothing compared to the revolutionary effects produced in the more traditional empires of Austria-Hungary, Germany, and Russia. Revolution, and in most cases civil war, swept through their successor states.

If the first stage of the mental and social transformation that was taking place was the deleterious effect of propagandistically inflated moral claims, and the second was that of social upheaval, the third was that of ideological confrontation, aggravated by the failure of the League of Nations to provide a framework for the universal peace that it seemed vaingloriously to have promised. But in considering those confrontations—notably the competitive rise of Fascism (here taken loosely to include Nazism) on the one hand, and Communism on the other—one must step back a bit.

World War I was itself a symptom of a deep malaise in the European society of which the constituent elements had deemed themselves to form a common civilization. It was not a war between states about interests—although there were plenty of conflicts of interest—and was not inevitable in any such terms. It is perhaps always important to bear in mind that the historical procedure of explaining effect by cause does not necessarily mean that such and such a cause inevitably produced such and such an effect. One might be tempted to think so in reading, for example, the magisterial work of the Italian historian Luigi Albertini, *The Origins of War of 1914,* but in fact, as computer experiments have shown (insofar as one can place any credence in computer experiments), there were plenty of alternative outcomes to the interacting crises that confronted the European states in the run-up to the war; and as late as the end of July 1914, war was the least likely of these. But computers, whether for good or ill, are not privy either to human passions or to human intelligence. The war was an outcome of both these forces, and had indeed been prophesied by a remarkable array of writers and poets in the years leading up to 1914—not all of them in Vienna, although that is where it is now fashionable to locate the evolution of the modern European consciousness.[5]

All the same, one remarkable Viennese writer, Karl Kraus, was already engaged on his discursive epic play *The Last Days of Mankind,* in anticipation of the self-destruction of civilization that was soon to come. He, and others like him (there were, incidentally, no others like him), stood out in sharp distinction from the *bien-pensant* liberal positivists of the nineteenth-century tradition. Their successors today read *The Guardian* and have muesli for breakfast. They assumed that the economic interdependence of the European system made war irrational—in which they were right—and therefore impossible—in which they were wrong. One of the chief proponents of this school of thought was Norman

Angell, whose book *The Great Illusion,* which adopted that line of argument, was published just five years before World War I broke out.

But if one looks back at the issues of *Die Fackel,* the journal that Karl Kraus published in the early years of this century, one can see his awareness of dark, irrational forces at work in European civilization, which were practically clamoring for disaster. And well before that, Nietzsche had written an uncannily accurate prophecy of the twentieth century. Struggling to cope with the death of God, men will, Nietzsche says, build societies that try more comprehensively than any before them to take care of their members, and to provide for the old, the poor, the sick, the disadvantaged. In the same passage he says: "There will be wars the like of which have never yet been seen on earth."[6] Nietzsche was not arguing that the welfare state is bound to fight terrible wars but rather that both the welfare state and the wars themselves are symptoms of a breakdown of all the beliefs to which humans had hitherto clung; and that the nineteenth-century belief in progress, which he emphatically did not share, was not substitute either for belief in God or for the courage to confront life without God. It is more than intellectual whimsy to suggest that if the Thirty Years' War had been a war about beliefs, World War I was a war about the lack thereof.

In any case the old, positivistic, rationalist optimism that had characterized the liberal belief in progress had already taken a severe intellectual knock or two well before the war broke out. Quite apart from the work of Nietzsche himself, Freud had become the center of much animated discussions after the publication of *The Interpretation of Dreams,* which suggested that humans were really wildly irrational. Einstein's special theory of relativity put an end once and for all to the comfortable view that the universe could be understood in terms of Newtonian physics. The first Cubist salon had made a nonsense of supposed realities of perception. Indeed, far from being a golden age of tranquillity before the deluge, the Edwardian era, the belle époque, and their counterparts elsewhere must have been very uncomfortable for anyone who had their wits about them.

Perhaps there were not many such; but certainly one can discern a generalized questioning of the old assumptions, even in what was now becoming the tabloid press. That phenomenon obviously owed its very existence to the spread of mass literacy—but mass literacy was not so much the sign of an educated society as a symbol of alienation on a grand scale. The popular press helped to fill a vacuum in religious belief or in deeply held values by appealing, in most countries at least, to a new kind of assertive jingoism. Nationalism became the means by which industrialized mass societies were able to masquerade as communities in the absence of more traditional beliefs[7]—but when the nation-state itself was destroyed by World War I or at least no longer commanded any unquestioning allegiance, the need to believe in *something* became increasingly acute. And in circumstances of social chaos, and apparent intellectual chaos too, when even "science" no longer appeared to make sense, new and strident ideologies had a terrible emotional appeal.

What the Spanish philosopher José Ortega y Gasset called *The Revolt of the Masses* rapidly took an ideological form, and the secular religions that the competing ideologies represented were soon to mobilize the masses into fighting more ruthless and destructive wars than anything hitherto known. The series of conflicts generally called World War II represented par excellence what Nietzsche had evocatively termed "the wars of the spirits." In many respects World War II can still be seen as a war between states, but underlying that was a war between societies and beliefs determined to destroy each other. The destruction of populations by each other was not merely some regrettable military necessity but an active principle, an aim in itself; and that extended not only to the overtly ideological combatants but also to such apparently nonideological belligerents as Britain and the United States—as can be seen in the Dresden communiqué quoted earlier. In that respect the war represented the final stage of the social and mental transformation that enabled the new technologies to be so murderous; and that is why it was suggested earlier that the nuclear weapon, offspring of World War II, was not so much a revolution as the logical culmination of the interacting social and technological transformations that had been going on for years.

The answer to the revolt of the masses was the weapon of ultimate mass destruction. But it wasn't quite the answer, as the circumstances make clear. The nuclear weapon was developed by the Western democracies—Britain and the United States and Canada, in that historical order.[8] The British began to develop it for fear that one ideological monster, Hitler, would do so first. Later on the United States joined in the search for the same reason, spurred by Einstein's famous letter to Roosevelt. Subsequently, the United States was to develop the thermonuclear weapon, in spite of Truman's initial reluctance, for fear that another ideological monster, Stalin, might get his hands on it first. In other words, these weapons of ultimate destruction came into existence as a reaction to the totalitarianism that might have authorized their extensive use.

But it was their nonuse that was to revolutionize strategic conduct even while it appeared that their very presence might help to keep totalitarianism at bay. It was these twin considerations that led to the autonomy of strategy that has characterized the nuclear age. The transformation of war between Napoleon and Hitler meant the almost complete breakdown of any systems of moral, legal, or political control. The implicit promise of the nuclear age was that strategic threats themselves could provide a new framework of control. But on what basis could that possibly work?

Notes

1. Michael Howard, *War in European History* (Oxford: Oxford University Press, 1976).

2. See Maurice Pearton, *The Knowledgeable State: Diplomacy, War, and Technology Since 1830* (London: Burnett Books, 1982).

3. See Sir Charles Webster and Noble Frankland, *The Strategic Air Offensive Against Germany,* vol. 4, *Annexes and Appendices* (London: HMSO, 1961).

4. See Paul Fussell, *The Great War and Modern Memory* (London: Oxford University Press, 1977).

5. For example, Friedrich Nietzsche in Germany, Andrey Biely in Russia, Robert Musil in Austria, Gerard de Nerval in France, and Gilbert K. Chesterton in England.

6. Friedrich Nietzsche, *On the Genealogy of Morals and Ecce Homo,* translated by Walter Kaufman and R. J. Hollingdale (New York: Random House, 1967), p. 327.

7. I have argued this at greater length in "The Twentieth Century as Self-Conscious History," in Nobutoshi Hagihara, Akira Iriye, Georges Nivat, and Philip Windsor, eds., *Experiencing the Twentieth Century* (Tokyo: University of Tokyo Press, 1985).

8. It should be made clear that although Canada was involved early on in the development of the nuclear weapon, the Canadian government took the deliberate decision in 1946 not to manufacture the Bomb.

6

The Evolution of Strategic Thinking: Stage One

The early pattern of strategic thought after World War II was dominated by U.S. assumptions and preoccupations. Indeed, these have helped to shape all other forms of thought about the strategic role of nuclear weapons ever since—either by reaction to U.S. views, or by imitation of them, or both. There are two reasons for this U.S. dominance. The first is straightforward, though not quite so straightforward as it might appear. The second is inherently more complicated.

The straightforward explanation can be summarized succinctly: in the immediate postwar years, the United States was the only power that possessed the Bomb. What use it chose to make of this instrument of mass destruction would inevitably determine the developments of international politics in many ways, including the confrontation with the Soviet Union and the assurances that the United States was able to offer its allies. Yet the historical reality was nowhere nearly so clear-cut as that. Quite apart from developments in the Soviet Union, which will be considered in Chapter 9, there is a fundamental paradox in the apparent U.S. monopoly of nuclear weapons. The first part of this paradox lies in the fact that the United States was *not* the only power to possess the atomic bomb in 1945. The Manhattan Project, the program that had developed the nuclear bomb in the United States, was not a purely U.S. undertaking, but depended on international agreement, and was indeed based on a free gift made by Britain to the United States of the details of the technique of fast-neutron bombardment that had been developed in London in 1942 (albeit by two German-Jewish refugee scientists). Before the war ended, the United States and the United Kingdom had agreed that neither government would use the nuclear bomb without the consent of the other—and in that sense, although the weapons dropped on Hiroshima and Nagasaki were dropped from U.S. aircraft, the atomic bombing of Japan was just as much a British as a U.S. responsibility. But in the course of the next couple of years, the United States arrogated to itself all control over nuclear weapons. Not to put too fine a point on it, the United States hijacked an international program—partly by congressional resolution and partly by executive decision—and made it a purely U.S. concern. The culmination of this process came when the British prime minister, Clement Attlee, visited Washington and reminded President Truman of what had been the agreement. After some initial stout denial that any such agreement existed, the U.S. government was later forced to concede the case. Dean Acheson, who was present at the time and was later to become U.S. secretary of state, makes this point in his memoirs.[1] In adopting this position, the United States effectively became the first country in the world to pursue a national nuclear weapons program, and by so doing initiated the process of nuclear proliferation that it has tried so hard to resist ever since. But why should that be part of a paradox?

The answer is that while this act of bad faith showed how keenly the U.S. government appreciated the importance of nuclear weapons (an appreciation that was also shown by the Baruch Plan, of which more later), it demonstrated at the same time an almost stupefying lack of seriousness in its original approach to the possession and use of the Bomb. In spite of Bernard Brodie's memorandum (as mentioned in Chapter 1), the majority of U.S. strategists, certainly the great majority of those in uniform, regarded the nuclear weapon as an answer to the problems of attrition, and little else. From now on it would be possible to flatten a city without incurring the loss of scores of expensive aircraft and expensively trained pilots and navigators. Otherwise, it didn't seem to make much difference. If one looks at the U.S. congressional debates in 1947 over the future of U.S. strategy, they are dominated by the question of universal military training (i.e., conscription) rather than by any nuclear considerations. Moreover, the United States was hardly bothering to produce the weapons themselves. It is possible to deduce from the memoirs of David Lilienthal, the first chairman of the Atomic Energy Commission, that by the time the Korean War broke out in 1950 the total number of weapons in the U.S. nuclear stockpile was still in single figures. There is also an illuminating passage concerning a meeting he had with President Truman, in the course of which it transpired that neither of them actually knew where the bombs were.[2] So on the one hand, the United States clearly took nuclear weapons extremely seriously, and on the other hand treated them in a manner that bordered on frivolity when it came either to their production or to their strategic application. It is possible, however, to resolve the paradox.

At one level, the resolution seems to lie in the fact that, so long as the United States had a monopoly of nuclear weapons, it would not be obliged to worry too much about their implications. That might help to explain the behavior of the United States toward Britain; but more importantly, it is also worth recalling in this connection that at the time even the most pessimistic intelligence estimates were suggesting that the Soviet Union would not be able to explode its own bomb before 1954. Even as the Cold War was developing, the United States might seem to have had a breathing space in which to address the formulation of nuclear policy. It is in that context, perhaps, that the Baruch Plan can be best understood. The plan was an offer, made in 1946, to create an international authority to supervise all forms of the application of nuclear energy. Under its terms, the United States would renounce the production of nuclear weapons if all other states did likewise. The plan was of course rejected by the ever mistrustful Stalin, and it is perfectly possible that such a rejection was foreseen. But there are no particular reasons to doubt its sincerity, and there are many reasons to believe that after Hiroshima and Nagasaki, President Truman was extremely reluctant to contemplate a future based on nuclear strategy. But such a future was of course to come about, and it was to be, as suggested earlier, the United States that dominated the formulation of nuclear strategy itself. It is here that the second and more complex set of considerations indicated above come into play.

To understand those, one must appreciate the general nature of the U.S. position in international politics after World War II. In a very short time the United States had been transformed from an isolationist country, anxious to keep its distance from the conflicts of other nations, into the most powerful participant in the international system. By 1943 it had come to assume the leading role in the formation of Allied strategy for the conduct of war. By 1944, with the Bretton Woods agreement, the U.S. economy assumed the role of the underwriter of the world economic system in the period of postwar recovery—and it would soon be clear that it would not only be the underwriter but also the generator. By 1945, Roosevelt was making plain his view that the future of the world would depend on the relations between the United States and the Soviet Union. Truman took office with a deep-seated aversion to the Soviet Union, which Roosevelt had not shared, but he did not dissent from that view. By 1947 the Truman Doctrine proclaimed the responsibility of the United

States for the global containment of Soviet power and the Communist ideology. By then, indeed, it was obvious that all forms of power—economic, political, military, technological—were concentrated to a higher degree in a single center than had been the case at any time since that of Antonine Rome. In fact it is hardly an exaggeration to say that in all essentials the United States was not just the most powerful participant in the system: the United States *was* the system. And in general, and in spite of some initial hesitations and some voices such as that of Senator Robert Taft, calling for a return to isolationism, the U.S. legislative and executive branches adopted this new role with enthusiasm.

In this context it seemed to be natural and proper that the United States as guarantor of global stability and recovery should have a monopoly of nuclear weapons. But a monopoly was not the same thing as an active strategy: it was more important that other countries should not possess them than that Washington should know what to do with those nuclear weapons it did possess. In that sense one might almost say that the absence of a strategy was America's first goal. But when it became clear that the future would indeed be concerned with nuclear strategy, it was taken for granted that the strategy would be American: just as global economic recovery depended on the dollar, so global security would depend on the U.S. nuclear bomb. Some writers have suggested that there is a high degree of semiconscious ethnocentrism in U.S. strategic thinking,[3] but while there is no doubt much truth in that, the early formulations of U.S. nuclear strategy were quite self-consciously and resolutely American, based first on the assumption of a nuclear monopoly and subsequently on a determination to maintain nuclear superiority into the indefinite future.

A conscious policy of nuclear deterrence, and a strategy directed toward that goal, nonetheless took some time to develop. Indeed it was not until 1954 that nuclear deterrence became officially integrated into U.S. foreign policy. When it did, it was on a global and comprehensive scale. But along the way, one can discern certain indicators pointing to that development.

The first of these was a commissioned report from what was then a recently established advisory body, the National Security Council (NSC). Generally known as NSC 68, the report was produced under the chairmanship of Paul Nitze, who was to be for many years one of the most influential figures in U.S. strategic policy, and subsequently in arms control negotiations. It advocated threatening the use of nuclear weapons to deter "Communist aggression" anywhere in the world. It was presented to the NSC in 1950 and foreshadowed much of the policy that was to be implemented in 1954. And even while deterrence had not yet become official, one can also see that at that time it was coming into operation. In 1948 the United States moved B-29 bombers to bases in Britain and Germany, which meant that Moscow was within their range. Stalin appears to have assumed, erroneously, that the bombers had nuclear weapons on board; and the negotiations over the Berlin Blockade, which were in progress at the time, quite suddenly assumed a tone of sweet reason. Nuclear deterrence was creeping into the conduct of international relations through the back door.

But it was in 1949 that a conscious and momentous decision had to be made, one that was to shape the future of strategic thinking. That year saw the explosion of the first Soviet atomic bomb, to the astonishment and dismay of everyone in Washington. But it also saw the successful testing at the Livermore laboratory in California of the fusion process that would make the hydrogen bomb a practical possibility. Its father, Edward Teller, was anxious that the United States should proceed to develop it at once, but Truman was extremely reluctant, and for very good reasons.

When the first nuclear weapon was successfully tested at Los Alamos in 1945, Robert Oppenheimer, the leader of the team that developed it, records that he recited to himself a line from the Bhagavad Gita: "I have become as death, the destroyer of worlds." Actually, that says more about Oppenheimer's ego than it does about the power of the atom bomb. Fearful though it is, its destructive power is relatively limited. But the H-bomb represents an exponential leap: it is as much more powerful than the A-bomb as the A-bomb is than conventional high explosives. It really could be the destroyer of worlds; and Teller's success led to much agonizing in the U.S. government, subsequently characterized as "the H-bomb debate."

Those who were against the production of thermonuclear weapons argued that if the United States went ahead, the Soviet Union would at some point inevitably follow suit and that the world would be doomed to a future in which its very existence depended on the confrontation between two (or even more) hostile powers. This was initially Truman's position. Those who were in favor adduced a variety of reasons, some of which were little more articulate than the proposition that "if we *can* do it, we *ought* to do it." But the clinching argument, and the one that finally persuaded Truman, lay in the question: "What if we don't do it and Stalin does?"

It is worth pausing for a moment here. The most unimaginably destructive weapon yet devised was not developed to serve any purpose at all except that of deterring the use of a similar weapon in other hands. After a long detour, in the course of which the H-bomb appeared to be capable of serving other purposes, it seems to have been acknowledged by both the United States and what is now Russia that deterrence was really all the H-bomb was good for anyway; and in 1992 both countries came to the logical conclusion that in that case they would be able by mutual consent to destroy the majority of their stockpiles (the START II agreement).[4] But in the interim it was the production of the H-bomb on both sides that made the problems of nuclear deterrence increasingly complicated.

That is looking ahead, however. At this stage, while the United States was fully committed to the containment of Soviet power, that commitment had been formulated primarily in economic and political terms.[5] Containment was now also to assume a military form with the formation of NATO, again in 1949. But the militarization of containment did not yet mean its nuclearization. The North Atlantic alliance will be discussed in Chapter 10, but one should emphasize here that while it represented U.S. commitment to come to the aid of Western Europe in the event of a Soviet attack, it was initially expected that any hostilities would be between conventional forces, the great bulk of which would be drawn from the European countries themselves. The alliance represented a revolution in U.S. foreign policy—the country whose first president had warned it against "entangling alliances" was now committed to the most entangling alliance in history—and a clear warning to the Soviet Union that it should not miscalculate. In contrast to the two previous world wars, the United States would join the next on Day One.[6] One might say that the United States was now engaged in an active policy of deterrence. But in spite of the experience of the Berlin Blockade, deterrence was not based on nuclear weapons. What changed everything was the Korean War.

The North Korean invasion of the South in June 1950 was immediately seen as a test-case of U.S. resolve in containing Communist aggression. This was surprising in the sense that Korea had not been mentioned when Dean Acheson, by then secretary of state, had outlined what he called the U.S. "defense perimeter" a little while before. Nonetheless, U.S. (and other) forces were committed to Korea under the mandate of the United Nations, and rapidly succeeded in driving the North Koreans back. What followed was three years of bloody warfare, largely because the U.S. commander and his political masters, heedless as they were of Clausewitz's arguments about the culminating point of victory, and heedless too of Chinese warnings, invaded the North and so brought China into the war. It was when MacArthur was in danger of being overrun that he got the sack for advocating the use of nuclear weapons; and this episode clearly demonstrated that the United States was not yet prepared to turn military containment into nuclear containment. (There were other arguments: the United States had very few nuclear weapons anyway, and it wished to preserve those it had for possible use in the European theater in case Stalin saw the Korean War as a diversion of U.S. power to the East, which would give him the opportunity to attack the West. But the fact that MacArthur was sacked shows the importance that Truman attached to maintaining the principle that nuclear weapons should not be used.) Yet in the end the Korean War did much to determine U.S. reliance on nuclear deterrence to contain the Soviet Union in the future. There were several reasons.

In the first place, the war itself greatly stimulated the production of nuclear weapons in the United States. It also stimulated the production of aircraft, including long-range bombers. More immediately, the war led a U.S. president for the first time to threaten a country directly with nuclear attack. When the Chinese in their turn passed the culminating point of victory and seemed set to invade South Korea, Truman's successor, President Eisenhower, made it clear to them that the United States might after all "go nuclear." The threat, as indicated earlier, had a powerful effect and did much to hasten progress at the Panmunjon truce talks. What had been a matter of indirect assumption at the time of the Berlin Blockade was now a matter of open policy. In turn, that testified to the fact that the war was not only bloody but also highly expensive and increasingly unpopular: Eisenhower had, after all, been elected president because of his promise to bring the troops home from Korea. And if the United States were to hold to its commitment to the global containment of Communist aggression, which had led to the Korean War in the first place, the pressures would be strong to do so by other means than fighting conventional wars.

If one looks at the vast peripheries of China and the Soviet Union, and contemplates the myriad points of conflict that could lead to local wars involving one or other of them in a period as tense as the early years of the Cold War, it is easy to see that the United States was simply incapable of allocating forces for every contingency. In sum then, the Korean War began as a demonstration of containment by conventional means and ended as an instrumental argument for nuclear deterrence.

In November 1952 the United States successfully tested its first thermonuclear weapon on the Eniwetok atoll in the Pacific.[7] It now had a monopoly of the H-bomb, which was expected to last for several years, a rapidly growing stockpile of A-bombs, and a large fleet of bombers of intercontinental range deployed on bases in Japan, the Middle East, North Africa, and Western Europe. The Soviet Union, though it was in fact to detonate its own thermonuclear weapon much sooner than expected (the so-called Joe-4 test in August 1953), had no aircraft that were capable of reaching the United States.[8] In effect, therefore, the United States, while it now had no monopoly of nuclear weapons and was soon to lose its monopoly of thermonuclear weapons, did have the most important monopoly of all—that of the capability of attacking the Soviet Union from a variety of angles while remaining invulnerable itself. It was in this context that a new policy of global containment of Soviet power by strategic nuclear threat came to be formulated.

That policy reflected many of the recommendations of NSC 68, but it was expressed in a manner at once more vague and more comprehensive than that of the earlier document. It was outlined first in a speech by Eisenhower's secretary of state, John Foster Dulles, in January 1954, and then more magisterially in an article he wrote in the influential U.S. quarterly *Foreign Affairs* in April of that year.[9] (The same journal had published George Kennan's original proposals for the political and economic containment of Soviet power in 1947.[10] A comparison of the two articles provides an illuminating summary of how far strategic principles had now come to dominate the formulation of foreign policy, and in such a very short time.) The new U.S. strategy rapidly became known as "massive retaliation."

Although Dulles does use the word "massive" in describing U.S. retaliatory power in the event of Soviet aggression, the principal characteristic of the new strategy was not that it was committed to the mass destruction of the Soviet Union if hostilities broke out, but that the United States had the ability and the intention to retaliate in places and in a manner of its own choosing. In the event of another attack like that in Korea, it would not necessarily respond by fighting on the ground but would attack instead according to political or budgetary taste. "Arbitrary retaliation" would have been a better term for it—but the import is clear in either event: from now on, the Soviet Union would not be able to calculate the risks it ran if it sponsored or took part in aggression anywhere in the world. It might risk the destruction of its industrial heartland in the Donbass basin, or even of Moscow itself, for the sake of comparatively minor gains in the global power struggle elsewhere. The assumption was that if the Kremlin could not calculate the risks, it would not take them, and so deterrence would be effective. In this sense, massive retaliation brought into play one of the principles that remained central to the conduct of nuclear deterrence ever after—namely that the potential risk to an aggressor should always outweigh any conceivable gain the aggressor might have in mind. The operation of that principle was to become increasingly complicated, but at the time it all seemed beautifully simple. Given the ability of the United States to strike at the Soviet Union without risking any retaliation in return, it was surely self-evident that nuclear deterrence could be relied on as the main instrument of U.S. foreign policy.

It is difficult now to see massive retaliation in its contemporary context. Certainly, the idea that any war anywhere could instantly become a nuclear war was enough to horrify millions of people and was bound to make the United States appear aggressive in the extreme—an impression that was sometimes strengthened by the pronouncements of such people as the U.S. Air Force Chief of Staff General Curtis E. LeMay, whose approach to strategy might be summed up as "Aw, Hell, let's drop it." Equally, it is clear that Dulles had abandoned any notion of moral restraint in warfare, dour and self-righteous Presbyterian though he was. But that said, massive retaliation can yet be seen as a rational attempt to make deterrence work and to keep global peace at a bearable cost. It was also, clearly seen as an interim strategy, one that could only work so long as the United States remained invulnerable—and nobody in their senses could expect that to last for more than a few years. What has not been appreciated until recently is that the interim nature of this strategy had a further implication: Eisenhower was no friend of nuclear weapons; and he hoped that massive retaliation would bring the new leadership of the Soviet Union to negotiate nuclear disarmament while it was to its advantage to do so.[11] (That is not the effect it had, partly because of Dulles's repeated threats to take the Soviet Union to the brink of war.) In general, the new strategy was simple, rational in its own terms, and promised to be effective.

In a sense, it was. The years of the mid-1950s were replete with international crises, but throughout that period the Soviet leaders behaved with great caution, and even showed anxiety to reach agreements that they might otherwise not have pursued, as for example in the Geneva Accords on Indochina in 1954. But all the same, the new strategy had serious disadvantages. The first lay in a flawed assumption—that the "Communist bloc" represented a monolithic empire whose leaders took their orders from Moscow. It was not, and they did not—or at least only on occasion and over certain issues. In these circumstances it was bound to be difficult to deter some socialist hothead in Tartary from contemplating a military adventure by threatening to bomb Dniepropetrovsk—of which he had probably never heard. In that respect the policy of massive retaliation can hardly have been said to be credible. But that raises the second disadvantage.

In Soviet eyes it was all too credible. Was Russia's survival to be put at risk every time some hothead somewhere embarked on a course of action that the Americans might construe as Communist aggression? Faced with such an appalling prospect, the Soviet leaders would have to do everything they could to deter a U.S. attack. If they could not do so by threatening the United States, they would have to use such means as *were* available. In the words of Marilyn Monroe, "You've got to make the most of what you've got." And what they had were enormous land and air forces in western Russia and Eastern Europe. The threat of overrunning Western Europe could act as a counterbalance to the U.S. threat to attack the USSR. After all, and above all, it was Western Europe that the United States was seeking to defend when it formulated the policy of massive retaliation in the first place. It is easy to schematize this, and to say that the Soviet conventional forces acted as a counterdeterrent to U.S. nuclear forces. In a sense, that is quite true, and its implications will be discussed later in this book. But such a schema obscures the political reality of the time—which was that whenever a crisis of any significance erupted elsewhere in the world, the temptation to put Soviet forces in Europe on full alert was overwhelming. NATO was then bound to respond in kind, with the result that a crisis anywhere was also in danger of becoming a crisis in Europe itself, at the very heart of the East-West confrontation. Such a pattern of events did occur at the time of the coup in Iraq in 1958.

The third disadvantage of massive retaliation, therefore, arose from a combination of the first two: it was what might be called a "centralized aggregation of crisis"; and it is perhaps no accident that it was in this period that the misleading term "bipolarity" became fashionable. More generally, the Cold War might be said to have been characterized by the aggregation of crisis, while détente was later characterized by the disaggregation of crisis: this is to say that a crisis in one part of the world no longer necessarily affected the central relationship between the superpowers or the confrontation of forces in Europe.

These were some of the disadvantages of massive retaliation. But behind them all lay the overwhelming consideration that the strategy could only work so long as the United States remained invulnerable to Soviet retaliation. The result was that a strategic policy proclaimed in a fit of superabundant self-confidence rapidly produced a nervous obsession with the question of when the USSR actually would develop the capacity to hit back. The extent of U.S. (and indeed Western) nervousness was amply illustrated in the year after massive retaliation was first formulated. In 1955 the Soviet armed forces put on an air display at Sheremetovo airport near Moscow, to which Western military attachés were cordially invited. There, to their horror, they witnessed a fly-past of intercontinental bombers. In fact, the USSR had by then developed only a few prototypes, but as these flew over in one formation, disappeared, and reappeared in another formation from a different point of the horizon, the attachés just kept on counting. Only a few months later the Senate Armed Services Committee, chaired by the influential senator Stuart Symington, had invented the "bomber gap." It appeared that not only was the Soviet Union now producing intercontinental bombers but that it was also doing so at a much faster rate than the United States. Such a piece of nonsense, to be echoed a short while later in Senator John F. Kennedy's mendacious election cries about a "missile gap," would be laughable were it not for the fact that it was also highly dangerous. The reason lies in the technological limitations of the period.

The bombers, and the first generation of missiles that were seen to make their appearance, were what strategic jargon calls "first-strike weapons." This is to say that they could not survive an attack, parked as they were on runways or, in the case of missiles, simply standing about in the open. (A small proportion of bombers was of course maintained on permanent airborne alert—but while that helped to maintain security it also increased the danger, as will shortly be apparent.) If a weapon cannot survive an attack, and if there is any reason to believe that such an attack is imminent, it becomes imperative to get one's own blow across first. Hence the term "first strike." The consequence is that nuclear war can easily occur without either side actually intending it, simply because the one misread the signs or misinterpreted the intentions of the other. In these circumstances, crises tended to acquire a different dynamic from those of earlier years. Aware of the terrible dangers they were in, leaders of both sides moved with great circumspection and caution: crises were slow in developing. But if a crisis was not resolved at an early stage, the reciprocal fear of being attacked first and the consequent determination to preempt that risk meant a sudden acceleration of tension and peril. This pattern of what is sometimes called "first-strike instability" prevailed throughout the late 1950s and early 1960s. Quite apart from crises, there was also the increased danger of accidental war. The plot of the film *Dr. Strangelove* is in part based on historical facts, and goes to show why keeping bombers on airborne patrol can be somewhat dangerous.

All these difficulties and dangers arose from the obsession with U.S. vulnerability, actual or potential, which the policy of massive retaliation had itself done much to generate. In fact, that policy came under critical fire almost from the day it saw the light, and was increasingly modified toward the end of the decade before being finally abandoned at the beginning of the next. But in its heyday it was the supreme expression of U.S. preeminence in the international order, indeed of the kind of assumption mentioned before that the United States *was* the order. Its economic role, its political and military commitments, its pledges to its allies: all seemed to come together in a policy that defined the United States as the guarantor of global peace and stability. The policy also defined the United States as the power that was able and willing to inflict massive destruction on its adversaries if its role as guarantor were challenged. To that extent it also defined deterrence as a policy based on the threat of all-out destruction. And it all seemed so *logical.*

The logic, which can be summed up in the proposition that the greater the risk, the more effective deterrence would be, was to persist for years. But it was to become more complicated. Seen from the standpoint of U.S. invulnerability, massive retaliation was a perfectly rational strategy in its own way. When the United States did become vulnerable, the response was to frame a strategy that was more complex but that still attempted to be rational. Later still, when it was generally agreed that nuclear war would mean the mutual destruction of the adversaries, deterrence could only work by being irrational. This progress from the simple/rational to the difficult/irrational will be examined further.

Notes

1. Dean Acheson, *Present at the Creation: My Years in the State Department* (New York: W. W. Norton, 1969), pp. 164–168, 314–321.

2. David Lilienthal, *The Journals of David E. Lilienthal,* vol. 2, *The Atomic Energy Years, 1945–1950* (New York: Harper & Row, 1964).

3. For example, Kenneth Booth, *Strategy and Ethnocentrism* (London: Croom Helm, 1979); and Colin S. Gray, *Nuclear Strategy and National Style* (Lanham, Md.: Hamilton Press, 1986).

4. Presidents George Bush and Boris Yeltsin signed up to START II ("Treaty on Further Reductions and Limitations of Strategic Offensive Arms") on January 3, 1993. The treaty builds on the foundations of START I ("Treaty on the Reduction and Limitation of Strategic Offensive Arms"), signed by Presidents Bush and Mikhail Gorbachev on July 31, 1991.

5. X, "The Sources of Soviet Conduct," *Foreign Affairs* 25, no. 4 (July 1947). Reprinted in *Foreign Affairs* 65, no. 4 (spring 1987).

6. See Lawrence Freedman, *The Evolution of Nuclear Strategy,* 2d ed. (Basingstoke: Macmillan in association with the International Institute for Strategic Studies, 1989).

7. The device tested in November 1952 was nondeliverable, but in the spring of 1954 the United States conducted a series of tests of "Superbombs" in the Pacific, including a deliverable one on March 1. See David Holloway, *Stalin and the Bomb* (New Haven: Yale University Press, 1994), p. 303.

8. According to Holloway, writing about the August 1953 test, "it is, to some degree, a matter of taste whether one calls it a thermonuclear bomb or a boosted weapon." In November 1955, however, the Soviet Union did test what was unquestionably a thermonuclear weapon. Holloway, *Stalin and the Bomb,* p. 308.

9. John Foster Dulles, "Policy for Security and Peace," *Foreign Affairs* 32, no. 3 (April 1954).

10. X, "The Sources of Soviet Conduct."

11. This is argued convincingly in a hitherto unpublished Ph.D. thesis by Rebecca Grant: "Eisenhower's Nuclear Strategy, 1953–58" (London School of Economics, 1989).

7

The Evolution of Strategic Thinking: Stage Two

In 1957 the United States proclaimed to an admiring world that it was about to place a satellite in space. This object, about the size of a grapefruit, was to be the first terrestrial artifact ever launched without returning immediately to earth. Meanwhile, without a word to anybody, the Soviet Union was preparing its own launch; and in fact the world's first artificial satellite, about the size of a football, was *Sputnik*. Its strategic significance was that it proved that the Soviet Union now had the ability to build intercontinental missiles. Its political significance was that not only did it catch the imagination of the world, but it also did much to terrify millions of Americans. For some years afterward, visitors to the United States were greeted in their hotel rooms with a card advising them of the whereabouts of the nearest fallout shelter in the event of nuclear attack. It was in this context that the strategy of massive retaliation came in for some radical reappraisal.

In fact, the whole idea of basing U.S. foreign policy on the threat to use nuclear weapons had already been heavily criticized in many academic institutions and strategic think tanks. In particular, Nelson Rockefeller had used his influence to bring together a number of prominent figures from "the Establishment" (although Americans would not call it that) to study the question, and their rapporteur, Henry Kissinger, published a book based on their conclusions, which made him famous.[1] Kissinger's *Nuclear Weapons and Foreign Policy* could not have appeared at a more auspicious time than in the year of *Sputnik;* and the impact of the book was the greater because it represented the views of many who were active in political and intellectual debate. It argues that nuclear threats are far too blunt and heavy an instrument for the conduct of a successful foreign policy and that their credibility is bound to erode—either because nobody can be expected to take them seriously if they are uttered over some minor issue, or because even if the issue had serious implications, every time such threats are made and then not acted on, it becomes harder to make them stick the next time. (The argument had been put more succinctly by Janos Kadar, the Hungarian party leader, in a famous phrase: "salami tactics." One might go to war for a whole salami, but not for a slice; but just keep slicing away, and you end up without war but with the entire salami.) The idea that hostile forces were slicing away at the U.S. world order and that crude threats of strategic nuclear war were no longer sufficient to keep them at bay meant that before long the policy of massive retaliation would have to be reappraised—not only at the intellectual or academic level but also at the political.

In fact, the process of reappraisal was already under way, though not in public. One of the most brilliant American operational analysts and mathematicians, Albert Wohlstetter, had been working for some time on a study commissioned by the best-known U.S. strategic think tank, the RAND Corporation, into the effectiveness of the Strategic Air Command (SAC). His findings were understandably and for some time kept secret, since they were pretty damning. The great strength of the SAC—its ability to attack the Soviet Union from a wide variety of angles and so to penetrate what were by now formidable Soviet air defenses—turned out also to be its greatest source of weakness. For to be able to coordinate complex bombing missions across a number of different time zones and climatic conditions requires highly trained air crews constantly on the alert. That in turn means innumerable training missions, which also means that not only the crews but also the aircraft themselves are liable to experience considerable fatigue. To deal with those problems, one needs an abundance of spare parts as well as a sufficiency of standby crews. Wohlstetter found that both were lacking. He also found that communications were inadequate. His general conclusion was that, on a good day, the SAC might be about one-third as effective as it was supposed to be. Air force generals and leading policymakers were thus made uncomfortably aware that just at the time when the United States was becoming vulnerable to the prospect of Soviet missile attack, its existing deterrent forces were scarcely adequate to maintain the threat of massive retaliation.[2]

What made things worse was that it was also at this time, in 1957, that NATO adopted a new strategic policy that linked any Soviet advance into Western Europe (if the Soviet forces did not call a halt after a breakthrough) to a rapid escalation to all-out nuclear war. Most such strategic policies take a long time to formulate and to be adopted, and this one was no exception, particularly since it involved the multinational diplomacy of an Atlantic alliance that had recently been expanded to include Germany. The premise of the threat of rapid escalation was clearly the relative invulnerability of the United States to Soviet attack (for even though the Soviet Union was building intercontinental bombers, it was now accepted that their numbers were small, while the United States and Canada were building extensive interception forces). In that respect, it was still credible to threaten rapid escalation in spite of the Soviet bombers. But it would hardly be credible when Soviet missiles could strike at the United States. Thus the new NATO policy, in itself a kind of subset of massive retaliation, was going out-of-date even before it could be implemented, and put further strains on the U.S. strategic position and on its credibility. These strains were to become increasingly evident in the politics of NATO over the next years, but what mattered at the time was that they gave a further impetus to the rethinking of U.S. strategic policy.

That process of rethinking began under the direction of Eisenhower's last secretary of defense, Thomas S. Gates, and culminated in 1961 with the announcement by his successor in the Kennedy administration, Robert McNamara, of an entirely new strategic policy. In spite of the fact that Gates had done much of the initial work, the policy rapidly came to be known as the McNamara Doctrine.

The doctrine was based on one major premise—which also dated back to 1957. It was then that the U.S. government first knew that the Polaris missile would work. The Polaris is launched from submarines operating at considerable depth from which they cannot be detected or attacked. In other words, they would, unlike the first generation of strategic missiles, be able to survive a first attack, and retaliate afterward. For this reason they were known as "second-strike missiles"; and the second-strike missile was to revolutionize strategic thinking.

From now on, anyone contemplating a nuclear attack would know for certain that there was no escape from terrible destruction, however successful that attack might be, or however much damage it might do. This meant that the appalling risks of the period when both sides relied on first-strike weapons could now be minimized. Under a first-strike regime there was the greatest possible incentive to get one's blow in first if it was feared that an attack was coming. The second-strike system provided the greatest possible incentive not to attack at all. Insofar as any system of nuclear deterrence can be said to be safe, this was it;

and it is to Eisenhower's eternal credit that at the time when he was under enormous pressure to close the so-called (and nonexistent) missile gap, he steadfastly refused to devote resources to building more first-strike weapons and chose instead to wait for the second-strike missiles to become operational. By 1961 they were.

Polaris was the most obvious form of the second-strike missile, but there was also another, based not at sea but on land. This was the Minuteman, named after a rather obnoxious genre of American guerrilla fighter during the War of Independence. (It is characteristic of the pattern of U.S. strategic and social thought during this period that, whereas one weapon of mass destruction should be named after a celestial body, the Pole Star, another should derive its legitimation from U.S. history. It is hardly an exaggeration to say that in the eyes of those associated with the Kennedy administration, the United States was taking over the universe. It was, after all, Kennedy who enthused his compatriots at this same time into spending millions of dollars in order to put an American on the Moon.) Anyway, the Minuteman could be made invulnerable to a first attack by being maintained in hardened silos; that is, pits surrounded by mightily reinforced concrete so as to withstand the blast of a nearby nuclear explosion, deep in the sides of mountains. And it had the advantage over Polaris of being considerably more accurate. It was the combination of these two systems with the strategic bomber force—the three generally referred to as the "strategic triad"—that provided the basis for the McNamara Doctrine.

But that doctrine also depended on numbers. U.S. intelligence had enormously overestimated the number of strategic missiles deployed by the Soviet Union. In fact, it was estimated in 1961 that there were over two hundred of these in place.[3] It is now known that in fact the Soviet Union did not at that time have a single operational intercontinental ballistic missile (ICBM). In response to this erroneous estimate, Washington decided to increase greatly its production of Minuteman missiles, and also, though perforce more slowly, of Polaris missiles.

The availability of the second-strike missile and the determination to achieve numerical superiority laid the foundations for the strategic program incorporated in the McNamara Doctrine. Compared with the apparently rational but crude ideas embodied in massive retaliation, it was the height of sophistication—even though it still aspired to making the credibility of the deterrent threat contingent on the demonstration that such a threat was still rational and even though the United States was now vulnerable to Soviet missile attack. It went as follows.

The basis of massive retaliation had been that if Soviet, or "Communist," forces attacked a country anywhere in the world that the United States regarded as important to its own security, Soviet cities would be put at risk of nuclear attack. In the era of U.S. vulnerability, that was obviously no longer feasible. How then to make a rational policy of deterrence stick? The answer lay in a bold stroke of lateral thinking. From now on, the United States proclaimed, it would not strike at Soviet cities in the event of strategic war between the superpowers. It would instead attack military targets, preferably those far removed from population centers, such as missile sites, bomber bases, command and communication centers, and so on. In doing so it would seek to spare as much of the population of the Soviet Union as possible, while neutralizing the great majority of its strategic nuclear forces.[4] There was no expectation of course that all strategic missiles or bomber bases would be eliminated. (Apart from anything else, the USSR at that time had a fairly primitive version of the cruise missile based on submarines; and though the submarine had to surface in order to fire them and was therefore vulnerable to air or sea attack, there was no doubt that the cruise missile could have done severe damage to the huge urban conglomerations on the eastern and western seaboards of the United States.) But what purpose would Soviet retaliation have served? Hitherto, the United States would have spared Soviet cities, but if U.S. cities were attacked in return for the (presumably Minuteman and bomber attack) on military installations, the Polaris could be called upon to devastate Soviet cities—it did not have to be all that accurate to do so. If on the other hand the Soviet forces had chosen to use up their few remaining military instruments against U.S. military bases, they would still leave the United States with a lot of surplus strategic potential (in particular Polaris again) with which it could do what it liked.

In other words, there would be no point in Soviet retaliation to a U.S. attack on the USSR's strategic installations: the country would merely rediscover that its own cities and civilian population were hostages. The implicit monologue was one in which the United States said to the USSR: "In view of the fact that although we are vulnerable, we have second-strike forces and you have not, and we've got a very good strategy for you. It's called 'surrender.'" In the rather more ordered strategic jargon of the time, the overall strategy was known as "controlled response," and its instrumentality was known as "city avoidance." Military targets were distinguished from civilian targets in a kind of Orwellian Newspeak, the former being designated "counterforce" and the latter "countervalue." (Of course the whole assumption that one could distinguish between strategic destruction and civilian deaths presupposed that the wind would never blow; but never mind.)

This complex strategy formed the deterrent component of the McNamara Doctrine. It was a sophisticated answer to the problems created by U.S. vulnerability. Those problems, it should be emphasized, arose not because the United States would have any trouble in deterring an attack on the American homeland: once the second-strike system was in place, any potential aggressor would be powerfully aware that retaliation was inevitable. "Central deterrence," that is, deterring an attack on one's own country, was simple enough. What was difficult was "extended deterrence," that is, deterring an attack on friends or allies. But while this strategy sought to maintain the credibility of the nuclear threat in the manner outlined here, and was generally referred to as controlled response, the U.S. administration was anxious not to give the impression that it was contemplating a nuclear war. Indeed it was not; and McNamara in particular frequently made it clear that he was most anxious to avoid one even while remaining committed to the defense of America's allies. His preferred means of doing so was what he called "flexible response."

Flexible response was not in itself a strategy. It rather described a search for options—an attempt to multiply the choices available to the president, to NATO's Supreme Allied Commander in Europe, and to others in command of military forces: all with a view to avoiding or delaying the decision to "go nuclear." It involved substantial increases in conventional forces, in terms of both personnel and arms, the development of new forms of equipment, and the retraining of forces for a wider variety of combat roles—including irregular warfare. And even though the number of tactical nuclear weapons increased overall, it also involved the withdrawal of some of the smaller tactical nuclear weapons that had been stationed in Europe (because it was considered too easy to use them too early) and a tightening of control, both procedural and technological, of those that remained. But flexible response never really developed in the way that McNamara had hoped. He tried in 1962 to persuade NATO to adopt it as official policy, but got nowhere. That was partly because of the cost implications—conventional forces are very much more expensive than nuclear weapons—and partly for political reasons. Germany in particular argued at this time that an expansion in the number of fighting troops would merely weaken the credibility of the nuclear threat and that, if controlled response was so sophisticated and so credible, why attenuate it with the measures associated with flexible response? In the end, in 1967, NATO did adopt it as official policy, but by then it had come to represent little more than a number of more sophisticated ways of "going nuclear."

In spite of McNamara's efforts, then, strategic thinking and strategic policymaking continued to be dominated by the paradigm of nuclear deterrence; and nuclear deterrence was still judged in terms of the credibility of a rational threat. But the effects on the Soviet Union were not quite what was expected. The trouble was that the USSR could not, in effect, make any rational response to the new U.S. policy—especially since its leaders knew how few strategic missiles they had in reality.

Khrushchev therefore resorted to irrationality, declaring that Moscow would never wage nuclear war according to the "capitalist rules" and that if Washington did launch a nuclear attack on Soviet military installations, the USSR would retaliate against "industrial and administrative targets"—that is, cities. This was the first time that any nuclear power openly relied on irrationality as a way of creating credibility. It was to become generalized within a few years. But Khrushchev could also make an indirect and more rational response. Just as, during the days of massive retaliation, the Soviet Union could hope to ward off a U.S. attack by threatening to overrun Western Europe so now they could play the "hostage Europe" card again, only this time in nuclear terms. For by now the Soviet Union possessed an extensive arsenal of medium- and intermediate-range missiles—about seven hundred of them. That was enough and to spare for all the major European cities, and Khrushchev did not hesitate to press the point home. He sent an official note to the Italian government, remarking on the beauties of Italy's landscape and the glories of its art treasures, adding, however, that it would be a great pity if all that were to be destroyed because of some act of folly on the part of the United States. Denmark received a similar note, though without reference to art treasures. In the middle of an otherwise perfectly civilized evening at the Bolshoi ballet, the British ambassador was summoned to Khrushchev's box to be told that it would take just fifteen Soviet missiles to destroy his entire island.

Such tricks were not frivolous. They could turn the earlier implicit U.S. monologue that ended with the word "surrender" into a dialogue in which the Soviet Union could reply by saying: "For every Soviet military site that you destroy, we will destroy a European city. If you respond by attacking Soviet cities we will have no further incentives for restraint and will unleash everything we have against American cities. If, on the other hand, you still avoid our civilian population in the hope of saving yours, then your whole strategy of extended deterrence will be exposed as a sham. So we've got a very good strategy for you: don't start." In other words, the astringent rationality of controlled response, given that it was designed to solve the problems of extended deterrence, was not by any means as effective as it looked.

But there was a third response available to the USSR, combining some elements of the irrationality of the first and the indirect rationality of the second. That was to persuade the leader of a friendly island just off the U.S. coast to play host to Soviet intermediate-range missiles. If these could be slipped into Cuba, they would, according to what President Kennedy was subsequently to say, have been able to reach targets in two-thirds of the territory of the United States.[5] That would have made no difference to the actual logic of controlled response, since the United States would still have its second-strike weapons, but it would have made simultaneous first attack against Soviet systems in both Cuba and the USSR enormously more difficult and certainly would have multiplied enormously the risks from an irrational Soviet act, which any U.S. president would be forced to contemplate.

This is not the place to go into a detailed analysis of the Cuban missile crisis, which has been extensively written about and almost constantly reinterpreted ever since. But two points are worth making. The first is that a strategy that was designed to impose the rules of stable behavior on the Soviet Union in fact produced the most intense and dangerous crisis that the world has yet lived through. To date, there have been fifteen meetings of the surviving protagonists of the crisis on both sides, and as they have explored each other's moves, reactions, and interpretations at the time, it has become abundantly and increasingly clear that a nuclear war was very narrowly averted. How this situation came about is obviously a complicated story, but one thing is clear: It was foolhardy in the extreme for Khrushchev to try to place missiles in Cuba, let alone to hope to do so undetected; and the fact that he was driven to such desperate measures indicates that the U.S. administration had broken one of the fundamental rules of Clausewitz. In confronting the Soviet Union it had passed the culminating point of victory. Partly because of faulty intelligence, partly because of the greatly accelerated production of second-strike missiles to which that led, it had so alarmed the Soviet leadership that what seemed to be "victory" in deterrence nearly led to the universal defeat of nuclear war.

The second point is that when the crisis broke, President Kennedy threw all the careful constructions of the McNamara Doctrine out the window and reinvoked all the obsolete ideas of massive retaliation, warning the Soviet Union that a single missile launched from Cuba at any point in the Western Hemisphere would unleash the full retaliatory might of the United States. Kennedy acquired enormous prestige from his handling of the crisis—and McNamara was later famously to remark that "There is no such thing as strategy any more, there is only crisis management." But the skill and restraint Kennedy is supposed to have shown (though the subsequent meetings of the protagonists cast some doubt on that) were deployed within the context of this crude and unrestrained threat. Whether it reflected a deliberate decision to maximize the danger so that in the end the crisis would become more manageable, or whether it reflected a semiconscious conclusion that nuclear war, once begun, is probably uncontrollable anyway, remains an open question. Certainly most military commanders and senior officials in defense ministries are convinced that any nuclear war, however limited the original scope might be, would very rapidly run out of control and speed up the escalator to Armageddon.[6] Be that as it may, if the Cuban missile crisis was in any sense a test of the strategy of controlled response, it failed the test.

Nonetheless, the requirements of extended deterrence remained, and for the time being the strategic answer was still deemed to lie in controlled response and counterforce targeting. But the context was now enormously different. The leaders of both superpowers had stared into the abyss. The complicated arcana of nuclear deterrence, the subjects of so many intellectually satisfying conferences and seminars, had threatened to become hideous reality. Bobby Kennedy's memoirs of the crisis, *Thirteen Days,* portray a president driven to the brink of breakdown by fear of an imminent nuclear war, indeed convinced at one stage that it was coming. Khrushchev's own memoirs, *Khrushchev Remembers,* make no secret of his own terror; and he was quite forthcoming at the time. He announced on Soviet television that the USSR had not responded to the U.S. "provocation." This was wrongly interpreted by most Western observers as a bit of a cheek—after all, whose provocation had it been anyway?—but in fact the phrase meant something quite different in Russian literature, referring to the deliberate insult designed to force the injured party to challenge the provocateur to duel. In such a case the choice is between risking death or retreating with dishonor. Khrushchev was telling the Soviet people that their country had retreated with dishonor rather than risk being wiped out; and he hardly seems to have appreciated the noises that were being made in Washington to the effect that skillful crisis management had left him a way of retreating without losing face.

In any event, the Cuban missile crisis had served to impress on both powers and their leaders the need for conducting their strategic relationship within a political context. Adversaries they might be, enemies even, but from now on they realized that it was vital to cooperate in preventing a nuclear war. In retrospect, one might say that the chief criticism to be leveled at the strategy of controlled response was that it was drawn up without any reference to the political context of the impact it might have on the other side. It was the supreme expression of the autonomy of strategy discussed earlier.

Yet there is a paradox here. It is certainly the case that after the Cuban missile crisis, both U.S. and Soviet leaders began to see their security as being ultimately defined in terms of their political relationship; and one might say that this represented a shift away from the autonomy of the strategy that had been so clearly articulated in the McNamara Doctrine. But that political relationship was itself defined in strategic terms. Strategic considerations were now the driving force of politics, as a string of agreements that followed the crisis readily showed: the installation of the "hot line" between the White House and the Kremlin (June 1963), the Nuclear Test Ban Treaty (August 1963), the Nonproliferation Treaty (July 1968), and ultimately the beginning of the Strategic Arms Limitation Talks (SALT), which Henry Kissinger defined as the key to the superpower relationship.[7] By the end of the decade, one might say that strategy had taken over politics; and that was to create endless difficulties both in the interpretation of détente and in the negotiations on arms control.

Nonetheless, it was a welcome development that the moves toward détente and some degree of superpower understanding occurred before the Soviet Union developed its own second-strike missiles. Once that happened, it was obvious that the United States was no longer in a position to impose the rules of the game through a U.S. interpretation of what was rational. It would henceforth be clear that any threat to go to nuclear war was irrational. It was also to become clear that the earlier identification of U.S. power with the world order could no longer be sustained. At the time, the Cuban crisis seemed to represent the apogee of that identification. In retrospect it looks much more like the moment at which the search for an alternative system began.

Notes

1. Henry Kissinger, *Nuclear Weapons and Foreign Policy* (New York: Harper and Bros. for the Council on Foreign Relations, 1957).

2. For the background to the "SAC vulnerability" studies undertaken by Wohlstetter and his team of colleagues at RAND in the early and middle 1950s,

see Fred Kaplan, *The Wizards of Armageddon* (New York: Simon and Schuster, 1983), especially chap. 6.

3. The third annual estimate of the Institute for Strategic Studies, *The Military Balance 1961–62,* turned out to be disastrously wrong in this respect.

4. The threat to Soviet missile sites presupposed of course that the United States knew exactly where the Soviet missiles were based, even while not knowing that none of them actually existed.

5. The highly expert U.S. magazine *U.S. Space Air Digest* was to accuse Kennedy within a week of gross exaggeration.

6. For a detailed discussion of these arguments, see Paul Bracken, *The Command and Control of Nuclear Weapons* (New Haven: Yale University Press, 1983).

7. The Strategic Arms Limitation Talks commenced in Helsinki on November 17, 1969, after a delay caused by the Soviet invasion of Czechoslovakia in 1968.

8

The Evolution of Strategic Thinking: Stage Three

By 1965 it was clear that the Soviet Union had begun to deploy its own second-strike missiles. These were mainly land-based, since for many years Soviet submarine technology lagged far behind that of the United States or of other Western countries. But for the time being at least, the Soviet Union was invulnerable to U.S. attack, which made it apparent that the period of counterforce strategy had come to an end. McNamara, who continued to serve as secretary of defense under President Johnson after the assassination of President Kennedy, was discreet at first in announcing its demise. He dropped hints to that effect in a testimony to the Senate Armed Services Committee early in the year, but it was a little while before he announced that the relationship of the two superpowers was now one of "mutual assured destruction," or MAD as it was soon to be termed. MAD was not in any sense a strategy; it was simply a statement of fact: namely that the United States and the Soviet Union could each destroy the other in a nuclear war, whichever attacked first. But the implication was that it could also become some kind of strategic regime under which both parties pursued a common policy of avoiding nuclear war. If so, MAD would be sane. If, however, that were to be the case, what would become of deterrence? The fact that both powers could wipe each other out did not mean that all the problems that the McNamara Doctrine had sought to address had now gone away. It meant rather that they had become insoluble. It was the reaction to this state of affairs that led to a revolution in strategic thinking, far more comprehensive than any seen so far.

In the past, the credibility of the threat implicit under nuclear deterrence had depended on being able to demonstrate to an opponent that it was rational to use nuclear weapons. Simple in the case of massive retaliation, complex in the case of controlled response, but rational all the same. Now that this rationality was impossible the credibility of a nuclear threat depended on demonstrating that whoever uttered it was irrational, irrational indeed to the point of lunacy. The implicit dialogue now went like this: "You touch Berlin and we'll nuke you." "But if you nuke us we'll nuke you back." "We'll still nuke you." "You're crazy!" "That's right—we're crazy and you'd better believe it."

There is considerable force to such an approach: it is, after all, very difficult to argue with a madman. And even if one believes that the declaration of irrationality is a bluff, the risks at stake are so enormous that the slightest doubt is likely to prevail over the stoutest conviction. But what does it all depend on? Clearly, if both parties are irrational, being crazy is not much help: one simply cannot guess at the other party's reactions. The efficacy of such a strategy therefore depends on the assumption that the other party is actually rational. Nuclear deterrence therefore turns into a four-way dialogue—the irrational talking to the rational both ways around. This is what Thomas Schelling calls "the rational use of irrationality." This means that if MAD is sane, it depends on being mad in the first place. It all seems a bit remote, but in fact these propositions came to operate in the real world.

On the night of the Soviet invasion of Czechoslovakia, the Soviet ambassadors in Washington, London, Paris, and Bonn each asked for urgent appointments with the respective foreign ministries there. They delivered identical messages, of which the first half was reassuring: that this was a crisis internal to the Warsaw Pact, that Soviet troop movements were part of an attempt to deal with that crisis, and that there was no threat to NATO or to Western Europe. The second half of the message was to the effect that: "And if you interfere we'll blow you off the map."[1] Later on, President Nixon laid much emphasis on the importance of ensuring that the Kremlin found U.S. behavior unpredictable, so as to reinforce the credibility of the U.S. deterrent threat.

Yet one should beware of being too convincing: if an adversary *is* convinced that one is genuinely insane, he could conclude, particularly in a crisis, that he could come under attack at any time; and in those circumstances, whatever the dangers of MAD, he might decide that his best chance of survival lay in attacking first. Irrationality therefore has to be selective. It is possible to make a convincing display of irrationality in some areas and over some issues while remaining wearily sane over others. Hence the importance of what, in this period, was increasingly discussed in terms of "commitment."

One of the reasons that the United States persisted for so long in fighting in Vietnam was the fear that if it withdrew and was seen to abandon its South Vietnamese protégé, it would weaken the credibility of U.S. commitments everywhere else. But in fact the process of withdrawal from Vietnam helped to sort out the genuine U.S. commitments from other areas of interest or (perhaps mistaken) engagement. It demonstrated that, effectively, one can only establish a commitment by already having it. It must be historically, psychologically, and even emotionally based.

In that sense, the commitments of the United States might be said to have been to its NATO allies, to Israel, and to Japan and South Korea (in the case of the latter, the commitment was almost entirely due to the fact that U.S. troops were stationed there). As for the Soviet Union, its commitments were probably restricted to the other members of the Warsaw Pact and to Cuba. These defined the areas of selective irrationality that helped to maintain the structure of deterrence in the era of mutual assured destruction; and throughout the many crises of the late 1970s and the 1980s, they remained remarkably stable and free from threat. But if what is implied here is true—namely that it is impossible to establish a credible commitment overnight—what about other areas where very important interests might be at stake, but where the simple threat of behaving irrationally would just not be credible?

Another incident that occurred at the time of the Soviet invasion of Czechoslovakia might help to illustrate the answer to that question. It appears that there were pressures on the Soviet leadership from the higher levels of the military command to complete the job of tidying up the Warsaw Pact and reasserting Soviet control in Eastern Europe by invading Romania too. Certainly President Johnson thought so, since he made a speech in San Antonio, Texas, referring to such an eventuality. Now, Romania lay within the Soviet area of commitment, and there was nothing the United States could do to prevent such an invasion without risking the nuclear war it had declined to risk in the case of Czechoslovakia. But Romania was also adjacent to Yugoslavia, and President Tito, while carefully ambiguous about what Yugoslavia would do, made it very clear that he regarded any Soviet invasion of Romania as a threat to the integrity or even survival of Yugoslavia itself. And Yugoslavia, though not an area of U.S. commitment, was certainly an area in which the United States and NATO had very powerful interests: Yugoslav neutrality was of immense strategic importance to NATO. How then could President Johnson hope to avert a Soviet threat to Yugoslavia?

What he said in his speech was that he had heard "rumors" (by which he presumably meant intelligence reports) that the Soviet Union was contemplating the invasion of Romania and that if this were true, it would pose a threat to Yugoslavia. He therefore *pleaded* with the Soviet leaders "not to unleash the dogs of war." Apart from showing that someone among the Johnson speechmakers could quote Shakespeare, this was an adroit position to take. If the president had bluntly threatened the use of nuclear weapons over the invasion of Romania, the Soviet Union would almost have felt bound to go ahead: the United States was not going to dictate to Moscow what it could or couldn't do in the Warsaw Pact. But by confining himself to the possibility that Yugoslavia might be drawn in, by implying very strongly that in that case the United States would come to its aid, he was making a different and altogether more credible threat—that is, that fighting could start, and that once it started there was no knowing where it would end. This is what, to quote Thomas Schelling again, might be called "the threat to lose control."

MAD therefore introduced two different principles into the continuing attempts to shore up the system of nuclear deterrence: that of irrationality at the core, and that of the threat to lose control at the periphery. Each was highly effective; and in the case of the latter it meant that the two superpowers were exceedingly careful to avoid any direct confrontation with each other. For whereas lesser powers can afford to back down or accept defeat, and even superpowers can do the same in conflict with lesser powers, they cannot do so in direct confrontation with each other. The United States might decide that it can only use diplomatic means to secure the return of the USS *Pueblo* after it has been seized by North Korea. The Soviet Union might decide to be philosophical when Soviet pilots in Soviet aircraft are shot down by Israeli pilots during the War of Attrition between Egypt and Israel in 1969–1970. In neither case is the credibility of their power at stake. But it would be very much at stake if either of them retreated in the face of the other—particularly so for a Soviet Union that was determined never to undergo the humiliation of the Cuban crisis again. The price that had to be paid for maintaining the credibility of commitment under the regime of MAD was that the threat to lose control became very dangerous indeed. And that puts a different gloss on the interpretation of mutual assured destruction itself.

For MAD can be interpreted in one of two ways. The first might be called the "psychological" interpretation, the second the "logical." The psychological interpretation is that since both powers are aware of the dangers of nuclear war arising from any conflicts anywhere, they will do their utmost not only to avoid confrontation, but also to cooperate in the settlement of other conflicts before they themselves might be drawn in, and will in general work together to try to ensure international stability. In such an interpretation, MAD provides the framework for a collaborative regime between the superpowers. The logical interpretation, however, looks very different. Logically speaking, since it is clear that neither power is going to risk a nuclear war, the world outside the central areas of commitment becomes safe for conflict. In circumstances where both powers avoid direct confrontation, other conflicts, wherever they might be, can be turned to advantage in a global power struggle. Whoever has the greater mobility, the longer reach, a local tactical advantage, or even the stronger will, can intervene—can support ideological allies, encourage proxies, or even commit troops and forces with impunity. In such an interpretation, MAD provides the framework for increased bloodletting in an intensified competition for global supremacy.

The difference between these two interpretations is not only categorical, it is also chronological. Under the first interpretation, which prevailed from the late 1960s into the early years of the following decade, the world witnessed the beginning of the SALT talks, superpower cooperation in ending the War of Attrition in the Middle East, the agreement on Berlin that brought to an end a dispute that had on earlier occasions threatened a third world war, and an increasing extension of bilateral relations in the economic and technological spheres. The culmination of this process of increasing cooperation came with Leonid Brezhnev's visit to Washington in June 1973, when he and President Nixon signed an agreement by which the two powers undertook, among other things, to give each other notice of any developments anywhere in the world that could provide a potential cause of conflict between them, and to cooperate in seeking a peaceful resolution.

The age of the second interpretation almost certainly began in October of 1973, when Egypt and Syria launched their surprise attack on Israel. An Arab-Israeli war was certainly something that could lead to superpower conflict—and the Soviet leaders knew it was coming but did not inform Washington. They probably did not know for certain until a very short time beforehand, possibly only four days.[2] That is admittedly not very long, but after all what is a hotline for? The October War produced a sudden and tremendous upsurge in Soviet-U.S. rivalry for the control of the outcome, so much so that at one point, U.S. forces worldwide were placed on nuclear alert, for the first and only time since the Cuban crisis eleven years earlier. In all probability, that was partly bravado, partly what appears to have been an elaborate double cross whereby Henry Kissinger was maneuvering both the Soviet Union and Israel into place so that the United States could emerge as the sole mediator of the subsequent disengagement agreements between the Israeli and Arab forces. But in any event, what it signaled was the new intensity of the Soviet-U.S. rivalry. That was, no doubt, due at least to some degree to the failure of the Soviet Union to have warned the United States beforehand of what was about to happen, but in more general terms it also marked the transition from the first to the second interpretation of MAD.

Of course, the United States won hands-down the competition for the control of the outcome of the October War. But that victory was also the beginning of a more intense competition between the two powers on a global scale, developing into what has since been widely termed "the second Cold War." In Central America, in Africa, in the Middle East, and in Southeast Asia, both intervened either directly or indirectly against each other's forces and protégés, and it would not be long before Zbigniew Brzezinski, the national security adviser and pet hawk of the Carter administration, was to speak of an "arc of crisis" ranging from the Horn of Africa to the Indo-China peninsula. His views seemed to be confirmed at the end of 1979 when Soviet forces invaded Afghanistan; and thereafter the Reagan administration was to engage in a renewed policy of containment of the Soviet Union—or as Reagan labeled it, "the evil empire"—but this time on a global scale. The consequences for arms control of this intensified competition will be discussed later, but in more general terms one might simply remark at this point that MAD did not seem to be so sane after all.

MAD, then, was an inherently ambiguous regime in which, for a time, the exigencies of strategic thinking seemed to promise all the blessings of détente, but in which later a pattern of a new, albeit indirect, confrontation evoked all the dangers of a new Cold War. Stable at the center, the world became increasingly unstable on the periphery. And as that development took place, both superpowers seemed to edge away from the idea of mutual assured destruction and to inch toward the possibility of trying to limit but also win some potential future nuclear war. In the U.S. case this took the form of a proliferation of new strategic "doctrines," as technological advances made it increasingly feasible to target intercontinental missiles with great precision. In the Soviet case, it took the form of a proliferation of new weapons, particularly intercontinental missiles whose sheer weight and numbers could make up for any deficiencies in accuracy, and intermediate-range missiles that *were* highly accurate and that could once again reinforce the old standby for Soviet policymakers of "hostage Europe." As mentioned earlier, the parallels with the neurotic mechanism in individual psychology are striking: the less that nuclear deterrence seemed to work, the more both strove to reinforce it. "MAD," after all, was quite an appropriate acronym.

But it is worth recalling that the term "MAD" was itself a U.S. invention. The Soviet preconceptions and the Soviet preoccupations were very different from those that were dominant in the United States. Although, in many respects, they tended to follow the patterns of U.S. strategic thinking, though usually trailing a few years behind, they had essentially different concerns; and in order to understand both the pattern of arms control negotiations and the confrontations that accompanied them, it is important to pay some attention at least to the nature of Soviet strategic assumptions.

Notes

1. Based on personal information from a minister who received one such Soviet ambassador at the time.
2. See Mohamed Heikal, *The Road to Ramadan* (London: Collins, 1975).

9

Patterns of Soviet Strategic Thought

U.S. strategic thinking developed out of an old experience of isolation from European quarrels that was transformed after World War II into a sense of global responsibility. However, that global responsibility was, initially at least, exercised on the basis of another historical tradition, that of U.S. invulnerability. One should not be too schematic about such things, but the Soviet historical experiences were almost exactly the opposite. Throughout its history, from the time of the Grand Duchy of Muscovy onward, Russia had been actively involved in European affairs. Moreover, it had been highly vulnerable to attack—first from the east in the form of the Golden Hordes of the Tatars, and subsequently of the Mongols, and later from the west. Traditionally, Russia had dealt with the problem of its acute vulnerability by expanding: to the point where by the end of the nineteenth century Muscovy had become the Russian Empire, whose borders by then incorporated Finland in the north, the Sakhalin Peninsula in the east and the Transcaucasian regions, snatched from the Turks, in the south. Yet the successor state of this expansionist empire, the Union of Soviet Socialist Republics, deliberately retreated into isolationism after World War I—relinquishing some of the old imperial provinces, such as Finland, the greater part of Poland, and the Baltic states, in the process.

The idea of a different form of expansionism, that of attempting to export the Bolshevik Revolution, was rejected first by Lenin as a tactic, and subsequently by Stalin as a principle in the name of "socialism in a single country" (the slogan in fact comes from Lenin not Stalin). But the German attack on the USSR in June 1941 catapulted the isolationist successor state into a different form of expansionism—one in which a confluence of geographical contiguity and ideological cohesion would ensure the security of the Soviet Union in the future. China to the east, the countries of what was to become the Warsaw Pact to the west: these would solve the ancient problems of vulnerability to the Golden Hordes on the one hand and Western aggression on the other. And yet the "socialist camp," as Stalin and Zhdanov termed it, remained isolated. That was partly out of Stalin's own volition. It was he, after all, who rejected the Baruch Plan and Marshall Aid. But it was also increasingly the case, as the U.S. policy of containment developed, that the traditionally vulnerable expansionist power, the Soviet Union, was becoming isolated by the traditionally invulnerable isolationist power, the United States.

It was within this historical context, conditioned by an acute sense of vulnerability, that the patterns of Soviet strategic thought developed. But they were conditioned by other factors too. The first was the ideological component, which it is convenient though not altogether accurate to divide into its Leninist and Stalinist elements. For Lenin, conflict between the socialist and capitalist systems was inevitable—which is hardly surprising since he had witnessed intervention against the Bolshevik Revolution by British, French, U.S., Polish, Czech, and Japanese forces. But that did not necessarily mean that future conflict should take the form of war; and Leninist thought on the relationship between the socialist and capitalist worlds was posited on the idea of advancing the revolution through the dialectical movement of history rather than on the relationship of the Soviet state to other states within the international system.[1] That could include reaching temporary agreements with the forces of capitalism—as for example during the period of the New Economic Policy—and could encompass "peaceful coexistence between states of different social systems" (this phrase is also Lenin's). In the Leninist framework, the relationship between the state and the revolution is complex, and that complexity was to continue into the Stalinist period and beyond, but at least the appeal of the latter did not depend on the power of the former. In the Stalinist framework, particularly after it became a matter of fundamental policy rather than a tactical expedient to create "socialism in a single country," everything was subordinate to building up the power of the Soviet state.

To that end Stalin turned the international revolutionary movement into an instrument of Soviet state policy through the agency of the Comintern. But he also sought normal state-to-state relations with other European countries in the 1930s, based on the principles of collective security and clearly designed to contain the growing power of Nazi Germany. When collective security failed, he tried another approach—the

Nazi-Soviet Pact, intended to stave off war in the East by turning the Third Reich against the West. Obviously, that did not work for long; and the result of Hitler's invasion in June 1941 was that the Soviet Union emerged from the war in many respects a ravaged and shattered country. But at the same time, it was treated as a superpower.

This new superpower in a sense combined the earlier features of Soviet development: as a state, it dealt with other states from a position of strength in spite of its own inherent weaknesses, and it exercised control over the countries of Eastern Europe through the ideology of the revolution. Moreover, Stalin transformed Lenin's thesis that conflict between the socialist and capitalist worlds was inevitable into the declaration that war itself was inevitable. But did this mean that Stalin had a revolutionary strategy?

The answer appears to have been that he had no strategy at all, beyond that of building up Soviet military might to the point where the armed forces of the USSR and the socialist camp would be able to repel any imperialist aggression. Stalinist strategic thinking was summed up in what he called the "permanently operating factors." These are of such stupefying banality, even if one tries to put a socialist/historical gloss on them, that they are hardly worth repeating: Numbers matter. The home base is important. And so forth. Wordsworth at his worst could have done better. But they are interesting for what Stalin regarded as unimportant. He minimized the value of surprise—which itself is not surprising after his experience in 1941. He also minimized the importance of nuclear weapons. Again, not surprising in view of the fact that at that time the United States possessed them and the Soviet Union did not. (In fact, the USSR had been working frantically on a program to develop nuclear weapons since 1943; and Solzhenitsyn probably owes his survival to the fact that he mendaciously claimed to be a nuclear physicist, and so secured a transfer from the death-regime labor camps to the relatively cushy surroundings of a *sharashka,* or scientific research prison of the kind he later described in *The First Circle.*) But in any event, the dismissal of nuclear weapons, the insistence on the permanently operating factors, and the fact that all discussion outside this framework, let alone dissent, was stifled, meant that the Soviet Union entered the nuclear age with no coherent approach to strategic thinking. In that sense it was doomed later to be largely reactive to developments in U.S. strategic thought and technology, even though its reactions were complicated by the legacy of revolution in its ideology.

Mention of U.S. technology here raises a different question, which also helped to condition the patterns of Soviet strategic thought. For very many years, and in most fields, the USSR lagged far behind the West in technological development; and the reasons were economic. They lay not only in the devastation wreaked by the Nazi attack on the USSR, but also in the system of centralized planning by which the Soviet economy was directed.

In theory, there is much to be said for centralized planning. In the first place, it allocates resources to the most important needs of society, and so is intended to maximize the socially beneficent effects of economic activity. Under capitalism, a product is tested, produced, and invested in only according to how much profit it is likely to generate—whether it be a skateboard or a new drug for the treatment of kidney ailments. (Although one should add that capitalism has never fully embraced the free market: if it had, cocaine and heroin would be readily available anywhere, and much cheaper too, as supply catered to demand. The socialist system merely generalizes what capitalist states regulate at the edges.) Moreover, the allocation of social priorities inherent in centralized planning also helps to eliminate the waste that is endemic to the capitalist system. Billions of dollars slushing around Wall Street, looking for outlets to invest in so as to produce millions more, whatever the cost in environmental terms or the depletion of natural or human resources, give way under centralized planning not only to the allocation of capital but also to a tidy economic system whereby the output in one sector of the economy becomes the input of the next, without the spendthrift intervention of the market—and without the boom and slump periods that are characteristic of the business cycle. Instead, not only does the output from agriculture become the input for industrial workers at prices deemed to be tolerable by the planning agency, but also the output within one elementary industrial sector (e.g., nuts and bolts) becomes the input for more sophisticated industries—until, in the end, chemical fertilizers and tractors assembled by machine tools return to the land to boost agricultural production still further. The whole economy can grow at a high and predictable rate; and socialism becomes synonymous with the creation of wealth. But real, socially beneficial wealth, not skateboards.

That is the theory. But in practice it obviously depends on the reliability of output in each individual sector to make sure that all the others can calculate their own input of resources and plan accordingly. There is, after all, no independent bank, no insurance company, no stock exchange to which it is possible to turn in order to raise the capital to buy in what is needed if things begin to go wrong. And under strict centralized planning, there is nowhere to buy from, except abroad in such an eventuality—and with neither a convertible ruble nor any available hard currency, it is impossible to buy from abroad in any case. The whole system is therefore liable to collapse unless output is absolutely certain and constant. No strikes may be tolerated, no influenza is permitted, hangovers are the prerogative of the class enemy. Every citizen, every collective farm, every factory: all must "fulfill their norm," as the saying used to go. In these circumstances, it is hardly surprising that Stalin, probably yielding to his natural inclinations, turned the whole system of centralized planning into a massive reign of terror, in which those who resisted collectivization or simply failed to fulfill their norms could be summarily executed or, more likely, deported to the labor camps that rapidly became an integral part of the Soviet economy and in which people certainly fulfilled and exceeded their norms until they simply died. By now, it is probably impossible to say how many millions perished in this way.

Faced with such a prospect, and conscious that the requirements of the plan had not been met, mindful of loved ones and desperate to survive, what would most ordinary human beings do? They would, to the best of their ability, cheat—and the Soviet citizens were not exceptions. They became adept at cooking the books, at inventing nonexistent products, at ensuring that others became the scapegoats. These practices became so widespread that, even after Khrushchev had done away with most of Stalin's apparatus of terror, it became virtually impossible to know what was actually going on in the Soviet economy, especially as the higher and middle echelons of the party themselves became accomplices in the cheating. One dramatic instance of how extensive the cheating grew occurred when a Soviet military satellite went off course and discovered that two million hectares of the Republic of Uzbekistan, dedicated to the production of cotton and for which the Soviet central exchequer had been paying the republic for years, was still uncultivated desert. That was after Brezhnev's death, and it is perhaps symbolic of the whole system that his son-in-law was implicated in the scandal. In sum, Stalin's terror was instrumental in creating such a system of cheating that the workings of the Soviet economy fell increasingly into the hands of black marketeers and mafiosi gangs—frequently aided and abetted by the members of the party *nomenklatura*. This is a problem that first Gorbachev and subsequently Yeltsin found virtually impossible to deal with. The implications of this for Soviet strategic thought will be considered shortly.

But before that, it is worthwhile considering for a moment what would have happened if centralized planning had worked perfectly—if there had been no industrial action or sabotage, if influenza had been banished, and everybody was always at peak efficiency. Supposing, then, that one were a manager of an industrial enterprise producing, say, machine tools, and were approached by a bright young engineer who said: "On the back of this envelope I've got a beautiful plan for producing more efficient machine tools for two-thirds of the price in half the time. What do you say?" One examines the plan, questions her in detail (in the USSR engineers are at least as likely to be women as men), and finds that it is entirely feasible. At which point, the only response can be: "Brilliant, but there's nothing to be done." To go into a different mode of production would entail closing down the plant and retooling. That could simply not be done while many other sectors of the economy were dependent on the immediate output of this particular sector. The macroeconomic costs of such an act of innovation would simply be too high. Moreover, where would the capital be raised? In principle, all capital has already been allocated for up to five years ahead and, once again, there is no stock market on which shares can be floated and no bank from which to raise a loan.

In other words, the system of centralized planning *militates against technological innovation.* Capitalism, for all its faults, including that of constant exhortations to keep up with the Joneses (the consumer equivalent of fulfilling one's norm), depends on constant innovation. There is in fact a perhaps not-quite-ironclad law whereby the system of centralized planning dooms a socialist economy to fall further and further behind the capitalized West in technological advance. Indeed, the great Andrei Sakharov gained fame as a dissident (in contrast to his previous celebrity as the father of the Soviet H-bomb) precisely because he argued that centralized planning forced the Soviet Union to lag behind. It was out of his experience as a dissident in that capacity that he later became a tireless champion of the cause of human rights. What happens when the inherent inefficiency of centralized planning comes together with the systematic cheating that was the legacy of Stalin's terror? And what happens when they are matched against the relentless advance of Western technology?

One answer is obvious. The Soviet Union frequently tried to make up in quantity what it lacked in quality, from the massive production of tanks, artillery pieces, and medium-range aircraft after World War II, to the huge numbers of not-very-accurate missiles that were later deployed first against Western Europe and subsequently against the United States. For many years all these were technologically much inferior to anything produced in the West. From about the mid-1970s, one can see Soviet military technology catching up on and in some respects surpassing that of the United States (the USSR is the only country ever to have put a permanently manned space station into orbit), but it did so at great cost. More and more capital resources were allocated to the defense sector, and though there is some controversy among Western analysts as to how far that sector became in effect a different economy, functioning in different ways from the rest of the Soviet economic system, there is no doubt that the rate of technological innovation there was far superior to anything found elsewhere in Soviet society. That has two implications.

The first is that the sheer rate of capital expenditure on defense inhibited investment in other areas of activity. In the United States, military innovation was part of a broad-based innovation activity that was going on in society as a whole. This meant that civilian innovations could be drawn on for military application, saving a great deal of money that would otherwise have gone into research and development. The heat-proof nose cones of space rockets, which were designed to bring astronauts safely back to earth instead of burning up as they reentered the atmosphere, were derived, for example, from a ceramic alloy that was first produced for the American kitchen. There could be no such spin-offs in the Soviet Union because of the low rate of investment and innovation in the civilian sectors. Indeed, whereas in the United States civilian economic activity enriched the defense sector, in the Soviet Union economic activity directed toward the military sector impoverished civilian society. That raises the second implication.

For many years Soviet leaders seemed to have regarded Western technological superiority as a threat in itself, a contemporary version of the country's historical vulnerability.[2] Given the nature of the economic system, however, that merely impelled them to spend more and more on defense, even while they were talking détente. In turn that led many Western observers to question Soviet sincerity: how *could* the USSR be interested in détente or peace while it was devoting such an enormous proportion of its gross domestic product to the arms race? And if one were a resolute skeptic one could take the argument even further, and argue that the arms race itself should be used as a means of forcing the Soviet Union into bankruptcy. That was certainly the view taken by some of the supporters of President Reagan's Strategic Defense Initiative or "Star Wars" program. In other words, one of the consequences of the system of centralized planning was ultimately to intensify the arms race.

So much for the context, historical, ideological, and economic. What were the consequences for Soviet strategic thought? The first was a serious split between the patterns of thought at different levels. Stalin's insistence that war was inevitable obviously implied that the USSR was not in the business of deterrence—it is impossible to deter the inevitable—but rather engaged in preparing for victory when war came. That remained the stated objective of Soviet military doctrine well into the Gorbachev period, having survived a tumultuous debate about the operational role of different forces in the nuclear age in the period 1959–1960. Yet after Stalin's death in 1953 the idea of deterrence as the principal strategic objective of the Soviet Union emerged quite rapidly as part of the power struggle between Khrushchev and Stalin's initial heir, Malenkov.

Malenkov argued that nuclear weapons had changed the nature of war, that they were a fundamentally new historical development to which the works of Marx and Lenin provided no guide, and that it was the supreme duty of a socialist society to avoid their use in war. Khrushchev's position echoed that of Stalin. Without quite arguing that Marxism-Leninism protected the human organism from nuclear radiation, he did argue that nuclear weapons were not decisive in war, and indeed that if they were used a socialist society could recover whereas a capitalist one could not. However, once he had won his power struggle with Malenkov, Khrushchev promptly adopted the latter's arguments and emphasized that nuclear weapons now imposed the necessity of peaceful coexistence. He did not yet, however, use the word "deterrence." That was still an alien concept. But what appears to have developed was that the Soviet forces were preparing for victory in Europe *if* war came (not *when*) and that this was seen as a counterdeterrent to the U.S. nuclear threat.[3] This was of course the period of massive retaliation. So far, one can argue that there was no real split between the Soviet military doctrine of preparing for victory and an overall strategy of avoiding war. But a split was to develop in a short period, complicated by the internal politics of party strife.

Between 1955 and 1957, over a million men were demobilized from the Soviet armed forces. This was partly an outcome of the policy of peaceful coexistence, partly an attempt to reduce expenditure, and perhaps most importantly a part of Khrushchev's efforts to reform Soviet agriculture by getting more people onto the land in the "Virgin Lands" campaign. But Khrushchev's agricultural policies, as well as his attack on Stalinism, provoked severe disagreements in the Politburo, which in 1957 passed a vote of no confidence in him as First Secretary of the party. Effectively, he was sacked; but at this point he handily remembered the constitution of the party, which theoretically gives the ultimate power of decisions not to the Politburo but to the Central Committee.

And with the help of the defense minister, the immensely popular World War II hero Marshal Zhukov, he organized military air transport to fly the members of the Central Committee from every corner of the Soviet Union to Moscow—where they promptly reversed the Politburo decision. Khrushchev was restored to power by what was in effect a thinly disguised military coup, and proceeded to purge the Politburo of his opponents (including Malenkov), who were now dubbed "the antiparty group." Now, any politician worth his salt must know that if an immensely popular hero has just saved his skin, the only thing to do is get rid of him fast. Shortly afterward Zhukov was accused of "Bonapartism" and sent to languish in an obscure command. He was replaced by Marshal Malinovsky, an old comrade of Khrushchev's from the time of the Battle of Stalingrad, and it was he who presided over the debate that followed at the end of the decade over the role of the armed forces. But he could not be of much assistance to Khrushchev in executing policy, since the latter's treatment of Zhukov had made him deeply unpopular among the military leaders, who now set out simply to obstruct him.

What they were obstructing was Khrushchev's determination to achieve further reductions in the forces, particularly the army, and to rely on a policy of deterrence. Khrushchev first used the word "deterrence" in a speech in 1959, in which he described it as a Western term, but also applied it to the Soviet ability to strike deep at the imperialist heartland, the United States.[4] The trouble was that, at the time, the Soviet Union had no such ability: for the economic and technological reasons outlined above, the first generation of Soviet intercontinental missiles was an expensive failure. The idea of nuclear deterrence was therefore introduced into Soviet strategic thought and policy at a time when the chief makers of that policy were aware that it was a dangerous bluff. Under the circumstances, it is hardly surprising that many of them argued for the continued capacity to win a potential war, albeit as the best means of deterring one, rather than wager all on strategic nuclear deterrence per se. Malinovsky himself made frequent speeches to that effect. Eventually, a compromise of sorts was reached, prefigured at the Twenty-second Party Congress in 1960, and spelled out in a commissioned book edited by another World War II stalwart, Marshal Sokolovsky, which was rushed into print in June 1961. Khrushchev did not get the force reductions he sought, and war-winning remained integral to Soviet strategic planning, but on the other hand the framework of strategic policy was now accepted as being that of nuclear deterrence. In fact, the book, *Voennaya Strategiya* (Military Strategy), is a thoroughly muddled piece of work, but it and its subsequent editions remained the repository of

Soviet strategic orthodoxy for many years to come. This is understandable in view of the fact that at least it appeared to resolve the political dilemma between advocating a security policy based on victory and insisting that deterrence could and would work.

Unfortunately for Khrushchev, however, June 1961 was also the month in which McNamara made a commencement speech at the University of Ann Arbor, Michigan, in which he outlined for the first time in public the principles of flexible response, with particular emphasis on city avoidance and controlled response at the strategic level. It is hard to resist a twinge of sympathy for Khrushchev at this point: just when he might have thought that he had the internal debate reasonably sewn up, the U.S. secretary of defense told the world that Soviet ability to strike at the American heartland would make no effective difference to America's capacity to threaten nuclear war. Small wonder that under this circumstance Khrushchev reacted as he did—in the manner outlined in Chapter 7—and in doing so helped to create the Cuban missile crisis.

Even though, by the time of that crisis, the Soviet Union did possess some real intercontinental missiles, the outcome of the protracted maneuvers of threat and counterthreat was a humiliating defeat for Moscow. A policy of strategic nuclear deterrence, born in bluff and tested in a Caribbean confrontation, had proved disastrous from the Soviet point of view. From now on, the USSR would not only continue to expand its armed forces (particularly the naval forces as had already been planned) but also made strenuous efforts to achieve strategic parity with the United States. That applied especially to the development of second-strike systems.

The irony of course is that the United States "won" the Cuban crisis because of its superiority in conventional forces at sea; but the Soviet conclusion was that the United States must never again be in a position to threaten the USSR with nuclear war. Given the technological inadequacy of many Soviet systems at the time, this led, as indicated earlier, to a huge buildup of missile forces, whereby quantity was intended to compensate for inferior quality. That was to create increasingly complex problems in arms control negotiations—in particular when Soviet technological quality began to improve and was harnessed to the quantitative superiority that Moscow had acquired during the 1970s. But that is for Chapter 11. What is still at issue here is that, although one might say that in the aftermath of the Cuban crisis and in the context of a new political discourse between Washington and Moscow, the Soviet leadership had begun to speak the same strategic language as that of the United States, there still remained two impediments to any genuine understanding between them.

The first difficulty lay in the Soviet heritage of thinking about deterrence as being formulated primarily in the threat to win war, should it occur, and in subsequent problems encountered by U.S. and other Western analysts in distinguishing between the war-winning pronouncements of Soviet military doctrine and the apparent acceptance of the principles of deterrence by the Soviet political leadership. When seen in light of the fearsome buildup of Soviet weaponry during the period from the late 1960s to the early 1980s, it is not hard to appreciate that the task of interpretation must have sometimes seemed near-impossible.

The second difficulty lay in the Soviet interpretation of mutual assured destruction. While not, as emphasized earlier, a strategic doctrine, MAD nonetheless incorporates a revolution in strategic thought, which even Clausewitz might have found initially difficult to grasp. Its basic premise is: "In my vulnerability lies my security." Because either adversary knows that it can be effectively wiped out by the other, should it dare to attack, each also knows that the other is most unlikely to initiate hostilities. Both can therefore enjoy what might be called a "synthetic confidence" in each other's intentions. Seen from the standpoint of U.S. history, such an approach, while bold, is not too difficult to accept. From the standpoint of Russian and Soviet history, it is much more difficult to accept vulnerability as a form of security. Indeed, there has been a bias in Soviet thought not only toward war-winning strategies but also toward active defense. In the days of the Strategic Air Command and massive retaliation, it is more than understandable that the Soviet Union should have built very large interceptor forces, the PVO Strany, as they were known. It is less understandable, though both powers did it, that in the era of MAD and the second-strike missile, that either should develop antiballistic missiles (ABMs), and that is one indication that MAD took a long time to be accepted as a comprehensive regime. Nonetheless, the United States rapidly concluded that the deployment of ABMs would threaten the security and the synthetic confidence that was offered by mutual vulnerability. The Soviet leaders, both political and military, were hard to persuade. Their argument was that since ABMs were purely defensive and could not be used for any other purpose, there could not be anything wrong with them. The idea that an extensive ABM network could provide the cover for an eventual decision to launch a strategic attack, and the prospect that if ABMs were to be deployed the United States would be the first to get a reliable network in place, eventually convinced them that mutual vulnerability was preferable. By the time that an agreement was reached to that effect in 1971 (the SALT I agreement), the two powers seemed to have accepted the same principles of mutual deterrence; and it appeared that these could be stabilized and codified through subsequent agreements in the course of arms control negotiations.

Such hopes were not to be realized. For both political and technological reasons, arms control negotiations proved increasingly tortuous and frustrating. One might also add that the reasoning on which their conduct was based was inherently flawed. But in order to spell that out, it is first necessary to consider the nature and functioning of the principal alliances in the nuclear age.

Notes

1. See Margot Light, *The Soviet Theory of International Relations* (Brighton: Wheatsheaf Books, 1988). See also Geoffrey K. Roberts, *The Unholy Alliance: Stalin's Pact with Hitler* (London: Tauris, 1989).

2. See David Holloway, *The Soviet Union and the Arms Race,* 2d ed. (New Haven: Yale University Press, 1984).

3. See Raymond L. Garthoff, *How Russia Makes War* (London: Allen & Unwin, 1954).

4. In fact, there are two words for "deterrence" in the Russian usage: One, *scherzhivaniye,* suggests "containment," and is indicative of the legitimacy of Soviet deterrent practice in obviating a malevolent foreign attack. The other, *ustrasheniye,* is based on the Russian root for the word "fear." That is what foreigners do in trying to terrify the USSR. In other words, the idea of the legitimacy of mutual deterrence was something that the Soviet military and political discourse found very hard to swallow. One might also add, though it is only semi-relevant here, that the distinction between these two terms contains an uncanny nuclear/socialist echo of the Just War tradition and its categories of what applied between Christians and what applied toward infidels.

10

Alliances

The United States has scores of allies in many areas of the globe, and the old Soviet Union had some, like Cuba or Vietnam, that were far from its borders. But only two alliance systems were central to the conduct of international relations in the nuclear age: NATO and the Warsaw Pact; and this chapter will concentrate upon them. This is not to say, however, that they were parallel organizations operating in some symmetrical manner. They had certain superficial resemblances, but the differences were far more important.

The resemblances are clear. Each alliance was dominated by a superpower and was the arena of its hostile confrontation with the other. In one case, the superpower had a monopoly of nuclear weapons, and in the other an overwhelming preponderance of their possession, even though Britain and France had developed nuclear forces of their own. In both cases the alliance came to represent an area of commitment over which the superpower was prepared to risk nuclear war. But for all that, the alliances served different purposes and functioned differently. This will become clear as they are considered in turn.

NATO first, because NATO was founded first. From the time of the signature of the North Atlantic Treaty in 1949 it was clear that NATO was far more than an "alliance" in any normal sense of the word. A traditional alliance between two or more states is a subset of relations within the international system. It has its *casus foederis,* defining the conditions in which the alliance comes into play, and its *casus belli,* defining the conditions in which the High Contracting Parties are prepared to support each other in war. Outside those circumstances the allied powers will go their separate ways and pursue their separate interests within the system as a whole. NATO was not such an alliance. NATO *was* the international system.

In the final stages of World War II, Roosevelt had expected the future international system to depend on cooperation between the United States and the Soviet Union. There is not indication that he expected a close working relationship with Western Europe; neither at first did Harry Truman, in spite of his instinctive and growing aversion to the USSR. But as the policy of containment was formulated, and as its formulation came increasingly to be defined in military terms rather than political and economic terms, so the future of the international system as a whole was posited on the U.S. commitment to Europe and on European and U.S. cooperation in containing Communist expansion. Indeed, the United States attempted to use the NATO model for further alliances, designed to the same end and also involving the cooperation of European powers. In 1950 it put great pressure on Britain to create a Middle East Defense Organization; and when this failed because of Egyptian refusal to participate, it encouraged Britain instead to create the Baghdad Pact—of which the United States, though not a member (it restricted itself to observer status), was nonetheless effectively the banker. Later, Britain and France were both to become members of the U.S.-led Southeast Asia Treaty Organization. In these and other respects, NATO was the focal point of the postwar reorganization of the international system—and indeed it is interesting, if one reads the documents, to see how extensive was the debate about whether NATO should be confined to any specific geographical area or whether it should not be regarded simply as a global alliance. In the end, the NATO area was defined as the territory of its member states and the North Atlantic Ocean down to the tropic of Cancer. That was to the source of much acrimony later.

But at the beginning, NATO defined itself as more than an alliance. The preamble to the treaty refers to the common values on which the alliance was based. That was the first such preamble in history, and it underlay the U.S. readiness to remain committed to the defense of Western Europe—though it was many years before President Carter could remark that, for the first time in its history, all the member states of the alliance were now democracies. This insistence on common values also helps to explain why the North Atlantic Treaty in fact contains no casus belli. Instead, the famous Article 5 simply declares that all the members would regard an attack upon one as an attack upon all. That is not, as is commonly assumed, an automatic commitment to go to war in the event of aggression against a signatory state, but the fact that the assumption is so widespread and that it dominated NATO military planning for years is perhaps more important than the actual wording.

In political as well as military terms, NATO became the dominant forum of relations between the United States and Western Europe. That was increasingly the case when the alliance became an organization in 1950 with the establishment of a supranational headquarters (initially in Paris, now in Brussels) and of supranational commands: the Supreme Allied Commander, Europe (SACEUR), who commands all forces assigned to NATO in the European theater, and who has always been a U.S. general; the Supreme Allied Commander, Atlantic (SACLANT), whose headquarters are in Norfolk, Virginia, and who commands NATO's international naval operations—always a U.S. admiral; and the Commander-in-Chief Channel, who coordinates and controls NATO activity in the western approaches, the English Channel, and the southern areas of the North Sea, and who has always been a British admiral.[1] The fact that member states of the organization were willing to assign their forces, even in times of peace, to the command of a foreign supremo, or to earmark more forces for such command in the event of an emergency, indicated a very close degree of political confidence and collaboration. But even given such confidence, what was the pattern of NATO's development?

As indicated in Chapter 6, NATO depended on the U.S. commitment to Europe and on the assumption that if there were to be another war, the United States would join it on Day One, but it did not depend on the assumption of an automatic U.S. nuclear guarantee. The expectation was that the defense of Western Europe would be based on conventional forces, and that the bulk of these would be provided by the Europeans themselves. The fact that the two most important Supreme Allied Commanders were American was generally accepted in Europe as an earnest indication of the U.S. commitment, but it was not meant to suggest that U.S. forces would have the primary role in European defense. Indeed, at one of the more notable NATO summits, which took place in Lisbon in February 1952, the twelve original member states of NATO pledged themselves to create a force of ninety divisions, thirty on a permanent basis and sixty more in reserve, but ready to be filled out and deployed at a moment's notice. By far the great majority of these were to be European—and it is worth recalling that at this time, neither Germany, nor Greece or Turkey, were members of NATO, and that of the twelve founding states, one (Iceland) contributed no forces at all, while Britain, France, Belgium, and Portugal all had extensive overseas commitments. The "Lisbon force goals," as they were known, therefore represented a very substantial pledge of resources on the part of the European countries, which were only just beginning to recover from World War II.

In fact, it was too substantial, and the goals turned out to be utterly unrealistic. The process of economic recovery itself made great demands on manpower (it was at this time that European countries were beginning to *welcome* overseas immigrants!), and the creation of the welfare state in one form or another in most such countries also demanded heavy financial investment. Choices would have to be made. In the words of one British officer: "What did we want—real teeth on the Rhine or false teeth on the National Health Service?" In the event, the number of divisions in NATO's vitally important Central Area, which includes Germany, was never more than twenty-six.

But it was not only the Lisbon force goals that failed to materialize. A European political initiative, undertaken at the instigation of France in 1950, also came to nothing. That was the creation of a European Defense Community (EDC), which would have allowed for German rearmament within the framework of an integrated European supranational command (details of the relationship between the EDC and NATO were to be worked out later). Although it did not come into effect—partly because of Britain's initial refusal to join, and partly because of a subsequent change of mind on the part of France—the very fact that the idea of a European Defense Community could be floated at the time, well before there was any serious discussion of a European Economic Community (EEC), shows how far strategic assumptions and the pattern of strategic thinking had come to dominate international relations. But even so, the failure of the EDC and the competing claims on European resources meant that it would be very difficult to devise an adequate framework for the conventional defense of Western Europe.

Under the circumstances, it is hardly surprising that when the U.S. administration announced a policy of massive retaliation in the aftermath of the Korean War, it was welcomed by most European governments with a relief that could be considered smug or abject according to taste. The United States was now hog-tied into the defense of Western Europe in a manner that had not been foreseen at the time of NATO's foundation, and was committed to waging nuclear war on behalf of European countries. If massive retaliation was in many ways a cost-cutting exercise on the part of the U.S. administration, designed to avoid expensive future wars on the Korean model, it was doubly so for the Europeans. They could now have their defense on the (comparatively) cheap at the American taxpayer's expense—and that same taxpayer might be forgiven for arguing in subsequent years that the Europeans were enjoying something approaching a free ride. In fact, the argument, by the time it came to the political forefront in the 1970s and after, was quite erroneous, but one can see where it came from.

As suggested in Chapter 6, massive retaliation was not quite as simple as it looked. Given the disparities between the United States and the Soviet Union in air and nuclear power on the one hand, and land and armored power on the other, its workings tended to put Europe more at risk in a period of crisis than if the Europeans had had adequate conventional defenses. The lack of these would mean ultimately, and especially in the age of U.S. vulnerability, that the United States would have to face all the problems of extended deterrence and of the choice between "annihilation and surrender." But that was not how it appeared at the time: Europeans were content to rely upon an apparently credible U.S. guarantee, and the United States was content to supply it.

What complicated matters in the first instance was not, however, the question of increasing U.S. vulnerability but that of the West German accession to NATO in 1955. This entails fairly complex matters of German history and German politics at the time,[2] but it might suffice to say here that the outcome of German membership was a transformation of NATO strategy. In the past, NATO military planning, whatever the nuclear backup, had relied on the possibilities of a war of maneuver, in which NATO forces had retreated to the Rhine in the face of a Russian onslaught, only to regroup and counterattack, encircling the forward Soviet echelons. Militarily admirable in many respects (it avoided the risks of instant nuclear escalation and enabled NATO commanders to make use of their qualitative superiority over the sheer numbers of Soviet forces), it nonetheless meant that the decisive battles would be fought on German soil—with all the contingent loss of German lives and the destruction of the territory that would be entailed. No sensible German, given the doctrine of massive retaliation that by then prevailed, would tolerate such a prospect. The dominant view was instead that in return for German membership of NATO, the Americans and other allies should commit themselves to a "forward strategy," whereby West Germany would be defended on the Elbe, not rescued from the Rhine—after the initial devastation of a Soviet advance, followed by the subsequent devastation of an Allied counterattack.

This argument was accepted by the principal NATO powers—it appears indeed to have been part of an undeclared bargain whereby Germany, joining NATO through the hitherto almost moribund West European Union, undertook not to produce atomic, bacteriological, or chemical weapons. But bargain or not, the new forward strategy meant that from now on the risks of nuclear escalation would be greatly and rapidly increased. For the need to escalate would be determined not by any calculations about the eventual outcome of the war but by the amount of German territory that the alliance was losing to a Soviet advance. That was why the German government was subsequently opposed to the proposal for flexible response when McNamara made it—and also why, years later, a Supreme Allied Commander in the 1980s, General Bernard Rogers, warned that he would have to use nuclear weapons within seventy-two hours of a full-scale Soviet attack. And that was after NATO had done much to modernize and improve the effectiveness of its conventional forces under what was known as the Long-Term Defense Program of 1978.

Meanwhile, however, the effect of the forward strategy in political terms was that it became the paramount concern of the European powers to maintain the U.S. commitment. In turn that meant first the development of a close political relationship between the major NATO powers in confronting the Soviet Union, and second a series of political disputes as the period of confrontation gave way to the period of détente. These disputes will not be examined in any detail here, but it is important to understand their nature.

The U.S. commitment to Europe was based ultimately not on interest but on an interpretation of the values referred to in the preamble to the North Atlantic Treaty. There were plenty of interests, to be sure. Some seven hundred thousand American lives were at stake in the European theater (this figure includes families as well as forces). There were billions of U.S. dollars invested in Europe. But in the end a country does not go to nuclear war, and risk almost certain suicide, for the sake of interests. It can mourn its dead abroad, it can write off a large fortune and prosperous trading partners, and yet survive. But commitment implies a willingness to die, and that is a matter of value. Détente on the other hand was not and could not be a matter of value. It was concerned with limited agreements, designed to avoid nuclear war, between powers whose very nature was rooted in mutually hostile values. The twin imperatives of the nuclear age—a value-free détente and a commitment based on value—were frequently difficult to reconcile, and led to mutual suspicions between the European and U.S. wings of the alliance. Some Europeans, notably President de Gaulle, were wary of superpower deals done "over Europe's head" (and that was one reason why France left the organization, though not the alliance, in 1966), while some Americans, notably Henry Kissinger, pondered aloud about the possibility of withdrawing U.S. forces if the Europeans proved obstructive. An attempt was made in 1967 to combine NATO's functions as a Western alliance with those of becoming a forum for détente through the so-called Harmel Report, named after the Belgian foreign minister and chair of the committee that produced it. In the event, the attempt proved none-too-successful: matters were complicated further by the fact that at the superpower level détente meant an attempt to stabilize the status quo, whereas at the European level it meant an attempt to change it. In other words, Europeans hoped to reintroduce questions of value into the value-free framework of the overall East-West relationship—what the West German chancellor Willy Brandt called, apropos the German Ostpolitik, "transformation through rapprochement." In retrospect, it seems that the Harmel Report marked the time at which NATO was changing its nature: from being the foundation of the international system as it had been in its early years, it was now beginning to look and behave more like an alliance within the international system—even though many of the older characteristics, such as the importance of Article 5, remained.

The attempt at transformation through rapprochement was not particularly successful, partly because the East German government had no intention of being transformed, partly because the requirements of strategic stability outweighed hopes for potential change. But the failure to achieve transformation was also, in a sense, a success for another policy on which both Americans and Europeans were agreed. This was that though there might be separate dealings with the Soviet Union—the SALT process on the one hand, the Ostpolitik negotiations on the other—the Soviet Union would not be allowed to enjoy, as it were, two separate détentes, one with Americans and another with Europeans. When, for example, the Soviet Union proposed in 1969 holding a European Security Conference, of which the very name implied the exclusion of the United States, all the West European countries refused unless the United States and Canada were also to be invited. When the Soviet Union reluctantly agreed, it became the Conference on Security and Cooperation in Europe (CSCE), which at present is still alive and active as the Organization for Security and Cooperation in Europe. In the last analysis, then, and in spite of intermittent strains and tensions, NATO did hold together. But its later years were certainly marked by increasingly public quarrels. These centered on three issues.

The first was that of what the U.S. Congress called "burden-sharing." The second was that of what was more widely known in NATO circles as "out-of-area" operations. The third, and perhaps most important, was concerned with the policy and tactics that should be adopted toward the Soviet Union during the years of the so-called second Cold War, which has already been mentioned.

The issue of burden-sharing really reflected a widespread American belief (already mentioned) that the European members of the alliance had been enjoying something like a free ride for many years, and that it was time for them to contribute more. Such a view arose not only from anxieties about the growing U.S. budget deficit from the late 1970s onward, but also from a rather crude comparison of budgetary expenditure. If the U.S. defense budget were compared with that of the European members' defense budgets combined, it would be roughly true to say that the United States contributed 60 percent of the total and the Europeans the remainder, even though the European members' combined gross domestic product was greater than that of the United States. On the basis of such figures, it was tempting for U.S. politicians and diplomats to argue that Europeans should "pull their weight" if the U.S. commitment and presence in Europe were to be sustained. But the figures do rather overlook a number of considerations. First, the size of the U.S. defense budget does reflect the U.S. role as a global superpower, not merely the role of a NATO member. That position can hardly be said to have been forced on an unwilling United States. Second, nonbudgetary defense costs hardly entered into the calculation. For example, West Germany set aside very large tracts of potentially profitable agricultural land for NATO maneuvers on its territory, and also endured much nuisance and damage from the constant exercises of low-flying aircraft, all of which amounted to a considerable economic and social cost but did not count in the calculations of who was sharing what burden. The third consideration can be illustrated by a simple example: at one point the U.S. secretary of defense, Caspar Weinberger, received in Congress a delegation of governors and elected representatives of the state of New Jersey, who called upon him to protest against a cost-cutting exercise that involved the cancellation of the flights of two aircraft per week from Newark to the U.S. Rhine-Main base near Frankfurt in Germany. These aircraft were loaded to the gunwales with American iceberg lettuces destined for U.S. post exchange (PX) stores in Germany, serving U.S. military personnel and their families. The sale of such lettuces made a tidy profit for the New Jersey farmers; but should the implicit assumption of the PX culture that German lettuces were not good enough to eat really be counted in terms of burden-sharing? In other words, it was a question not only of who spent how much but also of who spent how much on what—a question that was reinforced by the Pentagon's own office of audit, which revealed the gross overcharging by defense contractors of the American taxpayer for items that were only remotely related to defense, including lavatory seats at several thousand dollars each. In such circumstances, the West Germans, who effectively doubled their armored strength in the eight years between 1974 and 1981,[3] were unlikely to be impressed by U.S. accusations that they were not strictly fulfilling their commitment to increase their defense expenditure under the Long-Term Defense Program (agreed in 1978) by 3 percent a year in real terms. They tended to argue that they were simply more efficient. In any event, mutually suspicious resentments over burden-sharing became a regular feature of U.S.-European relations through the 1970s and into the 1980s, and did much to dent the image of interdependence that President Kennedy had proclaimed in 1963.

The second area of concern was that of out-of-area operations. The obligations entered into by the NATO member states had geographical limits. The United States, for example, was not obliged to consult its European allies (though it did in part do so) over its handling of the Cuban missile crisis because Cuba lies just outside the area defined as the "North Atlantic" in the treaty. In the earlier years of the alliance, such circumscription had tended to work to the political advantage of the United States—particularly when it came to keeping out of colonial wars fought by its European allies. It was also the case that most of the earlier crises in NATO were generated by the independent action of the Europeans in areas outside the sphere of the alliance—the Suez crisis being the prime example. (One might add that Britain and France drew opposite conclusions from that particular historical episode: the British deciding that they could never again act without U.S. support, and in their case that decision reigned until the Falklands crisis of 1982; the French deciding that they could never again rely on U.S. support and must in the future be able and prepared to act alone. Although never quite within their grasp, that has been a feature of the French government's approach to policy decisions ever since.) Later on, however, the out-of-area arguments tended to work the other way around. It was U.S. involvement in regions such as Central America or the Middle East that aroused the ire of many European governments. They frequently considered U.S. actions to be ill-advised or even downright aggressive, whether the matter was support for some of Israel's more curious activities or the invasion of Grenada. They also frequently complained about lack of consultation. The corresponding U.S. complaint—apparently well justified in the matter of how to react to the Soviet invasion of Afghanistan at the end of 1979—was that efforts were indeed made to consult on many occasions, but that the Europeans were singularly reluctant to return the call on the answerphone—a shorthand here for diplomatic procedures. Again, the disputes are too various and detailed to go into, but their rough outline might be described as a U.S. proposition on the one hand that if Europeans wished to maintain the U.S. commitment to Europe, they had better commit themselves to supporting U.S. policy elsewhere in the world, while the European response on the other hand might be said to have been (with the intermittent exception of Britain) that Europe had no intention of supporting policies with which it did not agree. That was yet one more indication of the manner in which NATO had degenerated from being the foundation-stone of the international system to an alliance within what was by now becoming an increasingly uncertain system, dominated by the changes and unpredictabilities of the superpower relationship.

It might be convenient at this point to refer back to Chapter 1, and to its contention that the world has never really been accurately described as a bipolar system. The problems and conundrums that arise when trying to treat recent history in this manner are reminiscent of those of Ptolemaic astronomy in dealing with a universe of which Earth was deemed to be the center. The procession of the equinoxes, the erratic movements of the planet Mercury: all these could be accounted for by the addition of increasingly complicated epicycles to the circular movement of the heavenly bodies around Earth itself. Similarly, the assumption that the systematic management of human destiny depended on the relationship between two superpowers, each of which had the capacity to snuff out that destiny, and each of which assumed that its European allies would have to go along with its designs, meant that the management of world affairs became more and more dependent on the way in which they could incorporate the epicycles of the fractious and localized decisions of a small country like Israel or an obdurate one like North Vietnam. In the jargon of the study of international relations, the need to incorporate such phenomena came to be known as "subsystem dominance." In the end, the phenomena and episodes of subsystem dominance led to an intensification of regional conflict between the superpowers, and to a new U.S. policy after the Soviet invasion of Afghanistan: one of global containment of Soviet power. It is in that context that the third area of dispute between the European and U.S. wings of the alliance can most readily be understood.

For many Americans, including the majority of senators, the invasion of Afghanistan provided the clinching evidence that the Soviet Union was simply not to be trusted; and it was for that reason that President Carter did not even bother to send the second SALT treaty to the

Senate for ratification: he knew that it did not stand a chance. It was also interpreted as part of a wider pattern of Soviet behavior, that evoked by Zbigniew Brzezinski's "arc of crisis": and under the first Reagan administration it became the paramount objective of U.S. policy to contain and reverse such behavior. European governments did not necessarily disagree: indeed the British government under Margaret Thatcher emphatically supported the U.S. position. But there were problems.

The first problem was one of interpretation. For example, the U.S. secretary of state, Alexander Haig, was readily inclined to conclude that the declaration of martial law in Poland in December 1981 was an act of indirect Soviet aggression. The German government—which the Polish deputy prime minister visited immediately after the declaration of martial law in order to explain the circumstances—was more inclined to see it as a matter arising out of the exigencies of the internal Polish situation, and, if anything, a measure designed to prevent Soviet intervention. That is only one instance of such differences of interpretation; but these led to disputes about the conduct of policy, about the diplomacy of the CSCE, about how far the Soviet Union should be "punished" or held to account for its behavior. That also raised the second problem.

For many Europeans, but for Germans in particular, the agreements reached in the early 1970s (the period of the first interpretation of MAD) represented solid and valuable achievements. Transformation through rapprochement might not have occurred, but nonetheless the establishment of diplomatic relations between the two Germanies, and between the Federal Republic and other East European counties, the Berlin agreement of 1972, the creation of a more or less reliable working relationship between Moscow and Bonn—one that might help to facilitate future solutions to the vexed problems of arms control: these represented the outcome of very hard work in the political, economic, and diplomatic fields, and were not likely to be jeopardized because of a deterioration in the global relationship between the superpowers. They were what the Germans called "the fruits of détente." Was the Berlin agreement to be endangered, was Poland to be threatened with a Soviet invasion because of a Western reaction to what had happened in Afghanistan? It was important, vital even, to differentiate between the appropriate policies for various matters and areas of concern.

In fact, there was nothing inherently incompatible between the U.S. and the European approaches to the Soviet Union. As in a double-hulled ship, it was perfectly possible to maintain an outer hull of global containment with an inner one of European détente. But the different interpretations of Soviet actions, sometimes combined with rhetorical bluster and different priorities in the field of arms control, often seemed to make the U.S.-European relationship more adversarial than amicable. Whatever one's interpretation of the Soviet invasion of Afghanistan (and there are a lot of ambiguities attached), it is hard not to feel some sympathy for any American politician, at a time when American taxpayers were paying four billion dollars to impose an agricultural embargo on the USSR, who might come across the communiqué issued by the West German chancellor Helmut Schmidt and the French president Valéry Giscard d'Estaing after a meeting in February 1980. It would not be an unfair summary of the communiqué to say that it declared that if the Soviet Union invaded Afghanistan again, it would be a serious blow to détente.[4] Understandably, members of the Senate Foreign Relations Committee were not pleased.

But what was also growing up at this time—the late 1970s and early 1980s—was a new sense of the relationship between the need for strategic containment and the possibilities of arms control. This reappraisal led, at best, to what might be described as a strained consensus among the different allies, and at other times produced strain without consensus. The implications of arms control questions will be discussed more fully in Chapter 11. But what they showed very clearly was that NATO was well able to hold together when the system of international relations depended on all-out confrontation with the Soviet Union, less well able to do so when an apparently bipolar world based on that confrontation gave way to an increasingly differentiated system, and found itself exposed to stresses and divisions when the questions of possible agreement with the USSR and the Warsaw Pact became matters of real instead of hypothetical policy. However, NATO, unlike the Warsaw Pact, survived the process of agreements. That, above all, shows the difference between the two alliances.

Earlier some mention was made of the obvious similarities between NATO and the Warsaw Pact. But their differences were, as suggested, more fundamental. These can be inferred in part from the different dates of their foundation. NATO, founded in 1949, very quickly became the principal forum of relations between the United States and Western Europe. The Warsaw Pact, founded six years later in 1955, never achieved that role in the relations between the Soviet Union and its East European members. That had already been established in the Council for Mutual Economic Assistance (COMECON), which was founded even before NATO and which provided the basis for coordination, not only of economic policies among the states that were now members of the Soviet empire, but also of a wide range of domestic and foreign policies too. In this respect, and for most of its history, the Warsaw Pact was an adjunct to COMECON. (NATO might also well have been an adjunct to an Atlantic Economic Community if the United States had been a founder member and had established it before the creation of the alliance. But the United States provided Marshall Aid to Europe instead; and while its subsequent behavior was seldom altruistic, it never sought to dominate the decisions of what did become the EEC in the way that the Soviet Union certainly sought for years to dominate COMECON.) That is the first difference between the two alliances, but another, and one equally fundamental, lies in the reason for their formation.

NATO was formed in response to what was perceived (probably mistakenly—as most historians agree) as a real military threat to Western Europe by a hostile superpower. Or else (as some historians argue) the idea of the threat was manipulated by certain politicians, primarily U.S. and British, so as to bring about the creation of the alliance. But its very foundation drew together all the threads of economic, political, and military cooperation between the United States and Western Europe, and the rationale at least was the necessity of confronting the Soviet threat of conquest.

The Warsaw Pact, on the other hand, was not founded to confront a hostile superpower, but in response to the emergence of a European power. The Soviet Union had long been anxious to prevent German membership of NATO—at one point in 1954 even offering to join the Atlantic alliance itself and thereby convert it into a collective security organization dedicated to the maintenance of German neutrality. (The proposal was greeted with some mirth in the Western chancelleries.) But it had also consistently warned that if West Germany ever did become a member of NATO, Moscow would immediately create a counter-alliance of its own. It fulfilled its promise very promptly in 1955. But why, one might ask, was German membership of NATO so alarming? And why bother to create the Warsaw Pact to deal with it, when the Soviet Union already had bilateral defense treaties with the East European countries and, for the most part, had Soviet forces stationed on their soil?

The answer cannot be seen in terms of any immediate military threat. After all, the Soviet Union was a nuclear power, whereas a condition for West German accession to NATO was that it would never manufacture nuclear weapons. And even though one day the Germans would no doubt produce an efficient army again, there were still twenty-six Soviet divisions on German soil, and they were likely to stay there for the foreseeable future. Even given the hideous and still recent memories of World War II, military anxieties can hardly have provided the principal Soviet motive. But there were other causes for concern.

The first lay in the fact that upon its accession to NATO, the Federal Republic became a sovereign state. Although it had managed its own affairs since 1949, and had conducted extensive foreign relations, in particular with France, it had lacked full sovereignty in the sense that the ultimate sovereign authority of the country lay not with the German government or people but with the occupying powers. In some respects and because of the terms of the Potsdam agreement, that was still to be formally the case for some years to come, especially if it came to a matter of who would decree a state of emergency. But in effect, that was a legal fiction. From now on the occupying forces were those of allies instead of occupiers, and they were dedicated to the defense of West Germany. To all intents and purposes, that state had become their sovereign equal. And one of the prerogatives of a sovereign state is that it can establish a foreign office and open embassies abroad.

That was a prospect to alarm the Soviet Union. By now the German economic miracle was in full swing, and Germany had traditionally dominated the markets and industries of Eastern Europe. The possibility that it might do so again, opening up embassies, sending trade missions, arranging credits, was something to which the Soviet empire was particularly vulnerable. The more so since it was a curious inversion of the traditional empire as analyzed by Lenin. In that analysis, the capitalist state needs ever expanding outlets for its manufactured goods, and so seeks captive markets in the colonies. In turn, it extracts cheap raw materials from these, and proceeds to convert them into more manufactured goods, which it then sells at a handsome profit. But in the empire of COMECON, it was the Soviet Union that exported the raw materials—oil, gas, even snow in the form of hydroelectric energy—and that received manufactured goods, notably from East Germany and Czechoslovakia, but also from all the countries with which it had had joint-stock company agreements. These were little more than a license for the USSR to exploit the economies of the East European countries—to whom West Germany, however, might now be able to offer a much better deal. And if one is a crude Marxist-Leninist of the kind produced by the Soviet system at the time, one fervently believes that the economic infrastructure determines the political superstructure, and that it will not therefore be very long before the counterrevolution sets in and all the states of the hard-won security buffer zone become bourgeois capitalist allies of the hostile West.

In that sense the emergence of West Germany as a sovereign state was a real potential threat to Soviet security interests, and it is certainly possible to argue that the Warsaw Pact was created primarily to control the foreign policy of the East European countries. But even so, why was it necessary to form an alliance when bilateral treaties already existed and when the Soviet Union was in the habit of simply giving orders that the other countries were in the habit of obeying? The answer lies in the fact that it was precisely at this time that Khrushchev was trying to break the habit.

Khrushchev had not yet made his famous "Secret Speech" denouncing Stalin, but the process of de-Stalinization was already under way. The joint-stock companies were being liquidated (although there was not yet an alternative economic system to take their place); the so-called comrade advisers, the KGB representatives who were sent to supervise the ministries of the interior in the various Eastern capitals, were being recalled; and in general "the thaw," as the Russians called it, had begun. Without the apparatus of Stalinism, it would be more difficult in the future simply to give orders; and the Warsaw Pact could be a useful instrument of policy.

There was perhaps one final consideration: the Soviet Union, while not necessarily fearful of German military power on its own, might well have been anxious about the potential emergence of a Washington-Bonn axis in NATO, which could have led to a major confrontation with the United States arising from a dispute with the Federal Republic over the conduct of its policies in Europe. Again, it is worth recalling that this was the period of massive retaliation.

Whether or not such anxieties played a part, it is clear that the Warsaw Pact was not so much a military alliance as a framework for Soviet foreign policy and the protection of Soviet interests. Its subsequent history bears that out. It was years before any integrated air defense system was established, years before multilateral military maneuvers took place (until 1961, all military exercises were bilateral at most, usually involving Soviet forces and those of whichever host country they happened to be in), and years before any attempt was made to modernize the forces of other Warsaw Pact countries to the point where they could make an effective contribution to what the Soviet military was planning. But for all that, the most striking feature of the Warsaw Pact is that it was an attempt to legitimize the management of foreign policy in terms of military security—even to the point where much of the language of the Warsaw Treaty deliberately echoes that of the North Atlantic Treaty. Other policy concerns were once again absorbed into and expressed in the terms of strategic confrontation—and that confrontation, as suggested earlier, vastly hindered the process of change in Eastern Europe.

There was, of course, one particular reason for this. Until West Germany joined NATO, the Soviet Union had been consistently in favor of German unification. The terms appear to have been variable, ranging from early political ambitions for a united Communist Germany in the early days of the Cold War[5]—perhaps up to the time of the Berlin Blockade—to aspirations for a neutral Germany between the two power blocs of the kind that Stalin proposed in an official note to the United States, Britain, and France in 1952. But from the moment that the Federal Republic did join NATO three years later, Moscow became an implacable opponent of unification: the idea that a unified Germany might be free to join NATO was too horrifying to contemplate. Since precisely that now became official U.S. policy, it was essential that the German Democratic Republic remain as firmly tied in to the Warsaw Pact, and the Soviet security system, as possible. And that meant that the Soviet security system could not change its political colors in a way that gave rise to any form of intra-German rapprochement.

So the Soviet Union hastened to recognize the Federal Republic in 1955, even while upgrading the status of the Democratic Republic to that of a fully sovereign state and ally within the Warsaw Pact. Two Germanies—each belonging to distinct and mutually hostile security systems—were now the best that Moscow could hope for. Meanwhile other states in Eastern Europe were to be discouraged from following Moscow's example: they should not entertain thoughts of engaging in diplomatic relations with Bonn. In fact, the Soviet leadership need hardly have worried. The Federal Republic, determined to pursue its own aim of ultimate reunification, declared in 1955—in the terms of the so-called Hallstein Doctrine—that it would regard as an unfriendly act the recognition of East Germany by any other state. When in 1957 Yugoslavia did recognize East Germany, the Federal Republic immediately broke off diplomatic relations with it. Nothing could have suited Moscow's book better. Since, perforce, all the members of the Warsaw Pact did have diplomatic relations with East Berlin, Bonn had now precluded itself, through this interpretation of the Hallstein Doctrine, from opening an embassy anywhere in Eastern Europe. So the German-German confrontation came to be the focal point of the confrontation between the two alliance systems and reinforced the propensity to interpret any possible change in Eastern Europe in terms of its potential threat to Soviet security.

The German question was dominant in the formation and development of the Warsaw Pact. But more generally, the history of that organization fell roughly into three phases. The first was the period between 1955 and 1960–1961. During that time, the pact scarcely existed in a military sense, but did serve to contain potential West German influence in the East, and to deal with some of the disputes about new COMECON policies after Khrushchev had launched his initiative for a new "socialist international division of labor" in 1958. (It was sometimes amazing to see how fast such disputes could be resolved once they were transferred from the economic agenda of the COMECON to the security agenda of the Warsaw Pact—though it did not always work like that. One reason for Romania's increasing defiance of the USSR after 1958 was precisely that it interpreted Soviet proposals for COMECON reform in terms of its national security and its own cherished version of Stalinism.)

The second phase began with the development of two crises at the beginning of the 1960s: that over Berlin vis-à-vis the West, which culminated in the building of the Berlin Wall in 1961, and that of the open eruption of the Sino-Soviet dispute in the East, which encouraged Albania directly, and Romania indirectly, to defy Soviet authority and Soviet policies. It is during this period that it is possible to discern the evolution of the Warsaw Pact into something approaching a genuine military alliance, with the beginnings of those elements of integration that had hitherto been entirely lacking. It is also worth noting that this was also the period of Khrushchev's attempts, ultimately futile though they were, to push through further measures of demobilization in the Soviet armed forces themselves. It was clearly to his advantage to stress the military potential of the Warsaw Pact countries. However, measures of modernization and integration were largely confined to the countries of what came to be known in the West as the Northern Tier: East Germany, Poland, and (at the time) Czechoslovakia. The others were left to degenerate into increasing obsolescence. But as the immediate crisis abated, and gave way to the détente of the mid-1960s, the pact also became increasingly important in terms of defining and regulating the conduct of its members vis-à-vis the West—and West Germany in particular. A clear instance of this can be found in the Karlovy Vary conference in Czechoslovakia in 1967, which occurred shortly after Romania, in another act of defiance, had opened diplomatic relations with West Germany (which thereby implicitly dropped the Hallstein Doctrine). The conclusion of this conference was to the effect that no other pact member would be allowed to establish such connections without the assent of East Germany and unless the relationship between the two German states had been sorted out first. In other words, the pact was by this time becoming the watchdog of détente.

But that raises the question of the third phase: whether the pact was also going to be the watchdog over the internal developments in the

East European states as détente progressed. At first, the answer had appeared to be no. Vaguely and vacillatingly committed to reform as the Soviet leadership seemed, it was also minded to allow its East European allies to develop their own internal reform programs to the extent that they saw fit, and to the extent that these were compatible with the overall interests of what was by then becoming fashionable to call the "Socialist Commonwealth." An occasional minatory nudge from Moscow would suffice to ensure that things did not get out of control. The evolution of the New Economic Mechanism in Hungary is a fair example of how matters were conducted at that time. But the sudden blossoming of the Prague Spring in Czechoslovakia in 1968 changed everything. That extraordinary historical moment, of which the nature was unforeseen even by its most central participants, of which the accelerating development was so noble, and of which the ultimate outcome was so tragic, represented in its more mundane aspects an attempt by the Czech leadership to play by all the historical rules that the Warsaw Pact seemed so far to have established. It was anxious constantly to reassure the Soviet Union and its other allies that it would not leave the pact, that it would not strike up a partnership, or even establish diplomatic relations with the Federal Republic of Germany. That was a theme to which the Czech foreign minister, Jiri Hayek, constantly returned. All that Czechoslovakia wanted was the capacity to conduct its own internal affairs in its own way. But whether seen from Moscow at the time or from Western academic seminars later on, the Prague Spring represented a unique challenge to the confluence of neorevolutionary ideology and Soviet state interests that by then had come to characterize the formation of policy in Moscow. If the party can exercise power only by the will and consent of the people, then the whole Leninist concept of the "vanguard party" is a nonsense, and the enormous sacrifices demanded had been in vain. And if Czechoslovakia, given its strategic location between the borders of Bavaria and those of the Ukraine, were permitted to go its own way, the Warsaw Pact could equally become a nonsense. In the end, and on either count, the Prague Spring had to be crushed.

It was. But central to the argument here, it was not the Soviet Union alone that invaded Czechoslovakia: the invasion included forces from all the other members of the Warsaw Pact except Romania—which was not allowed to play—and Albania, which by then had long ceased to be a member in any real terms and now took the opportunity of formally renouncing the pact altogether. But the fact that Moscow could press-gang the rest into joining the invasion seemed to mark the apogee of its management of East European policies—initially external, now apparently internal as well—through the pact. Certainly, a number of Soviet statements, both before and after the invasion of Czechoslovakia, seemed to confirm this. Collectively, they came to be known in the West as the Brezhnev Doctrine.

The principal tenet of the Brezhnev Doctrine was that while all states were sovereign equals in public international law, and as such had no right to interfere in each other's internal affairs, there was nonetheless a higher law, the law of socialism. When socialism was in danger in any one of the sovereign states in the Socialist Commonwealth, it was not only the right but also the duty of the others to intervene and protect it. This was like a production of the medieval teaching of natural law in modern dress; and just as once it had been the pope who judged whether a sovereign prince was guilty of infringing natural law and should be punished, so now it was Moscow that would clearly decide whether and where socialism was in danger. And it would be the Warsaw Pact that took remedial action.

There were three criteria of socialist solidarity. The first was "proletarian internationalism"—Sovspeak for toeing the line on foreign policy; the second was "socialist construction"—Sovspeak for adherence to Moscow's economic policies; and the third was the "leading role of the party"—which meant the leading role of the party. Between them, these three encompassed pretty well all the activities of the state, and from that time onward one might have expected the threat of Soviet military intervention to be at the forefront of East European calculations. Yet the third phase of the history of the Warsaw Pact, beginning in 1969, was really one of growing independence on the part of the East European states and a growing Soviet reluctance to intervene.

In 1969 the Soviet Union cordially invited other pact members to send "observers" to the scene of its border fighting with China along the river Ussuri. They all refused. In the same year the commander in chief of the Warsaw Pact—as always, a Soviet marshal—proposed the establishment of a rapid intervention force, to which all members would contribute and which would be ready to protect socialism wherever it was endangered anywhere in the commonwealth. That was rather like asking for contributions to a lottery in which the winner would be executed, and again the Soviet request met with a point-blank refusal. More generally, it is easy to see instances of defiance of each of the three criteria of the Brezhnev Doctrine. Romania did not bow to proletarian internationalism. Hungary did not sacrifice its economic policies on the altar of socialist construction. And in Poland, the leading role of the party became increasingly entangled in the complexities of a pluralist society.

Pact and party between them continued to hold down fundamental change, everywhere except for Poland's experiment with Solidarity, until the advent of Gorbachev in 1985. In the intervening years, the countries of the Northern Tier (no longer including Czechoslovakia) developed a formidable military alliance, and in that respect one might say that the Warsaw Pact was after all serving a military purpose as well as a political one. But this was also the period in which political and economic considerations were beginning to outweigh those of strategy in the conduct of relations between East and West. Apart from anything else, the Soviet Union needed German money, as had already become apparent when it allowed other East European states to establish diplomatic relations with the Federal Republic at the time of the Ostpolitik—and there might even be a case for saying that the success, albeit limited, of the Ostpolitik was one reason for the noninterventionist character that the Warsaw Pact had assumed in the third phase of its history. But it was Gorbachev who was explicitly to renounce the right of Soviet or of Warsaw Pact intervention in the affairs of any other member state. And that precipitated a wider irony.

Gorbachev's reforms led eventually to the East European revolutions of 1989. But by then much of his program had come to depend on the very things that the Warsaw Pact was originally established to prevent: Western, and particularly German, aid and investment. The "new thinking in international relations" that was part of his reform program also led him eventually to conclude that German reunification would be an acceptable price to pay for Soviet security, as it was now defined in terms of East-West cooperation rather than in terms of confrontation; much of the reason for that lay in the astonishing transformation of what was meant by "arms control" during the Gorbachev years.

Notes

1. This command structure has since been modified, with Commander in Chief Channel (CINCHAN) abolished and NATO's military structure now consisting of two strategic commands: Allied Command Europe (under SACEUR) and Allied Command Atlantic (under SACLANT). For the full details of NATO's current command structure, see *NATO Handbook 2000–01,* chap. 12.

2. I have tried to elucidate some of these considerations in "German Foreign Policy," in F. S. Northedge, ed., *The Foreign Policies of the Powers* (London: Faber, 1968). I returned to this theme at greater length in *Germany and the Management of Détente* (London: Chatto and Windus for the International Institute for Strategic Studies, 1971).

3. I went into these arguments in an Adelphi Paper for the IISS in 1981: *Germany and the Western Alliance: Lessons from the 1980 Crises,* Adelphi Paper no. 170 (London: International Institute for Strategic Studies, 1981).

4. The statement condemning the Soviet invasion warned that "détente would not stand up to another shock of the same order." Quoted in Melinda Liu and Scott Sullivan, "Paris and Bonn Take a Stand," *Newsweek,* February 18, 1980.

5. See Wolfgang Leonhard, *Child of the Revolution* (London: Collins, 1957) and *The Kremlin Since Stalin* (London: Oxford University Press, 1962).

11

Arms Control

Arms control is an approach to international relations that takes the existence of high levels of armaments for granted. In that sense it is not concerned with disarmament but rather with resolving the problems that disarmament could not cope with. It might help to explain the nature of arms control more clearly if the problems of disarmament are discussed briefly first.

At the beginning of this century, the European powers had been so long at peace that another war between them seemed an extraordinarily remote possibility. The first disarmament conferences were held with that in mind: it seemed pointless to squander money on armaments when nobody was going to fight anyway. The conferences were a failure—indeed the Anglo-German naval race intensified during that period—but the failure reflects imperial rivalries rather than any intent to go to war. All the same, some of the problems of disarmament, notably the difficulty of distinguishing between offensive and defensive weapons, were already becoming apparent. Later they were to be intensified as the purpose of disarmament changed. For after World War I, arms were widely regarded as the very cause of war, and the purpose of disarming therefore became that of preventing war rather than dispensing with an expensive luxury. But if disarmament was to be the means of preventing war, it became both more important than it had been in the past and also more radical in scope. The human propensity to fight means that if wars are to be prevented, arms would have to be cut to a very low level indeed. That has two implications.

The first is that on the way to achieving such very low levels, states are likely to be *more* concerned about their security than they would be with higher levels of armaments. They will insist on maintaining defensive weapons—for the time being. In some cases that presents no problems. An anti-aircraft gun cannot be used for anything except shooting down hostile aircraft. But in other cases the problems are formidable. A tank might be deployed in a defensive capacity, but it could rapidly assume an offensive role. In such cases, do numbers make a difference, and if so, what is the critical mass, and in what context? The postwar disarmament conferences came to grief on such problems, and on the wider but still related question of what constituted aggression.

The second implication is that, as disarmament became more radical, the measures of arms reduction would have to be checked with greater and greater severity. Obviously, a state that was abiding by its commitments and destroying its armaments would become increasingly vulnerable to a state that was cheating—through concealed production, through the diversion of peaceful programs to military ends, or through the hidden import of armaments from a third country, not necessarily party to any disarmament agreement. In the 1920s under the Rapallo Pact, Germany and the Soviet Union had what amounted to an agreement for Germany to circumvent the arms limitations imposed on it by the Treaty of Versailles. More recently, in the Middle East, it has become obvious that Iraq was engaged in the clandestine procurement of large numbers of weapons of mass destruction—using all three of the methods outlined here. In general, it is all too easy to cheat. Today, as the miniaturization of nuclear weapons advances, the problem of verification—of ensuring that an agreement not to make weapons, or to dispose of those already made, is being honored—is even more important. In fact, to abolish war by eliminating armaments would mean the creation of a *1984* kind of world in which endless teams of all-powerful inspectors equipped with the most intrusive gadgetry were entitled to probe under every bush and bed in order to ensure that nobody was cheating. Short of that, the problem of verification is insoluble—and though it was said earlier that arms control was in part an attempt to get to grips with the problems that disarmament could not solve, that problem also returned to haunt arms control negotiations in the age of Cold War confrontation.

These are some of the principal difficulties associated with disarmament. But there are others that have less to do with disarmament itself than with the political context in which it might be seen to operate. In the 1920s disarmament formed part of a trio in which the principles of collective security (the Locarno Pact), the identification and punishment of aggressors (through the League of Nations), and the renunciation of war as an instrument of policy (the Kellogg-Briand Pact) were all meant to further the pacific cause. But the collapse of such good intentions, and the rise of the Third Reich, discredited the general idea of disarmament, especially in Britain: the country's failure to *re*arm in the face of Hitler's policies became associated with appeasement and with Neville Chamberlain's abject behavior at Munich. After World War II, and as the Cold War began to intensify from about 1947, it was generally accepted, especially in Britain and the United States, that the best way to prevent a future conflict was to maintain a high level of armaments. In that sense, the wheel had come full circle.

This is not to say that disarmament now disappeared from the international agenda. It returned in 1960 with the convening of the UN's Ten-Nation Committee on Disarmament in Geneva, the result of a Soviet initiative. (Given the year, that probably represented yet another attempt by Khrushchev to gain acceptance for his proposed cuts in military manpower and expenditure.) At first composed of a few UN members, subsequently expanded to include more, and later degenerating into the kind of Irish fight in which anybody could join, its purpose has always been unclear.[1] In the early days, both superpowers tabled disarmament proposals, which neither can have expected the other to take seriously. But one might add more charitably that by its continued existence, the UN conference keeps aspirations alive and provides a meeting-point that might of itself help to change the political context in which more specific agreements can be reached. In this sense, it provided the forum for some valuable preliminary work on what was to become in 1993 an agreement to eliminate chemical weapons, to which many states have already appended their signatures. The problems of verification, however, remain in place.

Well before 1959, though, ideas about arms control were beginning to supplant notions of disarmament as the most effective way of preventing future war—particularly in the East-West context. Originating in U.S. academic writings, they rapidly gained a wider audience in which journalists, intellectuals, and politicians came together. Symptomatic of such developments was the foundation in London, in 1958, of the Institute for Strategic Studies—now the International Institute.[2] But if arms control takes the existence of large amounts of weaponry for granted—including nuclear weaponry—in what sense can it be said to attempt to prevent war? The answer lies in one word: stability.

Stability here means that in any armed confrontation between hostile powers or blocs, neither side should be tempted to seek an advantage by attacking its opponent first. That can apply at either the nuclear or the conventional level of armaments. (In negotiation, the question of which level should be tackled first is a matter of some complexity—but that question will be addressed later.) The attainment of stability clearly does not depend on the overall reduction of armaments: such a reduction could indeed entail the problems of a growing vulnerability of one state to another that were inherent in the problems of disarmament. Indeed, arms control might require an actual *increase* in the level of armaments in order to achieve stability. McNamara's advocacy of flexible response in 1962 certainly implied an increase in the level of NATO's conventional armed forces. But that example only illustrates the more general point: he had hoped to dissuade the Soviet Union from launching a conventional attack, which could have entailed the risks of nuclear war, by convincing it that it could not hope for a walkover at the lower level. In that respect his approach to flexible response, in itself an attempt to deal with some of the difficulties of extended deterrence, might be seen also as an exercise in arms control.

In other words, arms control is really nothing other than an attempt to prevent war through the stabilization of deterrence. It is concerned with the configuration and rationalization of armaments by both parties to any confrontation, such that war is the least likely outcome of their otherwise hostile relationship. Obviously, the most important single instance of such an approach is the development of the second-strike missile. Once that was in place, it became infinitely less likely (though never altogether excluded) that either superpower would seek to launch a "preemptive strike" against the other. But that development also illustrates another important feature of arms control. Disarmament, virtually by definition, depends on negotiation and agreement. Arms control measures can be adopted unilaterally: Eisenhower did not, after all, consult Khrushchev about whether he should deploy more first-strike missiles or wait instead until the second-strike generation became available. He simply took a sensible decision on his own.

But the difficulty here is that while in some circumstances it is possible for two contending powers to take sensible decisions on their own, while each expects and reciprocates an understanding of the other, it is also possible for them to anticipate the worst analysis of the other's intentions and to react accordingly. The central imperative of arms control—strategic stability—can therefore become an incentive to the intensification of the arms race. The arms race, however, cannot be defined in terms of the action-reaction phenomenon with which it is usually associated. If a power anticipates some action on the part of another, it might very well react before the event. When the United States was developing the antiballistic missile, it was soon argued on the basis of many technological precedents that if the Americans could do it, the Russians would one day be able to do it too. How then should the United States deal with the threat that would eventually be created by Soviet ABMs? The answer was to develop the MIRV (multiple independently targeted reentry vehicle—one of the more ungainly euphemisms of the nuclear age), whereby a single missile can carry a number of nuclear warheads, all to be released at different points of the trajectory, and each capable of destroying a different target. Sometimes known as the "bus-stop bomb," the MIRV was to complicate enormously future arms control negotiations. But at the time it was developed it was a reaction to the U.S. ABM program and to the *potential* of a Soviet one. At this point the United States was in effect running an arms race with itself.

A different way in which arms control can intensify the arms race lies in the accumulation of "bargaining chips." This is to say that when two powers are engaged in negotiations, either might sometimes develop weapons that it does not seriously intend to deploy but that can be used to extract concessions from the other side if it offers to give them up. The difficulty is that weapons systems, once developed, tend to take on a life of their own and it is not necessarily easy to give them up. A case in point is the cruise missile, which became world-famous in the Gulf War of 1990 but which Henry Kissinger has confessed that he regarded as a bargaining chip for the purpose of the SALT II negotiations. In general, many commentators have argued that in fact the SALT process stimulated that proliferation of weapons that it was supposed to bring under control.

These are some of the difficulties of arms control, whether it depends on unilateral decisions or on negotiated agreements. Now, it could be argued that increases in the numbers and types of weapons do not much matter if overall strategic stability is maintained. More and more weapons might be expensive and frequently unnecessary, but stability can operate just as well—perhaps even better—at higher levels of armament as at lower. There could be some force to that, particularly if the weapons produced on each side were pretty well parallel in their capability and purpose. But in the real world such attractive symmetries are not to be found; and as the level of armaments spirals ever upward, overall stability might be maintained, but the production of different kinds of weapons can well create dangerous pockets of instability within that framework. An example of this is the deployment by the Soviet Union in the late 1970s of the SS-20 missile, a highly accurate system of employing MIRV technology (which the USSR had by then developed) and capable of striking at every target of military significance between Sicily and Iceland. From the Soviet viewpoint, this was probably designed to counter the NATO threat of rapid nuclear escalation if war broke out in Europe. From the Western standpoint it represented the alarming prospect that under the cover of the SS-20s the USSR would be able to make much greater use of its superior conventional forces. Accordingly, after much heated debate, the United States deployed ground-launched cruise missiles at various sites in Europe (Greenham Common was one of them) and the particularly deadly Pershing II in Germany. The exceptional accuracy of the Pershing II, and the fact that its deployment in Germany meant that targets in the western Soviet Union were only found minutes away, so alarmed the Soviet authorities that they announced a "launch-on-warning" policy. This is to say that when the radar and computer systems indicated that missiles were coming, the buttons would immediately be pressed without any attempt at verifying whether the warning was accurate. This was a reversion to the worst perils of the first-strike period; and given the rotten state of Soviet computer technology, it threatened to make the European theater desperately unstable. And all that came out of the process of "stabilizing upward."

In order to maintain stability, therefore, especially in a period of crisis, it is important to keep numbers and types of weapons under control, even perhaps to reduce them, though it should be emphasized again that arms reduction is not of itself a purpose of arms control. In this context it is, however, a necessary technique. From that, it will be readily apparent that there is an inherent tension in arms control negotiations. The central purpose of making war less likely *might* demand a considerable array of weapons. That, to repeat, is arms control as stabilized deterrence. But to preserve stability might demand the reduction of weapons. How to strike a balance between these two considerations has been a problem that dogged arms control negotiations all the way through the 1970s and 1980s. Who gives up what and in return for which reductions on the other side is an extraordinarily difficult question, particularly when it comes to trading off different kinds of weapons—for example Soviet land-based missiles against U.S. submarine-launched missiles, which for some years involved competing criteria of numbers and accuracy.

That indicates one final complicating factor. As the 1970s advanced, both superpowers were making technological advances that permitted them to achieve a degree of accuracy in their targeting that was undreamed of a few years before.[3] That enabled them perhaps to use much smaller nuclear warheads, perhaps even to contemplate the use of conventional warheads. In consequence a subsidiary purpose of arms control began to creep into discussion and even negotiation: namely to make war less destructive if it did occur. But such a consideration flatly contradicted the primary purpose of making war less likely, because the less destructive a war might be, the easier it is to think of waging it. Indeed the first Reagan administration even began to discuss what it called a "countervailing strategy" ("to countervail" was a peculiar euphemism for "to prevail"), whereby an initial attack could destroy two thousand or more targets in the Soviet Union with pinpoint accuracy while allowing the society as a whole to survive. Not surprisingly, this made the conduct of negotiations more difficult. So, later on, did the realization on the part of the United States that Soviet systems were now becoming so accurate that they had the potential to destroy U.S. land-based missiles even in their hardened silos. It had looked for a time as if the dangers of war were receding. In the early 1980s they appeared to be advancing again as the policy of global containment coincided with technological advance. This was not something that the arms control process could cope with.

So much for difficulties and complications. Now for the progress report. Given the complexities, it is a miracle that any progress was made at all—and in effect there were only two moments of real progress, one being the first SALT agreement, signed in May 1972, which confirmed the concept of arms control as stabilized deterrence, and the second being the whole package of agreements on arms reductions of all kinds, reached between 1989 and 1993, which confirmed that arms control had changed its nature. To see why this was so, it is necessary to appreciate something of the structure of arms control negotiations.

There were three major sets of negotiations. The first, begun in November 1969, was the SALT talks, aimed at the limitation of strategic weapons and conducted between the two superpowers alone. "Strategic weapons" were defined as those (nuclear) systems by which either could attack the other from its own territory or from the oceans. The USSR originally argued that since it was vulnerable to attack by U.S. systems in continental Europe or the Mediterranean, these should also be included in the negotiating package, but the United States successfully resisted this, much to the relief of its European allies. (The Europeans were later to realize, however, that this had the effect of unhooking the European theater from the strategic relationship of the superpowers, an effect that was to give rise to considerable concern instead of relief when the Soviet Union began to deploy the SS-20s in Europe.)[4] The SALT talks concentrated at first on the question of antiballistic missiles and were later to try to reach agreement on the limitation of offensive systems. But it is revealing that McNamara's initial instructions to the U.S. negotiating team were that, when it went to Helsinki to begin the SALT process, it should seek to explore with its Soviet counterparts whether the two countries shared anything like a common approach to what was meant by "deterrence," rather than concentrate on weapons systems and numbers. This attempt was met with a point-blank Soviet refusal; and there are some indications that the Soviet attitude was another reflection of the distinction between Soviet strategic theory and military doctrine.[5] All the same, the United States was able to persuade the Soviet Union of the benefits of mutual vulnerability as a means of averting war, and the consequence was the agreement to limit the deployment of antiballistic missiles to strictly symbolic proportions. Each power would be allowed to deploy two ABM systems, one to protect a city and the other a missile launching site. Later this was reduced to one system each—and the Soviet Union did build up a chain of antimissile defenses around Moscow—even though these would hardly have proved effective against the advanced version of the U.S. Trident missile. (That was one reason for the British government's determination to buy the Trident.) As for the United States, it scarcely bothered, apart from some tentative deployment around a launch complex near Cheyenne, Wyoming.

The SALT I treaty was regarded, and rightly so in the context of stabilized deterrence, as a great success in redefining the nature of the superpower relationship. It was expected to lead to a further breakthrough in negotiating a more difficult question, that of the limitation of offensive weapons. SALT I had been negotiated in less than three years (1969–1971) and it was expected that SALT II would be concluded by 1974. In fact, an agreement was not reached until 1979, and by that time it was both politically and technologically out-of-date. This was in good measure due to the fact that the whole SALT process was inherently flawed, and that its purpose became increasingly unclear as negotiations proceeded. More of that later.

The second forum of arms control negotiations was what became known as the Mutual and Balanced Force Reductions (MBFR) talks. Begun in Vienna in 1973, they were concerned with the reduction of conventional forces in Europe, and were conducted between representative countries of both NATO and the Warsaw Pact. In this respect it is worth noting that while the Warsaw Pact was not the kind of alliance that NATO was, its very existence was nonetheless useful in providing what was potentially a valuable negotiating partner for the Western powers as a whole. Yet the cumbrous title of the talks indicated their central difficulty. They arose from a Soviet initiative subsequently amended by a NATO counterproposal. The Soviet Union had proposed talks on mutual force reductions—which would imply cuts of, say, 10 percent across the board in the first stage in aircraft, tanks, artillery, and so on, followed by further symmetrical cuts in later stages. But it hardly takes a mathematical genius to work out that if one side starts with a huge numerical advantage, the proportional advantage actually increases as the cuts proceed. It was for this reason that the NATO powers insisted that the word "balanced" be included in the terms of reference—meaning of course that reductions in conventional armaments should be greater on the side of the Warsaw Pact than on that of NATO.

Even though the USSR initially demurred, the principle was accepted, but that still left problems aplenty. Should the initial cuts be made among the forces that the superpowers had both deployed in Europe? Difficult, even if it were accepted that the cuts should be disproportionate, since it would still remain a geopolitical fact of life that it would be much easier for the USSR to reinforce its position than for the United States. Even so, the problem is not insoluble; and in spite of many arguments that reflected some of the old disputes inherent in disarmament negotiations, a tentative agreement was in sight when it foundered on a secondary problem. It was that of whether any successive reductions should be in that of the overall total of the European forces, or whether particular nations should reduce by proportionately more than others. Representatives of the Warsaw Pact would not, for example, have been particularly impressed if the Netherlands had offered to abolish all its land forces—which at that time had the somewhat unfair reputation of wearing hairnets and smoking pot. (In fact, NATO exercises have repeatedly shown them to be pretty efficient.) But they would have been very amenable to any suggestion, say, that Germany cut all its forces by 20 percent while leaving the Dutch entirely in place. That kind of "targeting" of individual national forces was something NATO was determined to resist, although it should follow from the principle of "balanced" force reductions that the Soviet Union was merely abiding by the rules that NATO had laid down.

Questions of that nature gave rise to another difficulty—namely that of how each side counts the other's effective forces. Is it proper to tally the clapped-out tanks of the Romanian army, which might have an estimated battle life of three minutes, in the same general category as the advanced T-72s of the Northern Tier? How does one measure "teeth-to-tail" effectiveness of the manpower on either side? If measurement depends on frequently faulty intelligence procedures, how can either side agree on the terms of measurement anyway?

All this is a rather elaborate way of saying that in spite of dedicated and sometimes imaginative negotiators and in spite of initial signs of goodwill, the MBFR talks got nowhere. They dragged on for years, but the best that can be said is that the foundations they established at least in terms of exploring the problems were later to be subsumed in the Conventional Armed Forces in Europe (CFE) agreement, signed in November 1990 and entered into force in 1992. But that was to be after arms control had changed its nature. CFE, as it became known, was a result of a wider change in the political relationship between East and West.

The third area of arms control negotiations was known, just to complicate matters, by two successive sets of initials. Each referred to the capabilities of intermediate-range nuclear missiles, and the negotiations were in a sense sandwiched between those on conventional forces on the one hand, and strategic missiles on the other. They were, so to speak, carved out of the original U.S. refusal to discuss European-based systems, which were capable of attacking the Soviet Union, within the ambit of the SALT talks. They began in 1978, at the time of the Carter administration in the United States. Their original designation went under the initials "LRTNF" (Long Range Theater Nuclear Forces) and it will be immediately apparent that these were designed primarily to counter the potential dangers created by the deployment of the Soviet SS-20 missiles. But they were also concerned with other medium-range missiles and nuclear bombers on both sides. Here again, they encountered familiar difficulties. What to count? Seaborne aircraft and cruise missiles on ships, which might be in the theater one month but not the next? Where to count? After all, if it was accepted that the European theater extended as far as the Urals, the Soviet Union could plausibly argue that it needed SS-20s east of the Urals to deter a hostile China; but the trouble was that such missiles, being mobile, could easily be rolled back west of the Urals at very short notice. For that and other reasons, the talks were rechristened under the Reagan administration and came to be known as the Mutual Force Reductions (MFR) talks, omitting all reference to the theater and widening their scope. In fact, agreement was very nearly reached. The two teams of negotiators did agree on the basic principles of counting and of the proportions of cuts in various categories. This was the famous "Walk in the Woods" formula (subsequently to be the improbable subject of a successful play), but it was rejected by the governments in both Washington and Moscow. That was partly because by then their mutual political mistrust had become acute, and partly because, or so at least report has it, President Reagan didn't understand it anyway.[6] Eventually, the Soviet Union walked out of the talks when the decision was made to deploy ground-launched cruise missiles and Pershing IIs in Europe; and negotiations were only resumed some time later in a very different political context.

It will soon become clear that the question of the political context was all-important. But first, it is worth considering the nature of these sets of negotiations. Partly for chronological reasons, in that the SALT talks were the first to start, and partly for reasons of superpower hegemony (the talks on medium-range forces profoundly affected the European countries but were conducted exclusively by the superpowers), the whole approach was gravely distorted. The assumptions seem to have been that if agreement could be reached at the strategic level, it would then be that much easier to get the medium-range balance "about right" and that on this basis it might be possible to deal with the much less important question of conventional armaments. But in fact a five-year-old would have been able to see at a glance that the fundamental problem was that of the imbalance in Europe of the conventional forces. It was this that drove NATO to a policy of nuclear escalation, thereby creating all the problems of the European theater, and it was these problems in turn that drove the strategic arms race. Nothing could demonstrate more clearly the mesmeric effects of a preoccupation with nuclear weapons than the way in which the hierarchy of dealing with the problems of arms control was in inverse order to the hierarchy of the problems themselves. As a consequence, many simply became insoluble, certainly within the political context of the time.

That raises a further consideration. When the SALT talks began, the United States was clearly well ahead of the Soviet Union in most areas of missile technology, and it intended to use this lead as a way of influencing Soviet behavior in other fields. Both President Nixon and Henry Kissinger were quite explicit about that, Nixon going so far as to hint broadly in his first foreign policy report to Congress (the "State of the World" message) that if the Soviet Union wished to reach a good SALT agreement it had better start behaving itself in the Middle East. In a sense that is understandable: one might see it as an attempt to translate the benign interpretation of MAD into arms control, and to use arms control to avoid the malign interpretation. But in another sense it was profoundly dangerous. If SALT, or the arms control process more generally, were to be the key to the conduct of international relations, then all kinds of other decisions all over the world would depend on whether the negotiations were going well or badly; and if they went badly, relations would deteriorate across the whole political spectrum. This is exactly what happened.

The SALT talks became increasingly difficult to manage or to bring to any conclusion. This was largely because the Soviet Union tended to compensate for U.S. MIRV technology and the greater and growing accuracy of U.S. missiles by building larger and larger numbers of new missiles of its own. (The Americans in contrast built no new land-based missiles at all from the later 1960s onward: they simply modernized and MIRVed those they already had.) Of itself, the dramatic increase in Soviet numbers need not have mattered overmuch, but as the growth in numbers gradually became wedded to greater accuracy, as the USSR began to develop MIRV technology, and as it began to produce a new generation of missile submarines that were much quieter than their predecessors (and so harder to detect and destroy), it began to appear that the older efforts to compensate for qualitative inferiority by quantitative superiority had created the basis of a disturbing new threat to the strategic equilibrium that the SALT talks themselves were attempting to codify and stabilize. These tendencies were already discernible, at least to Western intelligence, in the mid-1970s; and only one agreement was reached at that time to keep them in check. It was the so-called Vladivostok Interim Accord, signed by Gerald Ford and Leonid Brezhnev at the end of 1974. It limited the number of warheads that any one missile might carry to three—in itself a modest, even symbolic, measure, but one that had great significance for the future conduct of arms control, as will be discussed shortly. Otherwise, the wrangling became increasingly arcane, and the initial U.S. advantages that Washington had hoped to use to influence Soviet behavior in other fields were being inexorably eroded.

At the same time, political tensions increased—leading to the sense of global competition and confrontation that has already been indicated. A neat turning point in the whole process can be seen at the time of Henry Kissinger's visit to Moscow in an attempt to breathe new life into the SALT process in 1975. Asked by journalists when he left New York whether he intended to raise the subject of Angola (recently the subject of Cuban intervention) with President Brezhnev, he replied that he certainly did. Asked, once the discussions had been concluded in Moscow, whether he had done so, he answered that the SALT talks were far too important to be jeopardized by the question of Angola. And the final result of the whole process can be seen in President Carter's decision not to send the SALT II treaty to the Senate for ratification after the Soviet invasion of Afghanistan. What had begun life, at least in American eyes, as the instrument that determined the conduct of international relations, now ended all too obviously as the hostage to those relations.

That raises complicated questions. They can best be approached perhaps by a reconsideration of the Vladivostok agreement. The reason that such a modest measure had great potential significance was that neither superpower was able to check whether the other was in fact sticking to its word and limiting the number of warheads per missile to three. They had to *trust* each other. It was the question of trust that was to transform the nature of arms control negotiations later on. And it is also related to the matter of arms control as a means of determining political conduct.

The argument proceeds in separate stages. The first stage is the assumption that arms control can determine political conduct—what is known in the strategic jargon as "linkage." The general experience of the 1970s demonstrated that linkage so conceived cannot work. Worse, it tends to complicate the arms control process and to aggravate a deterioration of relations elsewhere. In such circumstances, many negotiators and specialists in the field of arms control came to argue with increasing vehemence that negotiations should not be linked to other political developments, but should concentrate on resolving functional problems without reference to what was happening in Afghanistan or anywhere else. But that raises the second stage.

If negotiations concentrate solely on solving functional problems, such as trading off the categories of who can throw what at whom and, in doing so, trying to achieve strategic stability without any reference to the wider set of political relations, then it becomes all the more important to arrive at agreements that can be checked out. After all, any agreement of which an element is to be based on trust depends on an assessment of whether the other side is *trustworthy*. And the question of trustworthiness depends on how one judges the other's record of political behavior. That would not be linkage in the original sense, but it would be linkage through the back door in the almost converse sense: that it is political behavior that determines what can and what cannot be achieved in arms control. Any attempt to eliminate such considerations and to concentrate on the purely functional issues therefore implies that agreements that are reached must be capable of independent and reliable verification. At this point the old ghost of disarmament talks returns to haunt the conduct of arms control.

Would the return of the ghost, however, mean that the feast of arms control (even if it was at best but nouvelle cuisine) was to be disrupted, as the anticipated banquet of disarmament had been? Politicians and press secretaries in the West tried to get around this difficulty by stressing that they were after agreements that, in the cant phrase, were "both significant and verifiable." But that raises the third stage. What is verifiable is not necessarily significant, and what is significant is frequently not verifiable. The number of warheads on a missile, how many times a reusable launcher can be pressed into service, the question of whether a cruise missile might be tipped with a nuclear weapon or conventional high explosive—all these are of vital importance in arms control negotiations, and yet, to put it mildly, extremely difficult to verify. The consequence is twofold. In the first place, so long as arms control negotiations are seen as being of great strategic importance, it matters that they are as hard-and-fast as possible. On the other hand, the attempt to make them hard-and-fast inevitably limits their scope. In the words of an exceptionally distinguished but extremely rueful American negotiator, shortly after an agreement had been reached on nuclear forces in Europe: "We could have had a much more significant agreement if only it hadn't been so goddamn important."[7] But of course, attempts are made to find a way around such difficulties, by extending the range of verification procedures. That is what is known as "intrusive verification."

To give an example: A submarine might be armed with cruise missiles capable of carrying nuclear or conventional warheads. Under the terms of a given agreement, those missiles are limited to conventional warheads alone. An inspection team is invited to check that this is so. But it is not good enough simply to examine the warheads. It is possible that, once the inspectors have departed, the conventional ones could be removed and replaced by nuclear weapons. To ensure that this is not the case, the inspectors will have to check on the size, weight, and fuel capacity of the missiles, since they will know that conventional warheads are heavier than their nuclear counterparts. They will also want to examine the gyro systems, and possibly the electronic maps that can be slotted in to guide the missile to its target, since it is obvious in most cases that a missile bearing a conventional warhead needs to be far more accurate than one carrying a nuclear charge. In other words, intrusive verification demands access to a great range of sensitive material, and possibly opens the door to industrial and strategic espionage.

There is an obvious paradox here. It can be summarized in the implicit dialogue: "I don't trust you, so if we are to have a substantial agreement, I must have the right to intrusive verification." "But that means you'll know all my secrets. Because *you* don't trust *me, I've* got to trust *you* with everything I have." That is the nature of the fourth stage of the process outlined here. Even the attempt to get away from questions of political trust, to rely on a functional and businesslike approach, and to extend the area of verification—all depend in the last resort on creating trust after all. The wheel comes full circle in the fourth stage.

These stages are not necessarily chronological—though they were in part—but their logic appeared to be pretty well ineluctable as the arms control negotiations outlined above moved from the 1970s into the 1980s. But at that same time the indispensable element of political trust virtually disappeared during the same period. That was in part because of the global confrontation of the so-called second Cold War. But there was also another reason.

In spite of President Reagan's instinctive distrust of the USSR, he seems to have entered office with every intention of reaching serious arms control agreements, particularly at the strategic level. Convinced that the arms race could no longer be allowed to "stabilize upward," the new administration attempted to radicalize negotiations, moving away from the old SALT talks, which, as the acronym suggests, were concerned merely with the *limitation* of strategic arms, to the new START process—that is, Strategic Arms *Reduction* Talks. Yet at the same time, the administration was about to make a decision that would throw the whole concept of "mutual deterrence" into confusion. In 1983, partly in response to pressure from significant sections of the American public (for example the Catholic bishops) who were finding the apparatus of annihilation ever more difficult to stomach, the president announced on television that the United States was about to launch what he called a Strategic Defense Initiative (SDI). This grandiose project was to provide the continental United States with a complete defense against missile attack by stationing interceptors in space. It would draw together a whole range of technologies, many of them as yet untried, at an enormous cost; but its advocates were confident that it would work and that the United States could afford it. It was seen by some as a technological answer to the moral problems of nuclear deterrence, by others as a measure designed to restore to the United States the invulnerability it had enjoyed when it first embarked on the policies of nuclear deterrence, and so to provide a reaffirmation of the credibility of extended deterrence. For the first group, the president among them, it did not represent any attempt to gain strategic superiority over the Soviet Union. For the second it emphatically did. And of course there were many who had no real idea of what the SDI was for but who just found the whole program technologically exciting or potentially profitable or both.

For the Soviet leaders the prospect was extremely alarming, and amounted to virtual proof that the United States was not negotiating in good faith. At the time of the ABM negotiations the Americans had dinned into them the benefits of mutual vulnerability; and that indeed had been the basis of the SALT I agreement. Now those same Americans, taking advantage once again of their superior technology, were proposing to change all the rules of the game and construct a system that would one day enable them, with impunity, to threaten the Soviet Union. It did nothing to reassure Moscow that President Reagan offered to share the SDI technology. Even if he were to be trusted (which in Soviet eyes he was certainly not), even if he were to share with them the last detail on the last blueprint, the Soviet leaders knew that for years and years to come, the USSR would not have the technological base to construct such a system and anyway would probably never be able to afford it. Besides, if the president's avowed aim was to enable both sides to move away from the threat of nuclear war, would it not be simpler and cheaper to do so by scrapping the bombs and missiles? This was the argument advanced by Gorbachev at his meeting with Reagan in Reykjavik in October 1986. But that alternative demands political trust, and as the Reykjavik summit showed, political trust was entirely lacking.

For some time to come the SDI blocked all other arms control negotiations, since the Soviet Union made concessions and agreements elsewhere conditional on the U.S. abandonment of the SDI. In fact the program was not abandoned until 1993, but the idea of providing a comprehensive defense of the United States was quietly forgotten. Instead, the SDI budget funded a number of advanced technological research projects, many of which have as much application to conventional forces on earth as they do to anything in space.

In spite of the SDI, however, the Reykjavik meeting can be said to have marked the moment at which political trust began to blossom—in spite of President Reagan's extraordinary public outburst at the time. The reason is that Gorbachev astounded the U.S. team by promptly accepting what one of them has candidly confessed was meant to be a wrecking proposal, namely the complete elimination of all medium- and intermediate-range nuclear missiles in Europe.[8] This "zero-zero option," as it was called, demanded far greater concessions from the USSR than from the United States; and the fact that Gorbachev was ready to accept it began to prompt speculation in Washington that the man was seriously to be trusted.

But there is a further implication. Once arms control negotiations were unhooked from the question of the SDI, the first significant agreement that was reached was indeed on the elimination of the theater missiles. Now, any thinking strategist could make a strong case that such an agreement represented a threat to European stability as hitherto conceived, because it actually weakened deterrence—potentially seriously. But most people would argue that stability and security were in fact enhanced because the very existence of the agreement indicated a new political rapprochement between parties that were now more intent on reaching understanding than on threatening war. In that context, and as the transformation of the Soviet Union under Gorbachev gathered momentum, it would soon become possible to address the fundamental question underlying all other arms control negotiations: namely the imbalance of conventional forces in Europe.

That this was possible was due to an extraordinary convergence of political change and institutional activity. The political change, again emanating from the transformation of the USSR, and of Eastern Europe, culminating in the annus mirabilis of 1989, expressed itself in the form of a real determination on the part of both East and West to escape from the straitjacket of the Cold War. The institutional activity was carried out by both the alliances discussed in the last chapter, and also within the forum of the CSCE. In the last days of its life the Warsaw Pact joined NATO in a joint declaration in proclaiming that the alliances were "no longer adversaries" and in affirming "that security is indivisible and that the security of each of their countries is inextricably linked to the security of all the states participating in the Conference on Security and Cooperation in Europe." That was in November 1990. What is interesting here is that by then the notion of an indivisible security had come to include that of the twelve neutral or nonaligned states that were also parties to the CSCE. But it is not too surprising, for by then the CSCE itself had also made an important contribution to the prospects for arms control and East-West understanding in Europe.

That contribution lay in the elaboration of what came to be known as "confidence- and security-building measures." Modest in themselves, focusing on such matters as the limitation in size of military maneuvers, prior notification of force movements, and the ability of representatives of either alliance to observe the exercises of the other, they yet did much to get around the problems of linkage and verification that had so bedeviled arms control negotiations. One might say that the idea of confidence-building measures represented the politicization of arms control, and was part of a process whereby, instead of arms control being the key to other political relations, those relations themselves became the key to arms control. This was a reversal of the position originally adopted by the United States at the beginning of the SALT process—but it also represented the lessons learned, albeit painfully, from the debacle of the SALT II treaty after the Soviet invasion of Afghanistan.

Obviously, all this is not to say that the codification of political understanding was an easy or uninterrupted process. Many a discussion between leading Warsaw Pact and NATO commanders, many a seminar addressed on either side of the old division by a visiting fireman from the other, ended if not in mutual recrimination, at least in headshaking and bewilderment. Not only that: allies themselves could be divided. When the withdrawal from Europe of medium-range nuclear forces had been agreed, the question arose as to whether that should be followed by the elimination of short-range nuclear weapons. West Germany, on whose soil most of these weapons were, almost by definition, positioned, was enthusiastic about the prospect. Britain, under Margaret Thatcher, was adamant in its opposition. The North Atlantic Council, along with various military committees, became the arena for much complicated diplomacy—including a subtext outside that arena of whether Britain and France would "compensate" for the abolition of the medium-range forces by collaborating on the production on an air-launched cruise missile. Old patterns of thought die hard.[9] But given all that, the fact is that Soviet military commanders and their Western counterparts did discuss such questions as the implications of Soviet military doctrine for the future security of Europe as a whole, and that, groping through the fog of historical suspicion, political leaders in both East and West were able to come to some understanding of what Gorbachev's rather vague phrase about "new thinking in international relations" might mean in practice and what measures of reciprocity that practice might require.

Accompanying, and spurred on by, these wider developments was the transformation in the nature and status of Germany—all of Germany. There is some evidence to suggest it was Gorbachev himself who proposed originally that the Berlin Wall be breached and ultimately dismantled—but that he did so in the hope of preserving the Democratic Republic as a separate and more or less viable state. The unexpected success of the West German dash for unification led to the absorption of the Democratic Republic into the territory and constitution of the Federal Republic. In effect, this was to signal the death knell of the Warsaw Pact, and indeed the transformation of NATO into a new and undefined entity. (After all, the original purpose of the Atlantic alliance had been to ensure that it kept Soviet forces out of NATO territory. Now, some four hundred thousand Soviet troops were still to be stationed, for the next few years at least, on the soil of a state that, after unification, was itself a NATO member.) But apart from the questions raised in this way about the future of NATO, the USSR had already agreed in bilateral negotiations to withdraw its forces from Czechoslovakia and Hungary by June 1991. In fact, the Warsaw Pact was officially dying, whatever the future status of Soviet forces in Germany.

The old Democratic Republic ceased to exist on October 3, 1990. Only six weeks later, the members of NATO and the remaining members of the Warsaw Pact signed the Treaty on Conventional Armed Forces in Europe. It is that treaty to which the joint declaration of the two alliances referred to above was an addendum, declaring that they were no longer adversaries but now partners. It is also the last (some might say the first) useful thing that the Warsaw Pact managed to achieve throughout its existence. Broadly speaking, the effect of the treaty, aimed as it was at establishing a genuine balance of conventional forces between the two alliances, was to eradicate the ability of the Soviet Union or its allies to mount a large-scale conventional attack on Western Europe without months and months of arduous preparation. In other words, to give the NATO states ample time to prepare for any such eventuality.

In the past the supreme strategic advantage of the USSR had been its ability to launch an attack on the West at short notice. That was what had forced the NATO powers to think of "going nuclear" very rapidly. And it was, ironically, dependent on that element of surprise that Stalin had discounted in his "permanently operating factors." Now it was to be relinquished.

The consequent irony is that such an agreement could only be reached through the untangling of all the assumptions that had been based on the Soviet Union's initial advantage—in particular the need to maintain deterrence through the threat of nuclear escalation. To say that this is ironic is to belabor a point already made: the entanglements of nuclear deterrence in Europe and of strategic deterrence more widely had been based on a failure to address the fundamental problem of the conventional imbalance. But historically speaking, it was only after some of these consequential matters had been tackled that the underlying cause of the problem could begin to be solved. Such comfort as may be derived from these ironies, however, lies in the fact that the near-insoluble problems of an arms control process, concerned only with the systemic and functional approaches to the question of stability, virtually forced upon the participants a reevaluation of their political relationship. It is doubtful whether that could have occurred without the transformation of the Soviet Union initiated by Gorbachev. But however flawed, he may appear to many as what Hegel would have termed a "world-historical figure," there can be little doubt that it was his reappraisal of the issues involved in the legacy he inherited that made it possible for such extraordinary changes to take place, and for the priorities to be realigned in a logical order.

Earlier it was suggested that there had been only two moments of real progress in arms control negotiations—the first being the SALT I treaty and the second the almost headlong rush of agreements that were reached between 1989 and 1993—if one is to include the chemical weapons agreement of that year. But the first might be summarized as a breakthrough within the original meaning of arms control: namely the stabilization of deterrence by mutual agreement among adversaries. The second, though, might be regarded as a transformation of arms control in the context of an entirely different political process from that that had informed the assumptions of the first.

Yet—final irony—it was that very transformation that enabled further agreements to be reached in terms of the negotiations that had been conducted on the old assumptions. That applies particularly to the START talks. The increasing scope and scale of the strategic missile reductions that these talks encompassed were breathtaking. Their provisions were in part able to solve some of the problems of verification, but it is probably fair to say that this was so only within the context of a new political confidence whereby each side found itself increasingly able to trust the other. Huge, radical cuts have been agreed on to-date in the strategic missile arsenals. To be sure, these agreements have been complicated by the fact that the old Soviet Union, America's partner in the START talks, no longer exists; and some of the successor states (Kazakhstan, Belarus, and Ukraine) maintain their nuclear systems even though they have agreed to hand them over to Russia as the successor state to the Soviet Union in its treaty relationships with the United States.[10] But so much admitted, the fact is that the argument advanced at Reykjavik has pretty well triumphed. If the ultimate objective of both parties to the Cold War conflict is to escape from the threat of mutual annihilation as the only way of ensuring stability, then it is easier, more sensible, and cheaper to do so by eliminating the means of such annihilation than by constructing elaborate defenses.

Once that logic is accepted, it becomes possible to agree that strategic nuclear missiles can be radically reduced—in the case of the second START agreement by 50 percent.[11] Problems of course remain: both the United States and Russia still worry about China; and Russia might feel that it still has to worry about Britain and France. But it is still true that both of these powers are at least officially committed to the elimination of all strategic nuclear weapons-systems within a very few years.

Two things follow from that. The first is whether they can sufficiently constitute a global partnership to deal with all the questions that might have brought them to the verge of war. The second is whether the somewhat decrepit but nonetheless reliable structures of the Cold War might have to be replaced by a much more pragmatic set of criteria. The criteria for that pragmatism lie at the heart of the decisions that might have to be made in the near future and might also have to draw on the older criteria of the moral, legal, and political forms of the control of war and strategy. In a sense, the transformation of arms control solved many of the old problems of the Cold War, but it also heightened the questions of how a new system, proclaiming itself as the successor to the Cold War, would be able to cope. And that also implied a reexamination of some of the other assumptions of the nuclear age. In particular, the triumph of arms control became the historical enemy of what had once seemed to be its handservant—the idea of Limited War.

Notes

1. The Ten-Nation Committee on Disarmament (TNCD) was followed by the Eighteen-Nation Committee on Disarmament (ENCD), the Conference of the Committee on Disarmament (CCD), and, eventually in 1979, simply the UN Conference on Disarmament (CD).

2. One of the earliest publications of the Institute for Strategic Studies (as it was named then) was Hedley Bull's book *The Control of the Arms Race: Disarmament and Arms Control in the Missile Age* (London: Weidenfeld & Nicolson for the Institute for Strategic Studies, 1961).

3. The unit of measurement of the accuracy of a missile is known as the circle of error probability (CEP). It is determined by measuring the distance by which missiles miss their targets during tests, and using the average of the distances as the radius for the circle. In the early days of ballistic missiles, the CEP was measured in kilometers. Later it was measured in hundreds of meters, and in some cases even meters alone.

4. See Helmut Schmidt's widely reported Alastair Buchan Memorial Lecture to the International Institute for Strategic Studies, October 1977, published in *Survival* 20, no. 1 (January/February 1978).

5. See John Newhouse, *Cold Dawn: The Story of SALT,* 2d ed. (Washington, D.C.: Pergamon-Brassey's International Defense, 1989).

6. Strobe Talbott, *Deadly Gambits: The Reagan Administration and the Stalemate in Nuclear Arms Control* (New York: Vintage Books, 1985).

7. At a conference sponsored by the Ditchley Foundation, April 1989.

8. The person who made this confession was Richard Perle.

9. Indeed, the United Kingdom and France have been discussing the prospects of nuclear collaboration on and off ever since.

10. Under the 1992 Lisbon START Protocol, Kazakhstan, Belarus, and Ukraine agreed to join the Nonproliferation Treaty (NPT) as non-nuclear-weapon states in "the shortest possible time." In separate letters to President George Bush, the leaders of the three republics also all agreed to destroy all former Soviet strategic weapons on their territories within the seven-year START reduction period. All three countries have stuck to their commitments and are now signatories to the NPT.

11. START II, ratified by the U.S. Senate in January 1996 and by the Russian State Duma in April 2000, calls for the reduction of U.S. and Russian strategic warheads to no more than 3,000 to 3,500 each. It also bans MIRVed ICBMs.

12

War All the Same

In the early years of the nuclear age, deterrence was widely thought of as the means of preventing all war—at least between the major powers in the international system. That is what Churchill had in mind when he spoke of "survival, the twin brother of annihilation, and peace, the sturdy child of terror." That, too, was the aim of the policy of massive retaliation. But as it became apparent that the threat to use nuclear weapons was increasingly difficult to implement, and that the credibility of such a threat was virtually zero outside the central areas of commitment, so policymakers had to face the question of what to do when important interests were at stake in a conflict but when nuclear posturing would be of no avail. The conclusion was that wars would still sometimes have to be fought, but that they would have to be controlled in such a manner that they would not escalate to nuclear war. In the past, war had been the ultima ratio of kings. This was no longer the case. The ultima ratio was now the avoidance of strategic nuclear exchange; but within that context war was still a resort of policy. How to fight it while avoiding the risks of escalation became a major preoccupation of strategic thinking.

That kind of war came to be termed "Limited War," the attempt being to distinguish it from all-out war. Although the term stuck, and there is no point in trying to avoid it, it is still rather misleading. It is perhaps more useful to think of Limited War as "controlled war." The analysis of its nature, speculation about how it might be fought, prescriptions for the future drawn from the lessons of the past (especially the Korean War) generated large quantities of writing in the late 1950s and early 1960s—much of it needlessly complicated. This was of course the same period as that in which thinking about arms control was also taking off; and it might be said that while arms control was an attempt to stabilize deterrence, Limited War was an attempt to stabilize the international system within that framework. This is what was meant at the end of the last chapter when Limited War was referred to as the "handmaiden" of arms control.

It will be clear that this reflects a thoroughly U.S. perspective on world affairs; and indeed most of the writing on the subject comes from the United States. Pretty ethnocentric stuff it is too, much of it based on the assumption that Limited War was really a problem for Washington, or at most the nuclear powers. Later discussion will suggest, however, that many of the questions and criteria of controlling war apply just as much when Tel-Aviv or Cairo is concerned as they do to Washington.

Before discussing these criteria further, it is as well to get one somewhat eccentric consideration out of the way. Some American writers have suggested in the past that it would be possible to consider Limited War between East and West in Europe, even involving the "limited" use of nuclear weapons.[1] That was presumably an attempt to sidestep the complexities of extended deterrence. But since military commanders with any experience of these matters are unanimous that it is virtually impossible to control nuclear escalation once it begins, such ruthlessly pious hopes can be discounted.

In the real world, the criteria for Limited War can be summarized as follows. First there is one criterion that provides the context for all the rest, and that is the limitation of objective. Obviously, if the objective of a war is to destroy the evil empire, there can be no hope of controlling it. If it is to resolve a dispute over something more tightly defined, then it begins to make sense to talk of Limited War. But a very difficult consideration lurks concealed there, which becomes more apparent when the second criterion, operating within the context of the first, is mentioned. That is the limitation of means.

So far, it sounds very Clausewitzian. It was Clausewitz who argued that the objective of a war should be clearly defined and adhered to, and that the means chosen should be appropriate at the end. But as Bernard Brodie very perceptively pointed out, the idea of Limited War actually represents an inversion of the Clausewitzian ends-means relationship.[2] For Clausewitz the definition of the ends came first, and to him that would have seemed self-evident. In the context of Limited War, the question of means is paramount—not because the means are chosen before the objective is defined, but because it is the *avoidance* of certain means (nuclear weapons) that determines the nature of the ends: what objectives can be fought for and what cannot. Not only does that complicate the question of the objective, it also mightily complicates the definition of victory, as will become apparent later.

The limitation of means is not confined exclusively of course to the avoidance of nuclear weapons. It can also take the form of not choosing other weapons of mass destruction: the United States made extensive use of CS gas and chemical defoliants in Vietnam, often with lethal side effects, but it did not deliberately try to gas the Viet Cong forces in, for example, the tunnel complex of Cu Chi. The limitation of means can also imply the avoidance of certain kinds of targets: in the many Arab-Israeli conflicts, Israel did not use its air superiority to bombard Arab cities—not, that is, until the bombing of Beirut after the invasion of Lebanon in 1982. Such forms of restraint might in part reflect the principles of discrimination of the Just War tradition, in part be directed toward the attainment of a settlement that adversaries can accept according to Clausewitzian principles; but above all they reflect the need to prevent the escalation of conflicts that, once started, could rapidly get out of control. That prompts two further considerations.

The first is that limited wars are not fought in a limited context. If they were, there would have been nothing to have prevented the United States from using nuclear weapons in Vietnam, particularly since the use of such weapons need not necessarily have brought about mass destruction. Many of the forces and supplies of the Viet Cong and the North Vietnamese army were infiltrated into South Vietnam through the remote mountain and forest tracks of what the Americans dubbed the "Ho Chi Minh Trail." The mountain passes in the early stages of the trail were scarcely inhabited, and it would have been easy to block them by using low-yield nuclear bombs without incurring any great loss of life. Why not just do it?

The answer lies not in any immediate effects such an action might have had but in the way it would have changed the international rules. The Soviet Union would not have responded by threatening to use nuclear weapons against the United States, but could very well have said: "Ah, very interesting. We now realize that it is permissible for us to use nuclear weapons against each other's smaller allies, and just to show that we've understood, we took out the Israeli positions in the Sinai Peninsula this morning." In other words, Limited War, however restricted the arena, is *fought in a global context.* For similar reasons Israel did not bomb Arab cities, quite apart from other considerations involved because it could have provoked Soviet intervention, which, again in the global context, would have been extremely dangerous. (And when it did bombard Beirut in 1982, the United States soon ordered it to stop. Menachem Begin was all defiance but stopped all the same.) It can be seen from this instance that the criteria of Limited War in the global context might apply to others, not just the superpowers. It should be added that other wars fought in areas or over issues that are remote from the global context of superpower interaction and the risk of nuclear escalation need not be limited at all: the participants can use all means available to massacre each other indefinitely.

The second consideration prompted by the ends-means relationship in Limited War is that, whereas Clausewitzian war had limitation and restraint imposed upon it by the forces of friction, those forces obviously do not apply when it is possible to kill millions thousands of miles away at the touch of a button. In those circumstances, restraint has to be voluntary, and crafted, so to speak, into the conduct of the war. This *is* a criterion that applies particularly when a superpower is involved.

So far, then, the primary limitation establishing the context of the rest is the limited objective, and following from it there is the limitation of means. What other forms of control are there? Of great importance is the limitation of theater. Wars can escalate geographically as well as vertically, as more and more countries get sucked in, and so can easily become impossible to direct or control. In the pre-nuclear age, World War I was a case in point. In the nuclear age, the limitation of theater can be vital. The classic example is the Korean War. Much of the writing on Limited War refers to Korea as the first real case of phenomenon, even though the concept itself did not exist at the time. In some respects, that is misleading: after all, the Korean War was brought to an end by the U.S. threat to use nuclear weapons. But in terms of the limitation of theater, the war really was a classic. It was fought on the Korean peninsula alone. U.S. forces did not bomb China, and China did not attack U.S. bases in Japan. There is no knowing what the consequences would have been if either had acted differently: and in that sense the Korean example became paradigmatic for all subsequent thinking about Limited War. Unfortunately, however, the question of limitation of theater is a little more complicated than this instance might suggest, as the case of the Vietnam War illustrates.

The last stages of some parts of the Ho Chi Minh Trail ran through Cambodian territory before entering South Vietnam. Moreover, Viet Cong forces established base camps in Cambodia, to which they would frequently withdraw after operations in Vietnam to rest and recuperate, and from which they would subsequently regroup to launch new attacks. In other words, Cambodian territory was part of the military theater of the Vietnam War. It was on this basis that President Nixon ordered the secret but massive bombing of Cambodia and the subsequent military invasion in December 1970. Yet although Cambodia was part of the military theater, it was in no sense part of the *political* theater of war. Its leader, Prince Sihanouk, even though bowing to force majeure in allowing the Viet Cong to make use of part of its territory, was determined to preserve his regime and his country by remaining neutral in the war, and indeed, so far as possible, in the wider East-West conflict of which it was a part. The U.S. invasion changed all that. It led to the overthrow of Sihanouk by the right-wing military dictator, General Lon Nol. His regime, repressive but receiving U.S. support, was in turn overthrown by the ferocious forces of the Khmer Rouge under Pol Pot, with the help of China. Quite apart from massacring some 20 percent of the entire Cambodian population, Pol Pot so incensed Vietnam (now united after the U.S. withdrawal) that it invaded Cambodia at the end of 1978. That action established the dominance of a Communist-ruled Vietnam over the entire Indo-China peninsula—the very outcome that the original U.S. intervention in Vietnam had sought to prevent. Nothing, of course, is easier than hindsight; and no one can say that President Nixon could have foreseen the consequences of his bombing and invasion of Cambodia—though there are many reasons (starting with common humanity) to say that these actions should never have been undertaken in the first place.[3] The point here, in the more restricted context of a discussion of strategic thinking, is precisely that the consequences of the U.S. invasion were unforeseeable because of the confusion between the military theater and the political theater of the Vietnam War. In that respect, the Korean paradigm provided a misleadingly simple example of the limitation of theater. Vietnam better illustrates its complexities.

The final form of limitation, one not much discussed in the voluminous writings on the subject but which can be very important in the attempt to control war, is limitation in time. The obvious classic example here, one involving only local powers but local powers operating again within a global context, is that of the Six Day War between Israel and three of its Arab neighbors (plus Iraqi forces). There are some suggestions, not yet possible to verify, that when Israel concluded after President Nasser had blockaded the Straits of Tiran that it would have to go to war, its government discussed the prospects with the United States. If the reports are well-founded, U.S. representatives assured their Israeli counterparts that they would be able to hold the ring for a few days, but impressed upon them the need for a rapid conclusion.

Whatever the truth of this, it is ben trovato. Some wars are just too dangerous to be allowed to drag on for long. In the case of the Six Day War, Israel's overwhelming victory seemed to confirm the efficacy of limitation in time. But it also served to mask another complication of which President Sadat of Egypt was probably well aware when he launched another war with Israel in October 1973. That difficulty relates to the problems of defining victory in Limited War, and will be discussed later.

Within the framework of limited objectives, then, mechanisms of control can be seen as those of limitation of means, of theater, and of time. None of them is simple, but the composite package sounds conceptually neat. At this point, however, any empirical observer might very well raise a potent objection. How was the Iran-Iraq War of 1980–1988 possible at all? It certainly occurred within a global context, which involved the competitive interests of the superpowers, the supplies of a strategically vital commodity, oil, and the security of an equally vital international waterway. If the criteria of Limited War encompass other agents than the superpowers, the Iran-Iraq War should have been impossible. It dragged on for eight years, both parties to the conflict used all the means they had at their disposal (culminating in Iraqi chemical weapons attacks on Iranian forces), and the territorial advances made by one side or another at various stages of the war threatened to break the bounds of the theater and to endanger the security of neighboring Arab states. Most important, the objectives of both parties to the conflict were quite unlimited: each aspired to overthrow the other's regime and entire system—and indeed, in the case of Iran, to go on from the destruction of Saddam Hussein's Iraq to the "liberation" of Jerusalem. How was such an *un*limited war possible at all?

There are two kinds of answer. The first refers to the self-evident fact that it is sometimes simply not possible for external powers, however mighty, to give orders to local countries that might be in themselves of considerable significance. Israel and Egypt could be persuaded to cease and desist from the War of Attrition in 1970 because each of them was beholden to its protecting superpower. But such considerations applied much less in the case of Iraq, and not at all in the case of Iran. They could threaten with relative impunity to set the world by the ears through their own local conflict. In such cases, tails can wag dogs. And what such a form of subsystem dominance means is that wars within the subsystem no longer take place in a global context and can very well become unlimited. This is something that much of the ethnocentric writing on Limited War frequently overlooks.

The second answer follows from the first, though in a somewhat paradoxical manner. The Iran-Iraq War, because of the considerations outlined above, was so potentially dangerous that everybody conspired to contain it and limit its effects. That involved not only intensive consultations between the superpowers, but also diplomatic initiatives encompassing Saudi Arabia, Israel, Jordan, and Syria, as well as others. Initially, the outbreak of war carried a very high risk of horizontal, geographical escalation in the Middle East, and subsequently a considerable risk of vertical escalation, had either superpower intervened. (That latter consideration had also been true in the case of the War of Attrition, but there the two had been able to exercise an influence that they lacked in the first Gulf War.) The paradox of this second answer therefore lies in the fact that sometimes the conflicts of the subsystem can so intensify the dangers of the global context that they force the world's major antagonists to collaborate.

All this suggests that it is as well to beware of generalizing too much about Limited War. It is a set of prescriptive ideas, rather than a deductive analysis, and as such it is frequently difficult to apply to the tangled disputes of the world. But even when the prescriptive ideas make sense, they still encounter formidable difficulties that arise from the inversion of Clausewitz's ends-means relationship, to which Bernard Brodie referred.

If the objective of Limited War is to be defined primarily in terms of the means one cannot use rather than in those of what it is desirable to achieve, how can a government or commander proceed to define the objective at all? Henry Kissinger famously declared about the Vietnam War (which for a good long time many prominent Americans regarded as an exercise in Limited War): "We would not have recognized victory if it were staring us in the face, because we did not know what our objectives were." There were of course many other reasons for the U.S. difficulty in defining the objectives of that war, starting with an act of bad faith by the Eisenhower administration in 1956, when it broke the terms of the agreement reached in Geneva in 1954, and going on through the attempts under Kennedy and Johnson to prop up an unsustainable South Vietnamese regime through ever greater U.S. involvement and relentless increases in the scale and scope of the conflict. That said, however, Kissinger's remark does illustrate the more general problem of defining an objective, and the case of Vietnam also helps to explain why it is so difficult.

If the United States regarded the Vietnam War as an exercise in Limited War, the Viet Cong and the North Vietnamese army emphatically did not. They were fighting an all-out war with the lower levels of force at their disposal and were unlikely to be impressed by the U.S. view that this was a Limited War when the United States was inflicting such destruction on Vietnam, particularly from the air, with the forces that were at its command. The conclusion that can be drawn here is that Limited War, to be effective, demands a certain "fit" between the objectives that both parties are fighting for, and possibly also a certain correspondence in the levels of force that they employ. Largely because of disparity of objectives, an immensely stronger power, using much greater force, lost in Vietnam to a much weaker one because the former thought of itself as fighting a Limited War while the latter did not. It is small wonder that after Vietnam, the ideas of Limited War lost much of their sex appeal in the U.S. strategic community.

Nothing could illustrate more clearly the difference between the Clausewitzian concept of war and the later notion of Limited War—in spite of the superficial similarities between the two. Clausewitz, as was stressed earlier, thought in terms of a European state order; and even though he regarded Napoleon as a mortal threat to that order, his assumption was still that the contending parties in the age in which he lived roughly knew and agreed on what they were fighting about. When opponents in our own epoch are fighting about what might be called the "historical future," it is exceedingly difficult to define, let alone agree on, the nature of the conflict. And that raises the final problem.

Without some underlying agreement about the nature of conflict, it can become very difficult for one side or the other to claim victory—and the fact that limited wars are fought within a global context compounds that difficulty. To elucidate: within such a context, there is no necessary correspondence between victory in battle and success in achieving the objective. Everything that Clausewitz wrote was dedicated to analyzing and clarifying the nature of such a correspondence. But that was because, for him, the state order provided the context. When, though, the context is one of fundamental conflict about what the order ought to be, and when it carries with it the risk of global annihilation, victory in battle no longer serves necessarily to accomplish any political end. The whole relationship between *Ziel* and *Zweck* has been lost.

To give an example: Before he launched the attack on Israel in October 1973, President Sadat indicated on numerous occasions that he hardly hoped to win. At one point he declared in public and perhaps with more than a touch of Arab rhetoric that he was prepared to lose a million men if necessary in order to liberate the Sinai Peninsula. Moreover, his subsequent conduct of the campaign, once Egyptian forces had captured the Israeli "Bar Lev line" (or most of it) along the Suez Canal, indicated that he had no intention of going for victory over Israel. Much to the fury of President Assad of Syria and of his own brilliant field commander, General Shazli, Sadat held the Egyptian forces back, and thereby gave those of Israel the opportunity to regroup and counterattack. While one can hardly say that this was his intention, it nonetheless remains that his overall intention was clear. It was not to defeat the Israeli forces per se but rather to invoke the global context—in other words to force superpower intervention. In the event, Israel won yet more dazzling victories, crossing the canal, threatening to capture Ismailia, and encircling the Egyptian Third Army at Suez. But it didn't matter. What was happening in the meantime was the extremely competitive superpower diplomacy that, as argued earlier, helped to transform the psychological interpretation of MAD into its logical interpretation, and in which the United States emerged as the clear winner. But how did it do so?

Obviously, Washington won the diplomatic battle with Moscow *because* it was the one superpower that had diplomatic (and even close) relations with Israel. As such, it was in a position to persuade Israel to withdraw its forces, in the initial disengagement agreements, first from the Egyptian territory they had occupied on the African side of the canal, then from a part of the Sinai Peninsula, and ultimately, under the Camp David agreements, from the whole—a victory that Sadat lived to see. (This is not particularly germane to the central argument here, but it might very well be suggested that there is an extraordinary continuity in policy between Sadat's attack on Israel in 1973 and his visit to Jerusalem in 1977.) What is germane, however, is that—again within the global context of superpower hostility coupled with the avoidance of nuclear war—Sadat knew very well how to translate defeat on the battlefield into political victory.

The loss of the relationship between military and political victory, between *Ziel* and *Zweck,* indicates the ultimate enigma that lies behind the apparently tidy formulae of Limited War. For Clausewitz, the nature of victory was defined in terms of the question: "*What* have we won?" In Limited War, the question becomes: "How do we know *whether* we have won?" Sometimes, when both parties roughly agree on the nature of the conflict, as in the case of Britain and Argentina in 1982, the answer can be fairly straightforward. Sometimes, when there are several layers to the conflict and the scope of the conflicting objectives is uncertain, as in the case of the Gulf War of 1991, it can be hard to know what victory actually means. The successive resolutions of the UN

Security Council during the crisis that preceded that war were ample testimony to the fact that the protagonists of the anti-Iraq coalition were uncertain of their ultimate aims. If the real aim was to eject the Iraqi forces from Kuwait, the subsequent course of the war can be seen as a classic Clausewitzian exercise culminating in a brilliant victory. But if the wider aims alluded to in successive UN resolutions were those of creating a new context for "peace and stability in the Middle East," then the campaign's objective would presumably have been to preserve a relatively strong Iraq while destroying its power to destabilize the region by toppling or at least fatally weakening the regime of Saddam Hussein. In the event, the campaign left a strong Saddam in place while fatally weakening Iraq. Its critics might contend that while Clausewitz warns the commander against going beyond the culminating point of victory, he fails to caution him against stopping short of that point. Presumably, it never occurred to him that anyone would. In short, for all its conformity to the ideas of Limited War, did the Gulf conflict result in victory for the coalition or not?

The fundamental enigma of Limited War, and the chancy applicability of the criteria it invokes, might make one wonder whether there is really much point in discussing it at all. Certainly, in terms of the ethnocentric ambitions, in the context of which it was conceived and has since been largely discussed—namely those of stabilizing the international system within the framework of stabilized deterrence—such a question is more than justified. But there is one last, neo-Clausewitzian word to be said on behalf of thinking and talking about Limited War. If war is ever to make sense or to have any justification, it can only be that of sorting out issues in dispute and helping to resolve conflicts. In that respect Limited War *can* sometimes serve a useful purpose. The criteria of victory might be less relevant than those of the limited objective. It can sometimes help to sort out, in those terms, what a conflict is about and what it is not about. Back to Sadat. His attack on Israel in 1973 served (and not, for once, paradoxically) to demonstrate to the Israeli political leadership and to Israeli public opinion that Egypt was not interested in "throwing Israel into the sea" but merely in recovering the territory it had lost in 1967. Unhappily, it took a war to enable the parties to the conflict to sort out the disastrous effects of Nasser's earlier rhetoric—but at least it did sort them out, and ultimately peace was possible. Surely, Clausewitz would have approved. All the same, the fact that it was a relatively minor power like Egypt that could engage in such an exercise, whereas a superpower like the United States had either clearly lost as in Vietnam or at best ambiguously succeeded as in the Gulf, might mean that there is a cautionary sting in the tail of ethnocentricity.

Limited War, then, *can* on occasion clarify conflicts and stabilize relationships within the system. What it does not set out to do, and probably could not do, is to change the course of history. After all, the whole idea was conceived by the strong in the terms of maintaining the status quo. Almost by definition, those who wished to change the status quo were the weak—in Frantz Fanon's words, "the wretched of the earth." And for a certain period of history after World War II, the war of the weak against the strong proved astonishingly successful, toppling empires and defeating superpowers. It presented the greatest challenge to the normal emergent patterns of strategic thinking that they had hitherto encountered. Guerrilla warfare was transformed during this time, from its history as a kind of adjunct of sideshow to "real" war, into a revolutionary strategy in its own right.

Notes

1. See Klaus Knorr and Thorton Read, eds., *Limited Strategic War* (London: Pall Mall Press, 1962).
2. See Bernard Brodie, *Strategy in the Missile Age* (Princeton: Princeton University Press, 1959).
3. See William Shawcross, *Sideshow: Kissinger, Nixon, and the Destruction of Cambodia* (London: Andre Deutsch, 1979).

13

Guerrilla

The tactics of guerrilla warfare are as old as history. Irregular forces, frequently part-time, have sought to ambush, harass, and intimidate the regular forces of a hostile government or occupying power, forcing them to disperse in various missions of hot pursuit, and wearing down their morale, until a proper army could arrive or be mustered to defeat them in the field. The word "guerrilla" itself entered the English language at the time of the Peninsular War in Spain, when, the Spanish army having been defeated by the invading French, the Spanish peasants engaged in a "little war" (the literal Spanish meaning of the word "guerrilla") to keep the French tied down until Sir Arthur Wellesley's British troops could engage them in regular combat. Goya's famous series of paintings, *The Horrors of War,* date from this time—and guerrilla warfare has generally been remarkable for its ferocity, especially the ferocity of the reprisals carried out by the regular forces under attack.

During World War II, guerrilla tactics contributed significantly to the victory of the Allied armies over the German occupation forces in Europe: General Eisenhower once remarked that the activities of the French resistance had been worth at least two divisions to him; and in Russia, Poland, and Yugoslavia, partisan forces were integral to the victory over Nazism. But it was above all in China that the tactics of *la guerrilla* became the strategy of the transformation of history.

More of that later. For the present, it is enough to note that other historical circumstances were highly propitious for the widespread adoption of guerrilla warfare—partly inspired by the Chinese example—by emergent nations struggling against their colonial masters. In part, these circumstances were what might be called "accidental." The war had vastly stimulated the production of armaments; and at its conclusion, huge quantities of weapons were left lying around the world. Arms were now available to the ordinary man in the jungle or the *bled* on an unprecedented scale. In other historical terms, the war had had effects that were more than simply accidental. Japan, by its initial victories over the British, French, Dutch, and U.S. forces in the Pacific and Southeast Asia, had demonstrated to the colonial world that the White Man could be defeated; and for all the brutality of its occupation of the same White Man's colonies, Japan gave a strong impetus to subsequent anticolonial movements. Indeed, that brutality itself was part of the impetus: in many territories, resistance to the Japanese occupation provided the basis for subsequent anticolonial struggles.

In one sense, this was nothing new. But what was perhaps new was the interaction of the history of China and Japan during World War II: the Japanese on the one hand defeating the white colonialists, but being defeated on the other hand by the tactical alliance in China between the forces of the Kuomintang under Chiang Kai-shek and Mao Tse-tung's Communist guerrillas—who in turn proceeded to conquer Chiang's armies once the Japanese defeat was ensured. By 1949, Chiang had fled to Taiwan and Mao ruled the whole of China. In the process, Mao had become what, in Max Weber's overused phrase, might be termed the "ideal type" of guerrilla commander and philosopher.

Since that time, the majority of aspiring guerrilla movements, right up to the Sendero Luminoso in Peru, have characterized themselves by reference to the thought and work of Mao. Reference becomes reverence when his aphorisms are quoted. Yet he wrote astonishingly little about guerrilla warfare—one can comb his collected works in vain for any sustained passage on the subject—and what he did write is frequently unilluminating. "When the enemy advances we retreat, when the enemy retreats we advance" is not only a maxim familiar to every soldier in history, but verges anyway on tautology. Nonetheless, Mao is central to the transformation of guerrilla warfare from a tactical adjunct to conventional war into a strategy in its own right, because he identified guerrilla with revolution, and revolution with guerrilla.

After the disastrous attempt at a proletarian uprising staged by the Chinese Communists in Shanghai in 1927, Mao concluded that the future of the Chinese Revolution lay not in the revolt of the urban proletariat but in the mobilization of the peasantry over a long term. It was this conclusion that informed his subsequent strategy from the Long March onward—and that also, incidentally, sowed the seeds of China's later break with the USSR. (Stalin simply could not stomach the idea that, contrary to Marxist orthodoxy, the revolution could be founded on any other force than that of the proletariat; and Mao, for all that he used Stalin as an emblem in his later quarrels with Khrushchev, had already broken with Stalinist conformity at the very time that Stalin was consolidating his power in the USSR.) That apart, the most significant effect of treating the peasantry as the foundation of the revolution is that the revolution itself, now transformed into guerrilla war, becomes a battle for time rather than territory. That is the real meaning of Mao's aphorism about retreat and advance.

When the Viet Cong and North Vietnamese forces launched a major military operation to drive the Americans out of Vietnam in early 1968, it proved a military disaster. In fact, the U.S. military won all the ensuing battles even though at the cost of very heavy destruction. But Bernard Brodie, as already indicated, characterized the Tet campaign as the decisive engagement of the war and indeed one of the turning points of twentieth-century history[1]—not because the Americans won the battles but because the campaign persuaded them that they could not ultimately win the war.

If the guerrilla forces are to win the battle of wills over time in circumstances of terrible destruction and at the cost of thousands upon thousands of lives, they must be driven by extraordinarily powerful idealism. In the case of China and Vietnam in particular, that idealism took the form of revolutionary consciousness. That implies that a guerrilla war acknowledges no limitation to its aims. It is an all-out war, fought usually against an enemy who is thinking in more limited terms (though that was not the case of Chiang Kai-shek). In such conditions the strong cannot hope to win a limited victory: there is no such thing when the weak are fighting a total war. In the end, the strong, at least when they are foreigners, have no real choice but to withdraw. The British, the French, the Americans, and the forces of the Soviet Union in Afghanistan have all learned the same lesson. But idealistic motivation is not enough in itself. The guerrilla forces must have the support of the people. They, to quote Mao again, "move among the people as a fish swims in the sea."

The people can help to hide the fighters, supply them with food and give them intelligence of what the enemy is up to, carry or transmit messages, and serve as a logistical base. General Vo Nugyen Giap, Vietnam's most famous commander, could not have won his momentous victory over the French forces at Dien Bien Phu unless local peasants had been willing to dismantle artillery pieces and struggle to pull them up a rugged, jungle-clad mountainside so that they could be reassembled at the top and rain down shells on the French positions below. That is what the support of the people means.

But gaining such support is ambiguous in its nature. It can be done by inducement and by the promise of social transformation. Or it can be done by intimidation amounting sometimes to downright terror. An example of the first lies in Mao's own instructions to his forces, including the precepts of always paying for what they took, always returning what they borrowed, and never showing discourtesy to women. The Viet Cong appear to have offered many examples of the second: contrary to widespread belief at the time, there is good evidence to suggest that they were deeply unpopular in Vietnam. Often, of course, the two tactics can be combined, particularly if the intimidation is selective. The execution of the landlord, the tax-farmer, or the informer can be popular measures, especially if combined with redistribution of land, health, education, and lessons in political awareness, sometimes including literacy.

All this indicates that the primary target of a guerrilla campaign is not the enemy forces but the power structures that they represent—including people's social attitudes: what the Italian Marxist philosopher Antonio Gramsci called "the hegemony." Indeed in prescribing the tactics that the Italian Communist Party should use in changing the Italian hegemony, he draws on the analogy of guerrilla war as a model. But *how* is such a war to be fought?

In the classical model, there are three stages. The first is that of sporadic action, of small bands carrying out small raids and ambushes, disappearing from the locality of one action only to pop up again somewhere miles away. Part of the objective here is to force the government or occupying troops to disperse as they attempt pursuit so that they become still more vulnerable to surprise attack. If they take reprisals against the civilian population, or even act in a nervous and trigger-happy manner, it does the guerrilla cause no harm; it serves merely to rally the people behind it. This is also a phase of intensive recruitment and training, as more arms are acquired, whether captured from the enemy or supplied from foreign sympathizers. In such conditions, the orthodox forces become increasingly uncertain as to what territory they can actually control or what support they can rely on. The old cliché about the French experience in Vietnam—that the French controlled whole areas by day but the Viet Minh controlled them by night—can be applied much more widely.

That leads to the second stage, in which the guerrilla forces do actually begin to take control of a territory or territories. It is here that the decisive battle for the support of the people is fought—at the level of the village but also, more gradually, of an entire region. The weapons in this battle have already been mentioned: measures promoting health, education, and welfare in the context of a promise of social transformation. If these measures are successful, it becomes possible for the guerrilla commanders gradually to link the areas they control and so to create a basis for mass mobilization. It is this that makes possible the transition to the third stage, that of full-scale open war.

In the end, the enemy's armies must be defeated in the field to demonstrate that the hegemony that they represented is now over. The conventional campaigns can be hugely destructive and highly protracted. The biggest battle in history was fought at Hsu Chow in December 1948, between the Chinese Communist and Nationalist armies. There, the casualties on the Nationalist side alone were equal to the entire casualties of the U.S. Civil War. But obviously, before contemplating any such terrible transition, the guerrilla commander must get the timing right. In Vietnam, General Giap did so against the French forces in 1954. But he was wrong in 1968 when he launched the Tet offensive. His reaction, however, to the U.S. victories was in effect to murmur, "Ah well, back to stage two." The offensive launched some seven years later against what appeared to be an increasingly competent South Vietnamese army, though one by now bereft of U.S. support, was entirely successful within a very short period.

So far, in the discussion both of the central characteristics and of the methods of guerrilla warfare, much has been made of the Chinese example and of the way in which Mao thought of revolution as war, and war as revolution. That is partly because in the twenty-two years from disaster in Shanghai to the final victory of 1949, China had become the locus classicus of the guerrilla, and partly because the Chinese example served as a model and inspiration in many other countries. But obviously, the determination, persistence, and courage of the guerrilla fighter do not have to be inspired by the idealism of the revolution. The sheer determination to be rid of colonial oppression, to establish a racial, national, or even personal dignity, can be an extremely powerful driving force. In some cases, as in those of Algeria, Angola, Mozambique, and what was Rhodesia, such aspirations could also form part of a revolutionary framework of thought and rhetoric, in which Marxist thought and existentialist sentiment embraced each other. In other instances, as in the National Organization of Cypriot Fighters (EOKA) campaign in Cyprus, nationalism was fuelled by counterrevolutionary emotions, verging, in the person of Costas Grivas at least, on the neofascist. In Afghanistan, the mujahidin were fighting against a regime that proclaimed its Marxist-Leninist credentials and was supported by the Soviet Union. They did so in the name of Islam and of a determination to reimpose the seventh century on the twentieth. But what these otherwise disparate phenomena have in common with the Chinese model is that all the campaigns concerned challenged the existing hegemony, promised a transformation of society, and brooked no compromise.

In most—perhaps all—these cases, the promises of social transformation were pretty hollow. The antagonism between the followers of the Soviet and East European models and the Chinese model in Rhodesia were founded at least as much in ancient tribal rivalries as they were in ideological disagreement. Competition between different mujahidin groups in Afghanistan might take the form of attempts to outdo each other in observance of Islamic conduct, but nonetheless relates very strongly to feuds and vendettas going back over centuries. And so on. Yet so long as there is an identifiable hegemony that can be challenged, so long as the enemy can be singled out and represented as the threat to "authentic" values, *la guerrilla* will flourish. It is the armed expression of the crisis of modernization in traditional society.

As such, guerrilla warfare seemed nigh-on invincible for many years. The reason is clear. During the period of colonialism, or in the case of China, of imperialist depredation and of Japanese conquest, it was the modern powers who had cast themselves as the traditional enemies. That provides a very potent social and intellectual focus. The traditional society can recast itself in opposition to what is being imposed upon it from outside, and in doing so can get to grips with crises, ineluctable in the contemporary world, in its own culture. But perhaps that also helps to explain why, after a period of apparent virtual invincibility and of bringing about vast historical changes, guerrilla warfare has tended to peter out. Not in the sense that there are no longer irregular rebellions going on, but in the sense that they are for the most part quite easy to contain and seem to accomplish very little.

That is perhaps a somewhat general and ambitious statement, and its implications will be considered shortly. But what it does suggest for the moment is that patterns of strategic thinking could not cope very well with the phenomena of the guerrilla—even though conventional thought and conventional forces did score some successes. Perhaps the most notable example was the British victory over the Communist insurgents in Malaya. Malaya, however, was something of a special case in that the insurgents were for the most part Chinese and found it difficult to win the support of the Malay people. They could try to do so by intimidation, but that enabled the British forces to assume the role of providing security rather than inflicting oppression. It was very hard to generalize from this experience, as the U.S. forces (and their British advisers) subsequently discovered in Vietnam. Nonetheless, strategic thinking did try to come to grips with guerrilla warfare, emphasizing what were called "low-intensity operations." There were three major schools of thought.

The first, the British approach, was really glorified common sense. It depended on competing with guerrilla forces in offering inducements to the people, ranging from land reform at the local level, to the promise, as in Malaya, of national independence. Military operations were small and discreet: the Special Air Service, for example, operated in units of no more than four men, who attempted to ambush the ambushers. Obviously that depended on good intelligence, which in turn demanded knowledge of the terrain and some linguistic proficiency. But those two conditions do rather depend on already being an imperial power; and if the main object of the guerrilla war is to drive the imperial power out, tactical success will not ultimately prevent the guerrilla forces from achieving their strategic objective.

The second approach, the American, was in part also dependent on "winning over hearts and minds" as the cant phrase has it. In Vietnam, special forces did go to remote areas of the country, carrying with them the finer products of the American way of life—from medicines to Coke. Many of the people involved in these operations were courageous, humane, and successful. But such activity was doomed when it was combined with a strategy that put immense emphasis on firepower, including aerial bombing. Indeed, one chilling strategic argument that was advanced in the United States at the time was that since the natural constituency of the guerrilla forces was rural and to be found in the villages, people should be bombed out of the villages and into the cities—the constituency of the South Vietnamese government. That is a guaranteed way of losing hearts and minds, and in general, the heavy use of air- and firepower is a poor way of countering guerrilla forces. (Even in Afghanistan, where the Soviet Union used airpower to devastating effect in the Panshir Valley, the mujahidin were able to go on fighting until the Americans provided them with Stinger missiles to bring the Soviet aircraft down.) Generally, what Vietnam demonstrated was that it is extremely difficult, if not impossible, to combine low-intensity tactics with the massive firepower of high-intensity war. Today, U.S. training concentrates on teaching the skills of low-intensity operations, and guerrilla warfare is appreciated as primarily a social phenomenon—and also as one into which U.S. forces should not, if possible, be drawn.

The French also drew conclusions from their defeat in Vietnam, and their approach is perhaps the most interesting of the three outlined here. It is that of *la guerre révolutionnaire,* which accepts the premise that the guerrilla war is war as revolution, and offers to compete with it by providing an alternative revolution, the "revolutionary war." The phrase was coined by Colonel Philippe Argoud of the Bureau of Psychological Warfare, which had considerable success in Algeria. (Argoud himself was later to be kidnapped in Munich by French intelligence agents, and imprisoned for the part he played in an attempt to assassinate de Gaulle.) The methods of "revolutionary war," it may be inferred, are not always humane: torture was commonplace in Algeria. But it also attempted a transformation of traditional society, including agricultural reform and the emancipation of women. Most important, volunteer and noncommissioned officers were sent to live in villages and patrol the *bled,* sharing the vulnerability of the peasants. But for all this, as de Gaulle discovered somewhat to his surprise, Algerian support for the Front Libération National (FLN) continued to grow; and the alternative revolution did not really provide an alternative at all. What can be said is that the French approach most comprehensively recognized the distinctive nature of guerrilla warfare in the contemporary era.

Given that, how can it be said, as was suggested earlier, that such a form of war has now tended to peter out? It should be stressed first that there have always been limitations on the potential of *la guerrilla.* There are certain geographical considerations that restrict its universal applicability. The war of wills over time demands a favorable terrain—remote mountainous areas or the cover provided by jungle or swampland that the guerrilla fighter knows but the enemy does not—if the promise to carry on indefinitely is to be kept. It is hard to imagine a successful guerrilla campaign being fought in the English Home Counties. That raises a second consideration.

Lin Biao, Mao's "trusted comrade in arms" until his disgrace and death, once said that guerrilla warfare was the war of the countryside of the world against the cities of the world. What he probably had in mind was the conflict as he saw it between the developing countries and the military machines of the industrialized powers. But to draw the analogy at all was to overlook the fact of the relentless global process of urbanization that has affected all countries, developed or not. And guerrilla warfare has proved extraordinarily difficult to sustain in an urban environment. Many attempts have been made, and governments and societies have discovered that they can be more vulnerable to attack at key points in the city than to anything that can be leveled at them in the countryside. But the organization of a revolutionary guerrilla movement is also more difficult in such circumstances, in that ideas and social problems are more diverse in the city and are harder to weld into the sense of common grievance and common purpose. In such circumstances, urban guerrillas tend to spend a lot of time on the run, and find it difficult to hold on to an area and demonstrate their alternative system. Frequently it is hard to distinguish their activities from those of terrorists who have no strategy at all. It is depressing to reflect that those Americans who argued during the Vietnam War that the village peasants should be bombed into the cities might have had a point after all: not in the sense that bombing accomplished anything but death and misery, but in the sense that those who migrate to the city do so in the hope of improving their lot within the system, not of changing it. If their hopes are disappointed, they might rise in revolution, and either be massacred as in Shanghai or succeed as in Tehran. But in neither case has it anything to do with guerrilla war—and the term "urban guerrilla" is virtually an oxymoron.

In addition to these geographical and social limitations there are others, primarily historical in nature. The first of these might be summed up in the words "Too soon." After the hybrid experience of guerrilla war and popular disaffection that brought Castro to power in Cuba, the hapless Che Guevara attempted to spread the gospel by establishing revolutionary *focos* in Latin America, starting in, of all places, Bolivia. Quite apart from the fact that he was betrayed, he seems to have stood no chance at all. Perhaps a society needs to have achieved a certain level of historical development before its members become susceptible to revolutionary ideas or are willing to undertake the grueling demands of guerrilla warfare. The Bolivian peasant emphatically was not.

The second historical limitation might be summarized in the words "Too late." That applies particularly to postcolonial societies in which, once the ideas of social transformation have been subsumed into the struggle for national liberation, once independence has been achieved, social expectations have all too often been bitterly disappointed and the unifying force of the struggle for independence has also disappeared. Successor regimes are able to claim a certain legitimacy, however corrupt or autocratic they might be, and it is very difficult to mobilize the people against them. Obviously, this is not always true: the people of Eritrea ultimately won in their struggle with the successive regimes in Addis Ababa—but for the Eritreans of course that was in any case the capital of a foreign power. Generally, it would appear to be the case that the success of nationalism leaves the aspirations of social revolution by the historical wayside.

There is a third kind of historical limitation that is technological in nature. It is now very much more difficult than it was even in the recent past to conduct a campaign based on guerrilla tactics. A whole army of new technological developments have made the guerrilla fighter much more vulnerable than before, at least when confronting a sophisticated enemy. Some arise directly from the U.S. experience in the Vietnam War, during which, to give an example, a number of chemical and other artificial sensors were developed that made it much easier to track the movements of guerrilla groups. It is possible to use such sensors to detect traces of human urine, so making the task of jungle tracking much less dependent on the cooperation of skilled local inhabitants. Other developments are not directly related to guerrilla warfare but can have a powerful bearing on it, particularly the computerization of intelligence information, which makes it possible to see in a flash potentially significant relationships between disparate facts that it would otherwise have taken a month to think of. At both the micro and the macro levels, technology has begun to strip away much of the natural cover that protected the guerrilla fighter in the past.

For all these reasons, the heyday of *la guerrilla* might well now be over. That said, however, the fact remains that at the very height of the Cold War and at the time of the deployment of thousands upon thousands of nuclear weapons that were meant in some manner to maintain a world order, it was guerrilla warfare that brought about vast historical changes that the nuclear threat was powerless to prevent. But the nature of the nuclear threat itself has not yet been fully considered.

Note

1. Bernard Brodie, "The Tet Offensive," in Noble Frankland and Christopher Dowling, eds., *Decisive Battles of the Twentieth Century* (London: Sidgwick and Jackson, 1976).

14

The Rationality and Ethics of Nuclear Deterrence

The nuclear threat embodied in the system of deterrence seemed both to justify and to encapsulate the autonomy of strategic thinking that was discussed in Chapter 1 of this book. The phenomena of *la guerrilla* had, all the same, challenged such a version of strategic autonomy at the very time when it seemed to reign supreme. The ability of "strategy" to impose the rules of social evolution and of the conduct of international relations, and to deal with the resultant conflicts within the context of Limited War, was *not* defined by the threat of global destruction, rather the reverse. Yet the Cold War, the idea of the superpower, the assumption of bipolarity—all these assumed that the criteria of international social history were to be determined by reference to the risk of global destruction.

It has already been argued that the reverse was the case—that, particularly since Gorbachev's accession to power in the USSR, the criteria of social developments came gradually to be seen as those that offered an escape from the hideously foreshortened perspective imposed on history by nuclear deterrence itself. But one might suggest further here that it was not only the victory of social, economic, and even human awareness over the pseudostability of the Cold War that inspired the search for alternative methods of conducting international relations; not only that Limited War had served to demonstrate how difficult it had become to define victory in conflict; not only that the successes of guerrilla war had exposed the limitations of a massively destructive threat; but also that the idea of nuclear deterrence itself was inherently erroneous, whether judged by either rational or ethical standards.

In fact, the either/or implications are misleading. It would be perfectly possible to make a case that if nuclear deterrence could be shown to be rational it might after all be judged to be ethical, even if it were to involve the risk of genocide. Many apologists of the "nuclear deterrent" have made such a case when arguing from elevated positions in U.S., British, French, and even Soviet governments (though the last was always dogged by the distinction between strategic policy and strategic doctrine) that "deterrence kept the peace" and that therefore the threat to commit genocide was in fact a highly effective instrument of saving not merely millions of lives, but the world itself. That position seemed to accept the ironic argument that the threat of global holocaust offered the best means of preventing a more localized or specifically targeted holocaust. But such an argument depends on the assumption that the system of deterrence "works," and can be seen to work—in other words that it is rational. This argument will be unpacked somewhat later; but before that it might be worthwhile to consider what the idea of rationality means in the first place.

What, after all, is rationality? Short of some idea of transcendental Reason within which any form of human activity—political, social, sexual, economic—can be judged, rationality must surely be defined in terms of a relationship between ends and means. If that basis is accepted, it becomes possible to ask how far the criteria of rationality can be applied to the conduct of two states operating a system of mutual nuclear deterrence.

Let us assume that each state is capable of totally destroying the other, whichever attacked first. But let us also assume that although they are hostile, each state is totally, totally rational. If that is the case, then it is in the interests of the one to attack the other and wipe it out completely. It can do this, not because the other lacks a retaliatory second-strike capability, but because it is rational. Being rational it would have concluded beforehand that there was no point in retaliating once it was dead, because the retaliation would serve no purpose at all: it would merely destroy several million innocent bystanders, without bringing the original victim back to life. But in the real world, states, or the people who govern them, are not as rational as that. They plan for pointless posthumous retaliation, and there is every reason to believe that this act of supreme irrationality, in which the second-strike means serve no discernible end, would actually be carried out. If deterrence "works" it does so because states know each other to be profoundly irrational actors in the ultimate theater of the absurd.

The proponents of nuclear deterrence would of course argue at this point that so long as all the parties concerned are aware of the underlying irrationality of the system, that very awareness imposes rational behavior on them; and that therefore the system, in its actual operation as distinct from the hypothesis of what would happen if it broke down, can be said to be rational. But this does not get away from the fact that the system depends *entirely* on the hypothesis of what would happen if it broke down. "Ah," the same proponent murmurs at this point, "but since there is no indication that it is ever really likely to break down, the hypothesis of irrational destruction need not concern us in our pursuit of rational policies such as arms control. We need to stabilize deterrence, not abandon it." But arguments of that nature do not stand up to any real scrutiny.

The first problem they encounter is one of straightforward logic. The idea that deterrence can deter war, at least between nuclear powers or alliances, is either a circular argument—deterrence works because it works—or else an unwarranted extrapolation from past experience into a generalization for the future. And even if it were *known* (which it is not) that it is the nuclear threat that kept the peace in Europe during the years of the Cold War, one can only say "deterrence has worked." To go on saying "deterrence works" is to make a statement that is either meaningless when not circular, or else that invites experimental challenge. According to the principles of the philosopher of science Sir Karl Popper, a general statement of that order must be capable of refutation if it is to have any meaning. Unfortunately there is only one way of testing the statement, and if experiment then refuted it, few would live to tell the tale. It is safer as well as more logical to regard it as meaningless.

The second difficulty is empirical. The stockpiling of large numbers of nuclear weapons is exceedingly dangerous.[1] Fortunately these dangers have receded as short-range and intermediate-range nuclear missiles have been withdrawn and destroyed and the complexities of keeping them ready for use while not being ready to use them have automatically been resolved. But the point here is that the command and control of nuclear weapons proved empirically to be very tricky, and it is simply impossible to say whether the probability of their use was always remote or sometimes high. All that is known for certain is, as mentioned before, that at the time of the Cuban missile crisis the world was considerably closer to nuclear war than even the major participants in the drama realized.

To summarize: the rational proponent of nuclear deterrence would concede that its effectiveness depends on the threat of ultimate irrationality but would still argue that a system of mutual deterrence imposes rational behavior and therefore works. Logically, that is an impossible argument to sustain. The proponent would also argue that the dangers of nuclear weapons ever being used are remote. Logically, it is impossible to project that argument into the future, while the empirical experience of the past suggests that whether such an eventuality is remote or not is at best impossible to determine.

It is within this context of fundamental irrationality and unknown risk that one can begin to approach the question of the ethics of nuclear deterrence. As already indicated, it is possible to make a case that the nuclear threat is ethical in the sense that the very effectiveness of the horror it invokes serves to keep the peace and save lives. That proposition is itself dubious, but let us accept it for the time being. In that case, what is the ethical proponent of the system actually arguing? It is surely, as much of the writing on the subject suggests,[2] that while it would be evil to carry out the threat of committing genocide, it is not immoral to make that threat in the cause of preserving peace. Such a distinction, however, needs some unpacking.

In the first place, while it *might* be morally acceptable to make the threat in order to keep the peace, and to do so without any intention of fulfilling it, is it still acceptable to do so when one has every intention of carrying it out if war did occur and escalation began? In the one case—that of having no intention of actually committing genocide—the ethical question becomes hostage to an empirical one: namely that nuclear deterrence is really a gigantic bluff—which is fine so long as no opponent realizes that it's a bluff or is tempted to call it. (That, as suggested in Chapter 7, seems to have been the position adopted by Robert McNamara.[3] But it is incidental here.) Yet does not the "ethical bluff," as one might call it, not only subordinate moral considerations to empirical considerations—"let's hope it works"—but also raise new questions, of themselves ethical in nature? That is to say, how far can it be deemed ethical to stake international peace on the tenuous credibility of a bluff instead of seeking an alternative policy? (To be fair, that is probably what McNamara was trying to do when proposing the strategy of flexible response in 1962, but by then the conduct of international relations had become so embedded in the system of nuclear deterrence that he really stood no chance.) In general, the ethical bluff approach raises as many moral questions as it seeks to answer. But that still leaves the other case to be considered—the case of what might be called "conditional intent."

Conditional intent implies that while one might hope to God that the day will never come, one is nonetheless prepared in the last resort to go to thermonuclear war. In one sense this can be seen as an answer to the dilemmas of the ethical bluff. This is to say that only if the adversary is certain that "we mean it," or at least has a pretty good inkling that "we might," will he desist from the kind of action that could provoke a war. In this sense, the ethical considerations are clearly subordinate from the outset to the empirical. But in another sense one might say that such an approach represents the triumph of the ethical over the empirical. This somewhat Delphic statement needs elucidation.

Hegel's parable of the Master and the Slave evokes two men locked in combat.[4] Each has a choice: whether to ensure the survival of the contingent organism, the body, by being prepared to surrender, or whether to preserve the freedom of the mind and will by being prepared to fight to the death if necessary and be killed. For Hegel, that latter choice represented the first moment of historical transcendence—the triumph of the conscious being over the condition of contingency. The rest of the parable becomes much more complicated as it continues; but for present purposes it might be said that this initial stage of what he was writing about finds its peculiar modern parody in the system of nuclear deterrence—aptly summed up in two slogans that were widespread in the 1950s and 1960s. The first, "Better dead than Red," represented the position of Hegel's eventual Master. The second, "Better Red than dead," represented that of the eventual Slave. But for Hegel, as the subsequent complex arguments of his parable testify, the interactive workings of these choices came to represent the work of the Spirit in human consciousness and the ultimate triumph of freedom. What never occurred to him, and what was historically impossible for him to foresee, was that the Spirit could actually commit suicide. But that is exactly what is implicit in the contemporary world: insofar as conditional intent represents the triumph of the ethical over the empirical—insofar as "Better dead than Red" became the prevailing slogan—the attempt to preserve values by threatening, even conditionally, a combination of genocide and suicide renders values meaningless and threatens the very existence of what Hegel would have identified as the Spirit.

Conditional intent, therefore, represents a conflation of two entirely contradictory ideas: on the one hand the triumph of the empirical over the ethical, on the other hand the triumph of the ethical considerations of value over the empirical considerations of survival—but in a form that is at best a parody of Hegel and that leaves no room for the meaning of value after all. This parodistic triumph removes the idea of value from the workings of history.[5]

Even then, it might still be possible to argue that conditional intent should be seen as a tool designed to preserve freedom and value after all. If the adversary is persuaded of its veracity, it need never be involved and civilization can flourish. Such an approach would be utilitarian in nature rather than signifying in itself a commitment to the triumph of value over survival. But its utility would clearly depend on the assumption that the tool is effective—that the adversary is indeed persuaded, that there are no insoluble problems about the command and control of nuclear weapons, and that accidents will not happen: in short, that the possibility of nuclear war is (once again) so remote that it is not worth worrying about in practice. This utilitarian approach, however, becomes, in its turn, a parody of a very different philosopher, this time not Hegel but Pascal.

Pascal was obsessed with the questions of religious faith and doubt, with the possibility of predestination of one's eternal soul, but also with the problems of what today would be called "probability theory" in mathematics. This combination of preoccupations led him to formulate his famous bet, which was in essence that the likelihood of the existence of God was extremely remote but that all the same it was worth staking one's life on it and living accordingly. In such a wager, there is everything to gain—eternal salvation itself—if the remote possibility turns out to be true, and nothing to lose if it does not. One is merely dead. The utilitarian approach to nuclear deterrence reverses this position. It suggests that, even though the world has everything to lose if faith in nuclear deterrence turns out to be misplaced, it is still worth betting on such a system because the possibility of nuclear war is minimal. Quite apart from the consideration that this assumption was empirically dubious, the bet involved reduces the gravest ethical questions that humankind has had yet to face to an exercise in probability theory. The least that can be said for Pascal is that he was trying to reconcile questions of probability with those of ethical choice. Conditional intent as a tool of nuclear deterrence reduces ethical choice to the question of what is or is not likely to happen. And that raises the latest observation.

Whether seen in terms of the parody of the Master-Slave relationship or in terms of the inversion of Pascal's bet, a decision to base security and value on a system of nuclear deterrence represents a form of existential suicide. For two reasons. The first is that human beings destroy themselves as human beings when they begin even to contemplate threatening the destruction of the human race in an attempt to ensure their survival or maintain their values. Survival itself, and the values that human societies hope to attach to it, lose all meaning in such a context. Second, deterrence condemns all human beings, not only those in the states endowed with nuclear weapons, to a permanent and indefinite fear of the future. Suppose it all goes wrong . . . ? Should we even have children . . . ? However distant, the outside possibility becomes a near neighbor in the dreams and relationships of people. Sociological research is lacking, but it would not be surprising if a distinct correlation were to be found between the explosion of the drug culture and the maturing of the generation that grew up accustomed to the threat of the Bomb. Whether that is the case or not, the threat itself ensured that survival, instead of being a condition for the articulation of value, became itself the ultimate value—with the result that dialogue between cultures or about values was virtually excluded from the conduct of international relations. That, as indicated earlier, was the nature of détente.

In conclusion, it seems extremely difficult to argue that the policy of nuclear deterrence can be either ethical or rational. If it were possible to show that it is rational, an ethical case might be conceivable. But it is not; and however many decent and well-intentioned men and women might argue that the nuclear threat is the best available ethical choice, the very nature of that threat ultimately destroys everything that is meant by the word "decency."

Notes

1. See Paul Bracken, *The Command and Control of Nuclear Weapons* (New Haven: Yale University Press, 1983).

2. See, for example, some contributors in Geoffrey Goodwin, ed., *Ethics and Nuclear Deterrence* (London: Croom Helm, 1982).

3. See McGeorge Bundy, George Kennan, and Gerard Smith, "Nuclear Weapons and the Atlantic Alliance," *Foreign Affairs* 60, no. 4 (spring 1982).

4. G.W.F. Hegel, *The Phenomenology of the Spirit* (Oxford: Oxford University Press, 1979).

5. Hayo B.E. Krombach, *Hegelian Reflections on the Idea of Nuclear War: Dialectical Thinking and the Dialectic of Mankind* (Basingstoke: Macmillan, 1991).

15

Beyond the Cold War

"The Cold War" is a strangely comforting phrase. It implied, obviously, that a real war was, and would be, successfully avoided. It implied too that the battle for the future of history between two hostile ideological and social systems would be fought out over a long term with weapons that were political and economic in nature (as George Kennan originally foresaw the policy of containment), or indeed social and ideological (as Khrushchev understood the terms of peaceful coexistence). And even though containment became first militarized and then nuclearized, the very threat of mutual devastation seemed nonetheless to promise that peaceful coexistence would continue. For millions of people, in spite of occasional nightmares and the vociferous opposition of such minorities as the Campaign for Nuclear Disarmament, it seemed perfectly sensible and acceptable to manipulate the prospect of destruction in order to prevent the use of force. "Peace," as the Strategic Air Command used to boast, "is our profession."

In such circumstances it is perhaps paradoxical but not surprising that while the conflict was conducted in terms to which the use of force was irrelevant, strategic considerations became, as was suggested at the very beginning of this book, predominant in the field of international relations. Strategic thinking became self-referring and self-legitimating; and the framework of nuclear deterrence became a reference point for the formulation of foreign policy. Yet as the years progressed, it became increasingly difficult to determine what it was that deterrence was actually supposed to deter.

In the early days of massive retaliation, it seems to have been expected that the nuclear threat would deter "Communist aggression" around the globe. But this rapidly proved illusory. Even at the height of peaceful coexistence, and in spite of massive retaliation, Khrushchev declared Soviet support for "just wars of national liberation," and such support was indeed forthcoming. Whether the wars led to liberation is another matter. The very fact that in the United States so much thought and energy were devoted to thinking about Limited War was itself an indication that American policymakers acknowledged that the early optimism of massive retaliation had been misplaced. And what this indicates is a fundamental category error.

The error lay in asking and answering the wrong question. The question that was answered was: "Who are we trying to deter?"—and the answer was: "The Communists," most particularly the Soviet Union and China. The question that was not asked in those early years, and that was only intermittently addressed later, was: "*What* are we trying to deter?"

For such lesser nuclear powers as Britain and France, the distinction between these two questions did not matter overmuch. Both were hoping to deter the Soviet Union, and both with the objective of avoiding a direct attack on their own territories. In spite of some rather grandiose statements to the contrary by General de Gaulle, those were the only terms in which the British or French nuclear forces were remotely credible. In spite of differences in their approach to the question of nuclear escalation on the European battlefield, the strategic policy of both countries can be summed up in the French concept of "proportional deterrence"—meaning that while each was fully aware that the Soviet Union had the power to wipe it out completely, it still had sufficient retaliatory power to inflict terrible losses on the USSR; and no Soviet government would risk incurring such destruction for the pleasure of destroying Britain or France. Under proportional deterrence there is no great need for the distinction between the "who" and the "what." But in the case of the major nuclear powers, and especially the United States with its manifold commitments, the distinction was vital.

As the question of "what" came to replace the question of "who," so the scope of deterrence narrowed. The process was gradual but inexorable, beginning with the questions raised in Henry Kissinger's *Nuclear Weapons and Foreign Policy,* continuing with the search for a more "flexible response," and moving into the areas of irrational commitment under MAD. Along the way, President Kennedy had already indicated in a famous speech at the time of the Berlin crisis in 1961 that the United States did not contemplate risking nuclear war over Berlin.[1] Later, changes in the targeting and deployment of U.S. nuclear weapons, such as those that occurred under Secretary of Defense James Schlesinger in 1974 (the so-called Schlesinger Doctrine), were indicative of an attempt to widen the scope of deterrence again. But the fact remained that the nuclear threat was becoming less and less effective as an instrument of policy and that wars multiplied around the globe. Yet in Europe, whatever the political upheavals, relations between East and West remained stable. This is not to say, as many commentators do, that during the Cold War, Europe enjoyed forty-five years or so of peace. One can hardly count the suppression of the Hungarian uprising or the invasion of Czechoslovakia as acts of peace. But it is to say that the menace of nuclear war came to be identified with the maintenance of peace. In other words, as the scope of deterrence narrowed, so its importance grew—and this does much to explain the furious frustration of the U.S. administrations when confronting the Soviet Union in the "second Cold War."

The underlying suggestion here is in fact that the system of deterrence gradually changed from being an instrument for the avoidance of war to becoming a framework for the containment of wars. The reason is not far to seek. Deterrence was institutionalized—and once something becomes an institution its nature changes. The guards in front of Buckingham Palace were originally posted there to repel the potential dangers of the mob. Today their principal function is that of attracting as big a mob of tourists as possible. And in a routine similar to that of the palace's changing of the guard, squadrons of the Soviet air force on the one hand and of the U.S. and British air forces on the other hand became accustomed to taking off from their respective bases in Germany virtually every day after lunch, flying toward each other's territory, and then peeling off to fly northward in something approaching close formation along the old East-West German border. Pilots even came to recognize each other and exchange greetings. That is institutionalization—and in that respect détente came to represent the institutionalization of deterrence. But for the very same reason, both deterrence and détente were impotent in preventing the spread of conflict almost around the globe.

Max Weber would have had no difficulty in recognizing such a phenomenon. It was part of what he refers to as "rationalization" (and also takes on many of the characteristics of what he discusses in another context as the process of "bureaucratization"). Deterrence became its own institution, its own form of rationality, its own bureaucracy—and was imprisoned, in Weber's famously tragic phrase, "in the Iron Cage of Reason." That iron cage represents the subordination of all other forms of international discourse to the autonomy of strategic thinking in the nuclear age.

The history of the nuclear age also demonstrates the increasing irrelevance of the assumptions that lie behind deterrence to the causes of conflict and of peace in the contemporary world. Not only, as has just been suggested, did its importance increase as its scope narrowed (and much of this obviously goes back to the malign interpretation of MAD), but this historical development also meant that the dangers of war actually seemed to increase rather than decrease as conflicts erupted in the "arc of crisis" and beyond even while opposing pilots exchanged friendly signals across the Elbe. In a well-known German political slogan of the early 1980s, aired as much by the right as the left in German politics, "Never again a world war starting on German soil." But the ironic footnote, not exclusive to the left, was: "But the next world war will be fought on German soil." It seemed to many as if the dangerous and horrifying conflicts of what in "deterrence" terms was the periphery might well command hostilities in what had hitherto been assumed to be a stable center.

That was not how it turned out. Partly because of the transformation of the Soviet Union, and (in consequence of that) partly because of the changes of the old criteria of arms control, the system of deterrence and the embedded threats of MAD lost their centrality in the conduct of international relations. Instead, the rapid thaw in the relations between the superpowers and between East and West led to a redefinition of those relations. But nothing could have proved more disillusioning than the results.

The end of the paradigm of deterrence in the conduct of international relations seemed to promise not only an end to those conflicts that had been engendered by the Cold War but also a new cooperation between the previous antagonists in resolving new ones. Using the UN Security Council as an instrument on some occasions, collaborating on a bilateral basis on others, the United States and the Soviet Union were able to agree on the withdrawal of Cuban forces from Angola and South African forces from Namibia, on what was in effect a U.S. intervention designed to bring an end to the Iran-Iraq War, and on the conditions for Vietnamese withdrawal from Cambodia and the installation of a transitional government in that country under UN protection. The Soviet Union decided unilaterally to withdraw its forces from Afghanistan, but it was part of a package of understandings reached with the United States.[2] Finally, in spite of much initial disagreement, Moscow and Washington sanctioned the UN-sponsored and U.S.-led intervention by multinational coalition forces after the Iraqi occupation of Kuwait in August 1990. It all looked very promising; and President Bush for one was tempted to proclaim a "New World Order." The stabilization and resolution of regional conflicts on the basis of superpower cooperation seemed to be the order of the day.

One cannot write this off altogether. There had been many conflicts that were prolonged or intensified by being drawn into the pattern of superpower confrontation; and once superpower involvement ceased, they proved surprisingly capable of resolution. But that said, most deadly quarrels in the world had, and continue to have, local roots that were not to be suppressed by some kind of superpower weed killer, whether administered through the UN or any other international agency. Their persistence betrays the hollowness of the assumptions behind what might be called "the superpower syndrome."

The cooperation of ancient adversaries has proved as unable to deal with the eruption of other conflicts as their previous antagonism had been. The idea of the New World Order was in fact a carryover of the old assumptions of the Cold War period into a new historical situation. During the Cold War, the conclusion was widely drawn that it was the superpower relationship that determined the fate of the rest of the world. That was true only in the sense that either of the two had the capacity to blow everybody else to smithereens. It was not true in the sense that this capacity gave them much ability to determine the outcome of developments elsewhere—as any citizen of Israel or of North Vietnam could have testified at the very height of Cold War rivalry in 1967. What is more plainly visible now, after the end of the Cold War, is that the very idea of the "superpower" was an epiphenomenon of the Cold War—and that, once this was over, the scope for influence of the old superpowers was in fact very restricted.

The implication here is that there are no more superpowers. That is partly just a way of saying that history has long been too damned complicated to be amenable to control by the threats of ultimate annihilation. But it is also to suggest something else: namely that the very word "superpower" carries a certain historical baggage with it.[3] Originally meant to distinguish the determinant powers of the post–World War II order from the traditional "Great Powers" that had dominated the world for the previous couple of centuries, it still reflected a view of power that was ultimately measured in terms of military might, and capable thereby of ruling history. Yet as the very history of the USSR has shown with startling clarity, and that of the United States in a rather more ambiguous fashion, military might is far from being a determinant of history. Instead, one might argue, the idea of the superpower refers not to how much power a country has but to what role it plays in the conduct of international affairs. While the Cold War assumptions were still in place, it was possible though probably always misguided (Mao Tse-tung would certainly have argued so) to analyze global developments in terms of the bipolar superpower relationship. Today it has become fashionable to say that there is only one superpower left—the United States. Yet although its physical power has not diminished, the United States is barely more capable of the superpower role than is Russia as the successor of the old Soviet Union. The role of superpower has vanished, and no actor can possibly hope to fill it. Where does that leave strategic thinking?

The short answer, as exemplified by the rapid collapse of any expectations of a New World Order, is that strategic thinking is now in a state of confusion and disarray. The "superpower"-led coalition that intervened after the Iraqi invasion of Kuwait did not topple the regime of Saddam Hussein nor remove his capacity to create new havoc in the Gulf and the Middle East more generally. The harrowing atrocities that have resulted from the breakup of what was once Yugoslavia led only to disagreements and recriminations among those powers that were supposed to have the military muscle to create or impose some kind of solution to the internecine conflict. Scores of wars between the autonomous and semiautonomous successor states followed the dissolution of the Soviet Union. The much-vaunted peace process in the Middle East, which was supposed to bring about a resolution to the Arab-Israeli conflict as a consequence (in some way or other) of the Gulf War, merely demonstrated yet again that peace was difficult and that tails wag dogs. That is by no means an exhaustive catalog. But it is enough to demonstrate that the era of strategic autonomy, in which considerations of strategy provided the parameters of economic and political relationships, has come to an end. Social questions, driven by ancient forces of religion or ethnic identity, or intensified by new problems of environmental degradation, have come to dominate international affairs—so much so that the great Anarch now seems set to rule.

That is itself in part a consequence of the earlier dominance of strategic assumptions. So much was repressed. To give but one example: handing over Soviet and Yugoslav prisoners, who had surrendered to the Western allies in the later stages of World War II, to almost certain death, was an act carried out by otherwise honorable men "for the sake of avoiding a third world war." And later, as both the threat of that war and the necessity of avoiding it became more imperative, so the scope of the psychological repression grew. In the end, the superpower relationship, characterized by Henry Kissinger's "awesome responsibility," became a device for avoiding those very confrontations of value from which the Cold War had originally arisen.

In that respect, détente as institutionalized deterrence (as discussed earlier in this chapter) was not, as many had hoped, a solution to the problems of what had been suppressed: it became part of the problem itself. Now, however, that questions of value have taken center stage (for example, the G-7 group of countries have agreed to be moderately generous in offering aid to Russia as it strives to become a working democracy), many other such questions have returned from their repression in a hideously vengeful form. The awesome responsibility of pursuing détente has turned into a terrible responsibility *for* dealing with its consequences. And at present, once the strategic considerations have been factored out, there are no tools readily at hand. All this is part—and only part—of the short answer to the questions of what now becomes strategic thinking.

The slightly longer answer might begin with different questions. In the past, attempts have been made to bring military and strategic activity under some form of control—the moral control of the Just War tradition, which began to merge into the legal control associated with Grotius and the Westphalian system, leading on to the political control advocated in particular by Clausewitz. In one sense the framework of strategic autonomy based on nuclear deterrence, designed as it was to avoid war between the powers central to the international system and to limit other wars elsewhere, *seemed* to answer all the sets of questions raised in those earlier attempts. In another sense it raises all the questions all over again, and makes them more starkly demanding than ever. How, and by what criteria, are the assumptions of strategic thinking that dominated the superpower relationship in the period of the Cold War to be brought back under control? How, in short, can strategy begin to divest itself of its ineffective autonomy?

Some tentative approaches to answering that question had already emerged in the last years of the Cold War. In the Federal Republic of Germany in particular, there was much discussion among politicians, officers, and intellectuals-at-large of how to address the problems of security in the new framework of analysis: one that considered the effects of military preparations on political relations and vice versa. Ultimately, it was realized that security lay in reaching political understanding; and military deployments should as far as possible be conducive to that end. This was the idea of the *Gesamtkonzept*—the "comprehensive" or "integrated" concept. Similar ideas can be discerned in exchanges of information and discussions of military doctrine between members of NATO and of the Warsaw Pact in the period that preceded the agreement on Conventional Armed Forces in Europe in 1990. This was part of the transformation of arms control that has been discussed earlier, and that indicated a new willingness to define strategic imperatives in political terms. But the *Gesamtkonzept* approach still depended on a recognizable and indeed familiar political context, one delineated by the Cold War. Today that context has been transformed and fragmented into a number of different contexts. It is hard to frame a comprehensive concept in this new situation.

Recognizing that, many academic strategists and strategic institutions have turned their attention to studies in regional security. They seek the causes of instability, they attempt to work out stable balance-of-power relations, and they consider whether military assistance or even intervention might be useful, and whether the United Nations has a role to play in particular regional conflicts. There is nothing specifically wrong with all that, but it does still depend largely on the assumption that strategic considerations are causal rather than consequential in nature. It is still part of the process of Weber's rationalization; and much of the effort represents an attempt to pour the old wine of strategic thinking into new, smaller, and intellectually fragile bottles. Precisely because strategic thinking was itself both the outcome and the instrument of an abnormal period of history, it is not appropriate for dealing with the many problems that have reemerged from beneath the surface of that abnormality. And the difficulty goes further.

The old context has fragmented, there is no global system, the superpower role is dead; but the scope for interaction between different developments around the world is now such that it becomes very difficult to define where a region starts and ends anyway. What is meant by "stability in the Middle East"? Where is the Middle East? Is Somalia, a member of the League of Arab States, to be included in it? If some Turkish or Iranian politicians get their way, it might soon be necessary to think of the Transcaucasian successor states of the old Soviet Union as part of the Middle East too. Conversely, is China one region or several? It might depend on which of China's neighbors one has in mind. In general, the idea of regional stability provides a pretty inadequate framework for the necessary transformation of strategic thinking.

Yet the prevalence of regional conflict in the world today also emphasizes that the only previous alternative to Cold War bipolarity—namely the Non-Aligned Movement—has also collapsed. Its potential was always greater than its ability to frame policy, but for a time it did seem to offer the promise of a different approach to the containment, or even resolution, of conflicts: one based on third-world consensus and on peaceful means. Yet perhaps, after all, the Non-Aligned Movement itself was as much an epiphenomenon of the Cold War as the superpower system.

Founded on hostility to that system, and in all appearance embracing a set of values that were irenic in nature, it nonetheless only flourished so long as superpower antagonism more or less maintained global order and ensured that the nonaligned states did not have to make awkward choices when it came to matching the requirements of value with the requirements of order. Today, of the original protagonists of the movement, India has been much involved in conflict, intervention, and repression (the latter especially in Kashmir), Yugoslavia has disappeared into hideous chaos, Indonesia until recently remained engaged in a campaign of imperialist brutality in East Timor, and only Egypt has survived as a country whose original credentials might still be said to be intact. (The irony here is that of all the founder members, Egypt was the only one to make an effective alliance, first with one superpower and then the other, and to bounce Israel into the peace process by invoking the prospect of superpower confrontation. The consequence of that irony is that Egypt's stability is threatened at present partly because of the very fact that it did make peace with Israel.) But the case of Egypt apart, the Non-Aligned Movement has collapsed along with the Cold War structure to which it objected and that was nonetheless its progenitor.

Is, then, the great Anarch really bound to hold sway? There is perhaps no intellectual answer to that question, rather the recognition of a moral imperative, acknowledged even obscurely by departments of state and international agencies: not to give way to counsels of despair. As already suggested, questions of value have now been admitted onto the agenda, and even into the financial accounting, of the conduct of international affairs. But what has not yet been admitted is that such questions actually revolutionize the whole agenda. Up to now, the G-7 group might be disposed to be generous to Russia (or might think so) in the interests of fostering Russian democracy; human rights might have become "official" in dealings between states (or between some at least). But all such signs of apparent progress have been indicative hitherto only of the breakdown of the old strategic, value-free structure of the paramount need to avoid nuclear war. In that sense the discourse on values has only crept sideways into the conduct of international relations. The real difficulty, however, is that this discourse has already come to the forefront in the form of war—between ethnic and historical groups, between different religious identities—even while the ex-superpowers and their respective blocs have begun to put the constraints of nuclear deterrence aside and to explore future forms of cooperation. That cooperation at the center is matched by an explosion of value conflicts almost everywhere else.

There are two phenomena inherent here. One is that of minor powers being able to recover their own freedom of action—even though some of the characteristics of the Cold War had given certain among them considerable freedom of action anyway. It is not so much the old minor powers as the new that have benefited from this new-found freedom. Witness, for example, the republics of the former Yugoslavia. The other phenomenon, more fundamental, is what might be called "the democratization of war."

Most wars today are fought not between states, but by groupings of people, banded together by a notion of common belonging that is itself contingent on hostility to other, similar groupings. In that sense, war has become the agent of identity, and identity has become the claim to democratic expression. The perhaps final paradox of the Cold War is becoming menacingly distinct; and the peculiar comfort that was attached to that phrase is no longer a comfort at all. Whether seen as a phrase of interpretation or as the description of an actual phenomenon, the Cold War was a conflict of values, commonly described at the time as an "ideological confrontation." Yet the protagonists in that conflict suppressed all discourse of value for the sake of survival. What has now happened is that this repressed discourse has returned, taking the form of war after war. In such a context, it is surely true to say, as did George Kennan, that nobody "won" the Cold War. The notion of democracy, far from having unequivocally triumphed, has itself become a battleground. Far from there being a New World Order, in which the rules of justice were somehow assumed to be incorporated, the conflict between justice and order is now at least as acute as it has ever been.[4] Outside the established democracies of the West, the process of achieving self-determination and democracy has itself become war. This interaction between the freedom of minor powers to act and the democratization of war, occurring as it has in a global context in which the old rules no longer apply—no superpower role—no viable nonaligned alternative—means that the traditional categories of strategic thinking are now barely applicable to the present situation of the world.

Yet as the old superpowers and their allies are beginning to discover the limitations of the old strategic imperatives, a number of other states, in some sense successors to the old Cold War system, have demonstrated their ambitions to acquire the old strategic panoply. In a highly restricted sense, it could perhaps be said that within the Cold War framework, the manipulation of the threats of mass destruction "worked": at least nuclear war did not happen. But because the possession of such means of destruction was widely seen as an indicator of status and responsibility ("a seat at the top table," as former British prime minister Sir Alec Douglas-Home once put it in an unwontedly vulgar phrase), the weapons themselves are still regarded as some kind of passport to international authority. As indicated earlier, the republics of the former Soviet Union, in particular the Ukraine, have shown themselves singularly reluctant to abandon their nuclear arsenals; and in many other countries the ambition to acquire nuclear weapons has become commonplace. This does not reflect any indication of their importance: the purposes that they might be deemed to serve are almost impossible to identify—and even when these might be thought to be apparent, for example in the case of Israel, the case hardly stands up to detailed scrutiny. All the same, and whatever the strategic irrelevance of nuclear weapons for most of the countries in the world, the pressures for nuclear proliferation seem to be remorseless. Why?

The answer appears to lie in the fact that the possession of nuclear weapons, whatever their apparent purpose, seems to confer a certain legitimacy upon the state, which might wear them on its coat of arms—legitimacy both in the sense of being capable of independent decision and destruction, and in the sense of being admitted to the international hierarchy. (Sir Alec Douglas-Home's "top table" remark had been preceded and perhaps outmatched by de Gaulle's telegram to the French nuclear team in the Sahara after the first nuclear test in 1960: "Hourrah pour la France!") But there is no real reason to suppose that such independence and such hierarchal legitimacy should be confined to the old Great Powers or the five permanent members of the UN Security Council. In the terms of the late and unlamented General Zia-ul-Haq of Pakistan: If there is a Western bomb, a Communist bomb, and a Jewish bomb, why should there not also be an Islamic bomb? In spite of the crudity of the categories (and in spite of the fact that the respective efforts of India and Pakistan might well be interpreted in terms of their confrontation on the subcontinent as a race to be last, in which the implicit dialogue is: "We *can* make nuclear weapons, but we won't do so unless you do"), such a statement represents a kind of aspiration to what one might call the "democratization of nuclear control." Why *should* the future survival of Earth, or even the regulation of the conflicts among its inhabitants, depend on the singular access to destructive power of those who are designed, by historical accident or by the kind of semi-dictatorship implied in the Nonproliferation Treaty, as exclusively permitted to wear the nuclear badge? In that sense, one might say, the trend toward nuclear proliferation is also a trend toward a democratization of the international system. But the implications are alarming in the extreme, particularly if they are taken in conjunction with the emergence of war as democratization, and democratization as war.

Brave New World Order! The worst possible outcome of these reflections is that war, as an instrument of the self-realization of democracy among those who were hitherto suppressed (and who are now engaged in their own atrocities), and nuclear proliferation, as one possible form of the democratization of the international system, might combine.

It is probably true to say that the articulation and realization of values have always been accompanied by war or the threat of war. That is not of course the same thing as saying that all wars have been about values. Yet two distinctions need to be borne very much in mind at this moment. The first is that war as part of the process of international democratization is not in itself necessarily concerned with any values other than those of the self-assertion of peoples or nations hitherto repressed. But the second is that *they* see such self-assertion very much as a question of value, even to the point where it becomes a moral imperative: witness the widespread popular support in the Arab world for Saddam Hussein's defiance of the Great Powers after the Iraqi occupation of Kuwait, of the prevalent sense among the Serbs that they were engaged in fulfilling some kind of historical duty. So the process of democratizing the international system through war came to be confused, in the post–Cold War period, with the ability not only to escape from earlier repression but also to rearticulate ancient values. Only this time, in a context in which the spread of nuclear weapons into more and more unconstrained hands became increasingly likely. And if the past is anything to go by, war when legitimized by morality is indeed more unconstrained than war fought for selfish or cynical reasons. Yet in the past, nuclear weapons were not available to help things along.

The confusion of the democratization of the international system with other questions of value, the tendency to articulate these through conflict, and the probability that weapons of mass destruction will become very more widely available—all these add up to a very alarming prospect. Some have argued that the spread of nuclear weapons in particular could have a stabilizing effect. This was a theme prosecuted by General Gallois in France in the 1960s, and more recently and in a more sophisticated form by Professor Kenneth Waltz in the United States.[5] But what both seem to presuppose is that either the possession of the Bomb *makes* one rational through the sheer awareness of its destructive power, or else that those who participate in present international activity are rational anyway. It is, however, very doubtful whether such assumptions would hold true of Saddam Hussein or Radovan Karadzic. In such a context, nuclear weapons do not, as the old patterns of strategic thinking derived from the Cold War might suggest, help to avoid or eliminate conflict; they only serve to make it infinitely more dangerous.

So, then, how to rethink strategic thinking? Old assumptions have disappeared, and the new process that is transforming the international system scarcely provides an answer: quite the contrary. One approach, obviously, is to reinvoke as far as possible the older traditions of moral, legal, and political control of war. As argued earlier, these have not disappeared, but coexist uneasily and in remnant form even in the contemporary world. Indeed, in some respects, their scope has even been extended.[6]

For all their failures, the UN and its agencies have shown themselves capable of redefining the old criteria in the modern age and of redrawing the map to take account of new contours. But—and this a very big *but*—the UN was founded on the assumption that war was and should be *abnormal*. And most modern strategic thinking has also accepted this assumption, even when concerned with the attempt to prevent war by the threat of all-out destruction.

The melancholy truth, however, appears to be that it is not war that is abnormal, but any sustained peace. In the terms once used by Kant, war might be described as a social form of unsociability. Yet even Kant aspired to the creation of a "Perpetual Peace" through the application of Reason and the reform of political constitutions. In the contemporary world, where historical and partial forms of rationality so frequently become the enemies of Reason, such luxuries are seldom permitted. The conclusion is that it is not war that needs explaining, or bringing under control, but international peace.

When both domestic societies and the international system have become so fragmented, it is an imperative requirement to bring peace under control. In the days of the Cold War, the strategic framework that threatened annihilation had become the successor to both the *ecumen* of the old Christian tradition and to Max Weber's Iron Cage of Reason in the post-Christian era. But in doing so, it also became vulnerable to all the interacting forces of separate and distinctive rationalities that amounted in the sum of their interaction to a comprehensive irrationality. In such circumstances, it became more difficult than ever to achieve the supreme abnormality of a human nature without war: war has been so integral to human nature throughout recorded history, so essential a requirement to the conduct and self-awareness of virtually every society, that the history of war in its social context has come to need a bold deconstruction and rethinking. There are precedents. Foucault, after all, did something similar in his *History of Sexuality,* which opened up the possibility of the abnormal (i.e., free) human being. But the abnormality of peace still needs a framework of thought.

There are two ways of approaching the abnormality of peace. The first is concerned with the origins and morphology of conflicts. It seeks to identify the patterns of conflict, whether at the domestic, the industrial, or the international level; and to inquire whether such patterns, once identified, can suggest techniques for resolving conflict itself. The attempt might be summarized as that of institutionalizing peace through the resolution of conflict. There are many intellectual institutes and university departments working along these lines today—predominantly in countries that have the Protestant ethic. They have produced interesting ideas that might even have helped on occasion to avert war. Indeed, some individuals and institutions claim to have done so. But they can hardly be said as yet to have developed a generalized framework of thought that helps to bring peace under control or distinguish its abnormality.

The second approach to the abnormality of peace might be called that of "international sociology." A word of caution is needed here. The word "sociology" today has far too many meanings. It can mean a form of philosophy—or perhaps rather signify that philosophy, when not concerned with linguistic logic-chopping, is rapidly becoming sociological in nature. It can also mean the degeneration of the whole field of thought into, as one leading British sociologist and interpreter of Weber has put it, "counting the number of feminist foot-fetishists in Dusseldorf."[7] International sociology in the present context means neither a branch of philosophy—though it draws on philosophical concepts—nor techniques of cross-category counting—though that can help. What it does mean is an attempt to examine the utility, or otherwise, of force within the complex interaction of international and social questions that characterizes the present world.[8] It seeks to move away from the question of how to harness war as an instrument of policy to the question of how to establish the international abnormality of peace. Unlike more conventional forms of strategic thought, it does seek to address the questions of the relationship values, relating them to the different kinds of contextual activity in which they are expressed. While not explicitly "deconstructive" in nature, it attempts to create alternative relationships between the communitarian demands of particular societies and the global demands of an international order. In the past that relationship took the form of war.

As a body of thought, it has enormous potential, partly because like all good sociology, it is ultimately tragic in nature. The more we understand ourselves, the less inclined we are toward complacency about our activities. And the less inclined we are to believe that terribly complex conflicts can be settled by nuclear threats. International sociology might not quite be Kant's Applied Reason and might not lead to his Perpetual Peace, but it does provide a better prospect than most for dealing with the conflicts that arise from the democratization of international society. Now that the autonomy of strategy in the nuclear age has come to an end, such a form of sociology can provide a fruitful and minatory framework for strategic thinking, precisely because of its inherently tragic nature.

The trouble with strategic thinking is that it was too optimistic. Many of its proponents attempted to cling to that optimism even in the face of disaster. In U.S. political discourse, for example, the horrors of the Vietnam War have been treated not in the obvious terms of tragedy—hubris, retribution, and expiation—but as a "syndrome" that had to be "got over." The Gulf War, and the much-vaunted expectations of a "New World Order" that followed from it, provided indications enough that such optimism remained in place. But its opposite is increasingly necessary: not pessimism but a proper sense of the tragic—starting with the assumption not that war is abnormal but that peace is difficult to achieve. If that becomes the future orientation of strategic thought, strategic assumptions can no longer provide a quick-fix solution to the tragic nature of human existence in international society. Instead, the understanding of tragedy can still be what, from the composition of the very earliest tragedies, it was meant to be: an act of liberation.

Notes

1. Said Kennedy: "I hear it said that West Berlin is militarily untenable. And so was Bastogne. And so, in fact, was Stalingrad. Any dangerous spot is tenable if men—brave men—will make it so." Radio and television report to the American people on the Berlin crisis, President John F. Kennedy, the White House, July 25, 1961.

2. These were semiformalized during a visit to Moscow by U.S. secretary of state George Schultz in 1988.

3. The term "superpower" was originally coined by Professor Robin Fox of Columbia University in 1943 when discussing the future after the end of World War II. (He included the United Kingdom along with the Dominions as one of the three superpowers of the future.)

4. Hedley Bull discusses this in *The Anarchical Society: A Study of Order in World Politics* (Basingstoke: Macmillan Press, 1977).

5. Kenneth N. Waltz, *The Spread of Nuclear Weapons: More May Be Better,* Adelphi Paper no. 171 (London: International Institute for Strategic Studies, 1981). Pierre Gallois, *The Balance of Terror: Strategy for the Nuclear Age* (Boston: Houghton Mifflin, 1961).

6. As in the 1977 Extension to the Geneva Protocol of 1949.

7. The words are those of Professor D. G. Macrae.

8. A number of the questions involved here are discussed in Amitai Etzioni, *Public Policy in a New Key* (New Brunswick, N.J.: Transaction, 1993).

Bibliography

Acheson, Dean. *Present at the Creation: My Years in the State Department.* New York: W. W. Norton, 1969.

Albertini, Luigi. *The Origins of the War of 1914.* London: Oxford University Press, 1965.

Angell, Sir Norman. *The Great Illusion.* New York: Arno Press, 1972.

Aron, Raymond. *Clausewitz: Philosopher of War.* London: Routledge & Kegan Paul, 1983.

Booth, Kenneth. *Strategy and Ethnocentrism.* London: Croom Helm, 1979.

Bracken, Paul. *The Command and Control of Nuclear Weapons.* New Haven: Yale University Press, 1983.

Brodie, Bernard. *Strategy in the Missile Age.* Princeton: Princeton University Press, 1959.

Buchan, Alistair, and Philip Windsor. *Arms and Stability in Europe.* London: Chatto and Windus, 1963.

Bull, Hedley. *The Anarchical Society: A Study of Order in World Politics.* Basingstoke: Macmillan Press, 1977.

———. *The Control of the Arms Race: Disarmament and Arms Control in the Missile Age.* London: Weidenfeld & Nicolson for the Institute for Strategic Studies, 1961.

Bull, Hedley, Benedict Kingsbury, and Adam Roberts. *Hugo Grotius and International Relations.* Oxford: Oxford University Press, 1990.

de Vattel, Emerich. *The Law of Nations: or, Principles of the Law of Nature, Applied to the Conduct and Affairs of Nations and Sovereigns.* New York: AMS Press, 1982.

de Wicquefort, Abraham. *The Embassador and His Functions.* Leicester: Leicester University Press, 1997.

Djilas, Milovan. *Wartime.* New York: Harcourt Brace Jovanovich, 1977.

Donelan, Michael, ed. *The Reason of States.* London: Allen & Unwin, 1978.

Douhet, Giulio. *The Command of the Air.* London: Faber and Faber, 1943.

Etzioni, Amitai. *Public Policy in a New Key.* New Brunswick, N.J.: Transaction, 1993.

Frankland, Noble, and Christopher Dowling, eds. *Decisive Battles of the Twentieth Century.* London: Sidgwick and Jackson, 1976.

Freedman, Lawrence. *The Evolution of Nuclear Strategy.* 2d ed. Basingstoke: Macmillan in association with the International Institute for Strategic Studies, 1989.

Fussell, Paul. *The Great War and Modern Memory.* London: Oxford University Press, 1977.

Gallois, Pierre. *The Balance of Terror: Strategy for the Nuclear Age.* Boston: Houghton Mifflin, 1961.

Garthoff, Raymond L. *How Russia Makes War.* London: Allen & Unwin, 1954.

Goodwin, Geoffrey, ed. *Ethics and Nuclear Deterrence.* London: Croom Helm, 1982.

Gray, Colin S. *Nuclear Strategy and National Style.* Lanham, Md.: Hamilton Press, 1986.

Hagihara, Nobutoshi, Akira Iriye, Georges Nivat, and Philip Windsor, eds. *Experiencing the Twentieth Century.* Tokyo: University of Tokyo Press, 1985.

Hastings, Max. *Bomber Command.* London: Pan Books, 1979.

Hegel, G.W.F. *The Phenomenology of the Spirit.* Oxford: Oxford University Press, 1979.

Heikal, Mohamed. *The Road to Ramadan.* London: Collins, 1975.

Holloway, David. *The Soviet Union and the Arms Race.* 2d ed. New Haven: Yale University Press, 1984.

———. *Stalin and the Bomb.* New Haven: Yale University Press, 1994.

Howard, Michael. *War in European History.* Oxford: Oxford University Press, 1976.

Howard, Michael, and Peter Paret, eds. *On War.* Princeton, N.J.: Princeton University Press, 1984.

Kaplan, Fred. *The Wizards of Armageddon.* New York: Simon and Schuster, 1983.

Kennedy, Robert F. *Thirteen Days: The Cuban Missile Crisis.* London: Pan Books, 1969.

Kissinger, Henry. *Nuclear Weapons and Foreign Policy.* New York: Harper & Bros. for the Council on Foreign Relations, 1957.

Knorr, Klaus, and Thorton Read, eds. *Limited Strategic War.* London: Pall Mall Press, 1962.

Krombach, Hayo B.E. *Hegelian Reflections on the Idea of Nuclear War: Dialectical Thinking and the Dialectic of Mankind.* Basingstoke: Macmillan, 1991.

Leonhard, Wolfgang. *Child of the Revolution.* London: Collins, 1957.

———. *The Kremlin Since Stalin.* London: Oxford University Press, 1962.

Light, Margot. *The Soviet Theory of International Relations.* Brighton: Wheatsheaf Books, 1988.

Lilienthal, David. *The Journals of David E. Lilienthal.* Vol. 2, *The Atomic Energy Years, 1945–1950.* New York: Harper & Row, 1964.

Mao Tse-tung. *Mao Tse-tung on Guerrilla Warfare.* New York: Praeger, 1961.

Newhouse, John. *Cold Dawn: The Story of SALT.* 2d ed. Washington, D.C.: Pergamon-Brassey's International Defense, 1989.

Nietzsche, Friedrich. *On the Genealogy of Morals and Ecce Homo.* Translated by Walter Kaufman and R. J. Hollingdale. New York: Random House, 1967.

Northedge, F. S., ed. *The Foreign Policies of the Powers.* London: Faber, 1968.

Ortega y Gasset, Jose. *The Revolt of the Masses.* Notre Dame, Ind.: University of Notre Dame Press, 1985.

Pearton, Maurice. *The Knowledgeable State: Diplomacy, War, and Technology Since 1830.* London: Burnett Books, 1982.

Poems of the Great War, 1914–1918. London: Penguin Books, 1998.

Roberts, Geoffrey K. *The Unholy Alliance: Stalin's Pact with Hitler.* London: Tauris, 1989.

Shawcross, William. *Sideshow: Kissinger, Nixon, and the Destruction of Cambodia.* London: Andre Deutsch, 1979.

Sokolovsky, V. D. *Voennaya Strategiya.* Moscow: Soviet Ministry of Defence, 1963.

Solzhenitsyn, Alexander. *The First Circle.* London: Collins and Harvill Press, 1968.

Sterne, Lawrence. *Tristram Shandy.* London: Everyman, 1991.

Talbott, Strobe. *Deadly Gambits: The Reagan Administration and the Stalemate in Nuclear Arms Control.* New York: Vintage Books, 1985.

Talbott, Strobe, ed. *Khrushchev Remembers.* London: Deutsch, 1971.

Truman, Harry S. *Memoirs.* Vol. 1, *Year of Decisions, 1945.* London: Hodder & Stoughton, 1955.

Waltz, Kenneth N. *The Spread of Nuclear Weapons: More May Be Better.* Adelphi Paper no. 171. London: International Institute for Strategic Studies, 1981.

Webster, Sir Charles, and Noble Frankland. *The Strategic Air Offensive Against Germany.* London: HMSO, 1961.

Windsor, Philip. *Germany and the Management of Détente.* London: Chatto and Windus for the International Institute for Strategic Studies, 1971.

———. *Germany and the Western Alliance: Lessons from the 1980 Crises.* Adelphi Paper no. 170. London: International Institute for Strategic Studies, 1981.

Index

About the Book

In this, his final book, Philip Windsor explores the emergence, meaning, and significance of the Cold War mentality. Tracing the evolution of strategic thinking from its origins in medieval Europe to the demise of the Cold War, he considers the peculiar character and autonomy that strategy acquired in the nuclear age.

Windsor is concerned with changes in our understanding of war and strategy—changes, he argues, that resulted less from technological innovation per se than from the combined effects of technological, social, and political transformations. This process culminated in the nuclear age, when strategic thinking became "self-referring and self-legitimating" and strategic considerations emerged as "the decisive force in the conduct of the politics of states and blocs."

Strategic Thinking addresses many of the themes that preoccupied Windsor throughout his academic career and on which his reflections threw such penetrating light: Soviet strategic thought, arms control, the role of alliances, the guerrilla phenomenon, and the rationality and ethics of nuclear deterrence. The final chapter explores the implications of the end of the Cold War for the future of strategic studies.

Philip Windsor (1935–2000) retired from the London School of Economics and Political Science in 1997. During his more than thirty years at LSE, he established a reputation as one of the most perceptive and thought-provoking thinkers in the field of international relations. **Mats Berdal** is director of studies at the International Institute for Strategic Studies. **Spyros Economides** is lecturer in international relations at LSE and a research associate of the IISS.